PIVOTAL POLITICS

PIVOTAL POLITICS,

A THEORY OF
U.S. LAWMAKING

Keith Krehbiel 1955-

THE UNIVERSITY OF CHICAGO PRESS
CHICAGO & LONDON

KEITH KREHBIEL is the Edward B. Rust Professor of Political
Science in the Graduate School of Business at Stanford
University. He is the author of *Information and Legislative
Organization* (1991) which received the APSA's Richard F. Fenno
Prize for best book on legislative politics in 1992.

The author gratefully acknowledges financial support from the National
Science Foundation no. SES-9022192.

The University of Chicago Press, Chicago 60637
The University of Chicago Press, Ltd., London
© 1998 by The University of Chicago
All rights reserved. Published 1998
Printed in the United States of America
07 06 05 04 03 02 01 00 99 98   1 2 3 4 5

ISBN: 0-226-45271-9 (cloth)
ISBN: 0-226-45272-7 (paper)

Library of Congress Cataloging-in-Publication Data

Krehbiel, Keith, 1955–
    Pivotal politics : a theory of U.S. lawmaking / Keith Krehbiel.
      p.   cm.
    Includes bibliographical references and index.
    ISBN 0-226-45271-9 (cloth). — ISBN 0-226-45272-7 (paper)
    1. Legislation—United States.   2. Separation of powers—United
States.   3. Law and politics.   I. Title.
    KF4945.K74   1997
    320.473′04—dc21   97-42848
                                                              CIP

To the Krehbiel supermajority—
Amy, Emily, and Sara

*an awesome force in stopping filibusters
and overriding vetoes*

❧ CONTENTS

✎ TABLES

This book is about conflict in the executive and legislative branches of government. How is such conflict resolved? Why is it so often not resolved, or resolved unsatisfactorily in the eyes of many participants and observers?

Somewhat ironically, the project originated in the judicial branch when, in the summer of 1993, I was called for jury duty. On day 1, I conjectured that I would be neither empaneled nor sent home, so I took a large supply of newspapers and magazines to the courthouse. As I observed that the jurors' waiting room was crowded yet curiously inactive, I read that politicians and journalists, too, were baffled by inactivity—albeit governmental stalemate of the executive-legislative type rather than the judicial type. Specifically, they tended overwhelmingly to be surprised that Bill Clinton and friends were stymied at nearly every turn in their efforts to change business as usual in Washington. My gut instinct was that the current events in Washington, while interesting, were not particularly surprising in light of the intentions of the framers of the U.S. Constitution. Additionally, Capitol Hill these days is a diverse, individualistic, rough-and-tumble place—a big domed ego farm in many respects—even (especially?) when the president's party is blessed (cursed?) with majorities in the House and Senate.

Having caught up with my periodicals on day 1 but feeling insecure about my casual intuitions regarding gridlock, I took a yellow pad of paper to the courthouse on day 2. My objective was modest—to suppress my trivial personal frustration with judicial gridlock by addressing a significant question about executive-legislative gridlock: Is there any simple analytic basis for expecting that a president with a heterogeneous and individualistic congressional majority will break gridlock, even under seemingly favorable conditions, such as after a 12-year run of divided government and a significant electoral success? The yellow-pad answer was simple (and perhaps simplistic) but unequivocal: No.

On day 3, the yellow pad yielded to a laptop computer. Courthouse officials eventually told me to go home and not to come back. In the meantime, I had gained an appreciation for judicial gridlock, for it had allowed me to begin and soon thereafter complete a manuscript titled "Institutional and Partisan Sources of Gridlock: A Theory of Unified and Divided Government." Although I was mostly satisfied with this manuscript as an admittedly basic but nonetheless useful theory, my professional peers were mostly dissatisfied[1]—or so it seemed approximately until the health-care stalemate underscored the reality of, and public befuddlement about, gridlock in unified government. In any event, it became clear that a necessary condition for engaging a broader audience with a simple theory about a complex process was to explore more systematically its empirical implications.

After two intervening years of business school as usual—and with a great deal of data collection on the side—focused exploration became possible in 1995–96 at the Center for Advanced Study in Behavioral Sciences. With the exception of the sad fact that the CASBS does not confer tenure, the working conditions were ideal there, so this book came to life.

Part One of the book lays out theoretical foundations pertinent to U.S. lawmaking. Chapter 1 identifies a need for a theory of lawmaking in U.S. national government that accounts for two basic facts: gridlock occurs usually but not always, and winning coalitions are almost always bipartisan and greater than minimum-majority sized. Chapter 2 presents a relatively nontechnical introduction to the formal model developed in the summer of 1993 and published in the *Journal of Theoretical Politics* in 1996. The model is called the "pivotal politics theory" because, in collective choice settings in which issues are well-defined, decision-makers' preferences are well-ordered, and rules of procedure are well-identified, a specific and identifiable decision maker is shown analytically to be pivotal to, or determinative of, the final policy choice. The theory is consistent with the basic facts identified in Chapter 1. This is only a starting point for more challenging questions, however, the most general of which is: Can complicated political situations and the behavior that ensues be represented usefully as a few pivot points on a line?

---

1. As an extreme but amusing example, a reviewer for a major journal asserted each of the following within a one-page review. (1) The model is too simple. (2) The model is awfully complicated. (3) The model doesn't tell us anything we don't already know from Gov 101. (4) The predictions of the model seem to be wrong.

Part Two addresses this question with a diverse assortment of empirical tests. Generally, the findings sum up to a claim that the theory is useful, not so much in spite of its simplicity as because of its simplicity. More specifically, Chapters 3 and 4 explore the predictions of the theory regarding variation in legislative productivity and coalition sizes, respectively. Chapters 5 and 6 test implications of the theory for behavior of filibuster pivots and veto pivots (and their spatial neighbors), respectively.

Part Three then turns to some novel applications of the theory. Chapter 7 inquires into whether presidential power can be measured by using some of the theoretical constructs and data from previous chapters. It can. Chapter 8 pushes this inquiry one step further to the question of whether measured presidential power has a partisan component. It does. Chapter 9 then makes some slight adjustments to the theory to assess the degree to which it can be applied usefully to the congressional budget process—an arena where complexities of the real-world processes stand in sharp contrast to the simplifying assumptions of the theory.

Part Four recapitulates the main argument and speculates about worthwhile future research that—unlike this project—might develop and test theories of lawmaking that go beyond basics.

Throughout the chapters, three stylistic preferences are evident and deserve a brief introduction and defense. First, because I try to reach a broad audience—including practicing political scientists, graduate students in training, smart undergraduates, and perhaps a few journalists—the exposition is somewhat layered. All of the aforementioned will be able to follow the main line of argument from the text alone. Dipping into footnotes, working through figures, and studying tables, however, are advised for those who desire a more comprehensive grasp of theories, methods, and related literatures.

Second, I have a strong preference for assessing more than one theory at a time whenever possible. The main advantage of testing different (and often competing) theories is that insights are gained regarding *comparative* strengths and weaknesses of approaches to understanding lawmaking. So, although I propose and focus consistently on one basic theory—pivotal politics—I am also on the lookout for other theories that may be better in some respects. Readers are hereby alerted to the disadvantage of this approach: the theory or theories of secondary interest often change from chapter to chapter because no single competing theory is testable across all chapters.

Third, I like to use a blend of formal, quantitative, and qualitative analyses. Other things being equal, systematic quantitative evidence paired with formally derived hypotheses seems to be the best recipe for scientific progress. Other things are not always equal, however, so most of the chapters include many real-world examples to add concreteness to the more systematic evidence.

Friends and colleagues contributed to this project in major ways. The long list begins with Bill Riker and Dick Fenno who, years ago, convinced me of the importance of working to bridge the gap between theory (narrowly construed) and data (broadly construed). More recently, assistance was obtained from John Aldrich, David Austen-Smith, Dave Baron, Rick Beth, Sarah Binder, David Brady, Chuck Cameron, John Cogan, Miles Davis, Daniel Diermeier, David Epstein, Tim Feddersen, Tom Gilligan, Tim Groseclose, Chuck Jones, Dan Kessler, Eric Lawrence, Bird Loomis, Forrest Maltzman, Nolan McCarty, Keith Poole, Doug Rivers, Eric Schickler, Steve Smith, and Jack Wright. More than any other set of interactions, conversations with David Mayhew at the Center were instrumental in stimulating new thoughts and providing reasons to rethink old ones. Arlene Saxonhouse and Bill Barnett also helped in ways that are hard to pinpoint but easy to appreciate.

As the project neared completion, Doug Arnold and David Mayhew provided extensive and extremely helpful comments on the first complete draft, as did an anonymous referee. Stanford's fine graduate students also contributed in a variety of ways inside the classroom and out. Cliff Carrubba, Scott Wilson, and Alan Wiseman are acknowledged for their capable and cheerful research assistance, while Brandice Canes and Craig Volden are singled out for exceptionally close, critical, and constructive readings of the near-final draft. Meanwhile, speaking of near-final drafts, Betsy Reid exhibited tireless proficiency at recycling through—and making countless corrections on—approximately a half-dozen drafts that I had the audacity to call penultimate.

Last but not least, special thanks go to Jeff Banks for a well-timed visit and conversation just prior to the final push, to Emily and Sara Krehbiel for their daily doses of good humor, to Paul Crabb and Ken Krehbiel for their daily doses of what we call humor, and, most of all, to Amy Krehbiel for her unfailing support and remarkable patience.

Keith Krehbiel

Stanford, California
May 1997

I

THEORETICAL
FOUNDATIONS

ONE

BASICS

It is often said that law is like sausage: those who like it should not watch it being made.[1] If so, then political scientists are gluttons for the grotesque. Long enamored with lawmaking, researchers of legislatures have amassed a fascinating set of case studies to help build an impressive edifice of knowledge about how bills become laws.[2]

In spite of the abundance of excellent descriptions of lawmaking in the United States Congress, however, there seems to be a shortage of good basic theories of lawmaking that incorporate presidential as well as congressional decision making. The objective of this book is to supply a theory that begins to satisfy this demand. With the exception of some minor twists and turns, the path of development is straightforward. I argue that numerous existing theories are limited in terms of their ability to explain basic facts about lawmaking in the United States. I propose a new and surprisingly simple theory of lawmaking that is consistent with the basic facts. I test the theory using macro- and microlevel data. I apply the theory to study otherwise elusive issues pertaining to presidents, power, and parties in U.S. national government. Finally, I speculate about how fruitful advances can be made beyond the basic theory of pivotal politics that is proposed, tested, and applied in this book.

---

1. The quotation is sometimes attributed to Otto Von Bismarck (Jones 1995).

2. Among many excellent case studies are Asbell 1978; Bailey 1950; Beer 1976; Jones 1975; Mann 1996; Redman 1973; Reid 1980; Waldman 1995; and Whalen and Whalen 1985.

BASIC FACTS

How might a short and simple summary of the many diverse and complex perspectives on U.S. lawmaking demonstrate the need for a new, basic theory? One approach is simply to identify basic facts of lawmaking, to survey extant theories (broadly defined), and to see whether their predictions are consistent with the facts. Two such facts pertain to gridlock and coalitions.

Gridlock

A 12-year streak of divided government from 1980 to 1992 corresponded remarkably well with a 12-year increase in the salience of the word *gridlock* in American political discourse. Examples are plentiful. In accepting the Republican nomination for the second term, President George Bush blamed "the gridlocked Democratic Congress" for the general inability of leaders in national government to negotiate their way out of a wide range of legislative impasses. Later, after the return to unified government, President Bill Clinton used the term under more hopeful circumstances. When the Senate passed a much-modified version of the Democrats' budget in 1993, President Clinton praised Senate leaders, saying, "Finally, we've done something to break the gridlock."[3]

The term *gridlock,* according to one etymological account, "first appeared in print in 1980 to describe a 'worst case scenario' for traffic in New York City, in which the grids or cross-patterns of the city literally locked, tying up traffic in all directions" (Dickson and Clancy 1993, 146). Transportation of the term into the political arena occurred soon thereafter, as gridlock came to refer to the persistent inability to enact major legislation when majorities on Capitol Hill and/or the president seem to prefer such enactments to the status quo. A more precise, analytic definition of political gridlock is given in Chapter 2. For introductory purposes, three items of clarification suffice.

First, although the modal form of finger pointing about the sources of gridlock suggests that the phenomenon is intricately related to interparty bickering, the core meaning of the concept itself is not inherently partisan. Because gridlock may characterize nonpartisan lawmaking as well as lawmaking in highly partisan environments, parties and partisanship should be viewed as hypothetical causes of gridlock rather than defining characteristics of gridlock.

---

3. David E. Rosenbaum, "Senate Approves First Step in President's Budget Plan," *New York Times,* March 26, 1993.

Second, although gridlock is a relatively new term, the class of political phenomena to which it applies is at least as old as separation-of-powers institutions of collective choice. Assorted synonyms for gridlock have been around since the Continental Congress, because passing important laws in the United States has never been easy. Grant McConnell, for instance, not only agrees that gridlock is a basic fact but also identifies another possible cause: "American institutions are studded with so many barriers to action that stalemate is the essential reality of the United States" (1966, 337). So, although occasional historic bursts of legislative productivity occur, such as Roosevelt's One Hundred Days, these are the exception—not the rule—in U.S. politics. As such, political stalemates were common well before the recent run of divided government turned gridlock into a trendy term.

Third, although the practical usage of the term is pejorative more often than not, the underlying phenomenon of gridlock is not necessarily a bad thing. Opponents of major policy change in a specific area obviously have an eye for the salutary attributes of stalemate. As Senate Majority Leader Bob Dole once quipped, "If you're against something, you'd better hope there is a little gridlock."[4] Less obviously, and in a fully nonpartisan vein, gridlock can be viewed as essentially the same thing as policy stability, in which case its normative attributes can be defended in the absence of partisanship and self-interest.[5]

The first basic fact of U.S. lawmaking is that gridlock occurs often but not always. Therefore, a good theory of lawmaking ought to have the property that *gridlock is common but not constant.* Better yet, a good theory of lawmaking should identify conditions under which gridlock is broken.

Large, Bipartisan Coalitions

A minimum sufficient condition for breaking gridlock—that is, for enacting laws—is that simple majorities in the Senate and House vote for a bill and that the president signs it. The constitutionally defined minimum winning coalition, then, is small: half the House (plus one), half the Senate

---

4. Safire 1993, 305.

5. Having identified the normative side of gridlock, I shall *not* proceed to take a normative stance on the goods versus evils associated with gridlock or policy stability. In effect, my view is that a necessary condition for any tight normative argument of this form is the development of a more basic and sound understanding of lawmaking than currently exists. In other words, positive questions (generically, "What is?") must precede normative questions ("What should be?"), and this study is a positive pursuit first and foremost.

(plus one), and the president. Practice departs from this theoretical minimum, however, in significant ways. Winning coalitions are normally much greater than minimum-majority sized, both at the level of roll call votes generally and votes on final passage more specifically. For example, David Mayhew (1974, 113) presents *Congressional Quarterly* data for the 1972 House and Senate, and his data show that in at least half of roll call votes winning margins were greater than 70 percent. Insofar as these data include many trivial votes, such as votes on approving yesterday's *Journal,* nonbinding "hurrah" resolutions, etc., they are perhaps not sufficiently selective. But even if the analysis is restricted to coalition sizes at the very end of the legislative process when votes are of the do-or-die sort, the finding is much the same. Consider, for example, all votes on final passage of laws enacted by the 102d and 103d Congresses (1991–94).[6] The average size of the winning coalition on these 324 votes is 79 percent. Furthermore, such coalitions are typically bipartisan. For example, we can ask: In what fraction of the votes did at least 40 percent of Republicans join at least 40 percent of Democrats in the winning coalition (or vice versa)? The answer is considerably over one-half: 68 percent to be precise.[7]

A second basic fact of U.S. lawmaking, then, concerns coalition sizes and partisanship. Specifically, a good theory of lawmaking ought to have the property that *winning coalitions are bipartisan and greater than minimum-majority sized.* Better yet, a good theory of lawmaking should identify covariates of coalition sizes.

BASIC TERMS

Three esteemed presidency scholars recently wrote, "Almost everyone agrees that research on the presidency should be more theoretical. *Theory,*

---

6. Notice that this includes one unified-government Congress and one divided-government Congress. To bias the estimate downward, I exclude all resolutions (which often generate so-called hurrah votes) and measures that require supermajority support for passage (e.g., Constitutional amendments and bill considered under suspension of the rules). I omit votes on amendments not because amendments are unimportant—many are, of course, key—but rather because of the inherent ambiguity of such votes given parliamentary situations. For example, does a large coalition of yes voters on an amendment mean that most legislators prefer the amendment over the bill, or that they prefer the amended bill over the status quo? The first possibility seems likely; the second possibility is significantly less clear. In the case of votes on final passage, however, the second possibility seems quite clear.

7. The 40 percent threshold is arbitrary, of course. For a 50 percent standard, the answer is 62 percent; for a 30 percent standard, the answer is 76 percent. For simplicity, I pooled House and Senate observations even though average sizes (and bipartisanship) is greater in the Senate than the House. These differences are explored more thoroughly in Chapter 4.

however, turns out to be a remarkably plastic term, so different authors have different agendas when making this assertion" (Edwards, Kessel, and Rockman 1993, 13). I agree, and I have an agenda.

Because the issue of what ought and ought not to be designated as a theory is recurring and controversial, it is helpful to clarify the issue at the outset, even though the distinctions that follow will become blurred from time to time. At first pass it is useful to differentiate between a deductive, *positive theory* and an inductive set of *empirical generalizations*. In the best instances, positive theories are explicit and formal, and their derived propositions are logically explicit and sound. In William Riker's (1977) terms, the quintessential feature of such propositions is that they are "theorems in a theory." Likewise, in the best instances, empirically derived generalizations are carefully drawn and based on a large number of systematically selected observations. If so, Riker calls these "well-verified generalizations."

In the absence of empirical verification, a theory is only a set of interrelated abstract symbols that may or may not clarify and illuminate real-world behavior and outcomes. In the absence of an explicit theory, well-verified empirical generalizations state what happens, but they offer little insight into why it happens. Either way, the metaphorical glass of scientific discovery is only half full.

In contrast, when theorems in a theory and well-verified generalizations coincide, a major goal of science is attained by the joint contributions of the theoretical and the empirical pursuits. The goal is *law-like statements*. As Riker summarizes:

> Law and axioms thus reinforce each other. The necessity of the inference makes the law seem reasonable, and the empirical validity of the law makes the axioms seem true. Thus, with a theory, there is a much stronger reason than mere observation to accept a scientific law. (1977, 15)

The methodological approach in this book is to try to fill the metaphorical glass by bringing deductive and inductive approaches together. Consequently, the topics covered will span theories (formal and informal) as well as empirical claims.

To call empirical claims *theories* in the absence of compatible deductive arguments is common but misleading. The manufacturing of empirical claims includes a wide range of inductive pursuits that, however useful, do not fit well under a rubric reserved for deductive activities, such as reasoning from first principles. Nevertheless, how others choose to use the term *theory* is not a major concern here as long as the methodological distinction between deduction and induction is clear. Toward this end, I shall use the term *theory* to refer to arguments—preferably but not necessarily formal—in which assumptions are posited, and conclusions, results, or propositions are derived. I shall refer to other, less consciously deductive claims as *empirical generalizations* (or, sometimes, as *schools of thought*). It bears repeating that these two sets of phenomena can, do, and, in the best cases, should overlap. Their methodological starting points, however, are different. Theories begin with assumptions. Empirical claims begin with observations.

BASIC THEORIES OR SCHOOLS OF THOUGHT

Although volumes have been written about what various theories and empirically based schools of thought say about gridlock and coalition sizes in U.S. lawmaking, a short discussion must suffice here. Table 1.1 summarizes the discussion. Its main conclusion is simply that no existing theory or school of thought provides a precise explanation for the basic facts concerning gridlock, coalition sizes, and variation therein.

Responsible Party Government

In the traditional normative theory of responsible party government, parties adopt well-defined and differentiated platforms, a unified government is elected, majority party members in government act cohesively to enact and implement the platform, policy outcomes are realized, and this process repeats (Schattschneider 1942; American Political Science Association 1950). In this theory, gridlock is rare to nonexistent because cohesive parties always enact the platforms on which they run.[8] Finally, although the theory does not directly assess the issue of sizes of coalitions, responsible parties with differentiated platforms surely would not coalesce in bipartisan fashion to pass legislation. This, in turn, seems to imply that winning coalitions will be equal to the size of the majority party.

In some respects, the theory of responsible party government is a dubious starting point. As noted, this theory was intended to be normative or prescriptive, not positive and descriptive. Moreover, its prescription was born out of a belief on the part of Schattschneider and most of the American

---

8. Alternatively, a strong necessary condition for gridlock is the absence of changes in preferences in the governing party.

Political Science Association committee that what should be true about U.S. lawmaking departed significantly from what was true about U.S. lawmaking. Postwar history continues to bear out this discrepancy. While U.S. parties adopt platforms in national conventions, their platforms are usually amorphous, frequently identical on many provisions, and hardly ever serve effectively as constraints during the campaign or after the election.[9] Furthermore, U.S. governments in the postwar period have been divided more often than unified, and parties in government have been cohesive and in opposition only under special circumstances.[10]

Conditional Party Government

A belief in the significance of parties in U.S. lawmaking plus a tacit concession about persistent mismatches between normative theories and empirical realities have recently given rise to a distinctively weakened notion of party government—not *responsible* party government in the traditional and broadest sense but rather *conditional* party government (Rohde 1991; Aldrich 1995, chap. 7; Aldrich and Rohde 1995). This perspective is clearly intended to be descriptive—not normative. In conditional party government theory, the condition for party strength is stated in terms of legislators' preferences. If the parties' members have distinctly different preferences across parties but homogeneous preferences within parties, then the majority party is predicted to be sufficiently strong to pass *skewed* or *noncentrist* outcomes.[11]

When the condition for conditional party government is met, gridlock will not occur for reasons comparable to those in responsible party government theory: the majority party is cohesive, disciplined, and decisive. Similarly, coalition sizes will be majority-party sized, because no rational minority-party member will join in passing *noncentrist* bills that favor the majority, and because the homogeneous majority-party members are in

9.   It was widely reported in 1996, for example, that the Republican candidate for the presidency, Senator Robert Dole, openly confessed not to have read the Republican platform. (Nor, of course, had most Democrats or Republicans read their party's platform.)

10.   For example, confining attention only to "significant enactments," Mayhew 1991 finds that most bills were passed by very large, bipartisan coalitions.

11.   "Skewed" is Aldrich and Rohde's term. "Noncentrist" is Dion and Huber's (1996). In either case, the baseline is the chamber median voter or, in Aldrich's (1995) case, a multidimensional but informally defined counterpart thereof.

Table 1.1
Theories or Schools of Thought and Their Implications

Theories or Schools of Thought (Authors)	Gridlock		
	Overall	In Unified Government	In Divided Government
Responsible party government (APSA, Schattschneider . . .)	Not likely	No	—
Conditional party government (Aldrich, Rohde)	Not likely	—	—
Divided v. unified government (Sundquist . . .)	Depends on government type	No	Yes
Median voter theory (Black)	Rare or nonexistent	—	—
Majoritarian chaos (McKelvey, Schofield . . .)	Rare or nonexistent	—	—
Stability-inducing theories (Shepsle . . .)	Common	—	—
Divide-the-dollar games (Baron and Ferejohn . . .)	Nonexistent	—	—
Reduced form theories			
Econ. theories of regulation (Stigler, Peltzman . . .)	Nonexistent	—	—
Electoral party competition (Downs)	Not likely	No	—
Balancing theory (Alesina, Fiorina, Rosenthal)	Rare or nonexistent	None	None

unanimous support of such bills. Therefore, coalitions also are purely partisan.

When the condition for conditional party government is not met, the predictions of the theory are less clear. This ambiguity is reflected in the following passage:

> Conditional party government depends on intra-party homogeneity (especially in the majority party) and on inter-party differences. If there is *much* diversity in preferences within a party, a *substantial* portion of the members will be *reluctant* to grant strong powers to the leadership, or to *resist* the vigorous exercise of existing powers, because of the realistic fear that they *may be* used to produce outcomes unsatisfactory to the members in question. (Aldrich and Rohde 1995, 18; italics added)

Coalitions		
Size	**Partisanship**	**Qualifications**
Majority-party sized	Partisan	Theory is normative and authors argued that the normative ideal was not attained.
Majority-party sized	Partisan	Domain of theory is unclear, especially when the condition for party government is not met (see Chap. 8).
Majority-party sized	Partisan	Argument is informal, so it is unclear what is assumed and what is derived.
Small	Bipartisan	Theory is nonpartisan, so coalitions are bipartisan whenever distributions of party preferences overlap.
Small	Bipartisan	Theory is nonpartisan, so coalitions are bipartisan whenever distributions of party preferences overlap.
?	Bipartisan	Multidimensionality of the choice space makes derivation of testable predictions difficult.
Small	Bipartisan	Unidimensional collective goods version of the theory has implications approximating those of median voter theory (see above).
?	?	Focus is on inputs and outputs more than lawmaking processes within government.
Majority-party sized	Partisan	Party implementation of electoral platforms is assumed, not derived. Lawmaking domain is questionable.
Small	Bipartisan	Domain is electoral choice; lawmaking theory is implicit and not central to the authors' interests.

I return to this problem in Chapter 8. For now it suffices to note that the interpretations offered for conditional party government assume that the condition *is* met.

Divided versus Unified Government

Another set of literature is relatively explicit about conditions for gridlock or its complement, legislative productivity. Arising during the recent 12-year run of divided government, these studies attribute gridlock to precisely that: split party control of the Congress and the White House.[12] The sup-

---

12. See, for example, Sundquist 1981, 1988; Cutler 1988; Kelly 1993; and countless journalists. When looking for the latter, however, look before 1995.

porting reasons for this relationship vary somewhat across works, but the common element in the body of work on divided versus unified government is that interparty jockeying for advantage in the electoral arena has behavioral manifestations in the governmental arena that negate opportunities for bipartisan coalition building. In other words, programmatic parties in government cannot cooperate effectively if government is divided. In contrast, unified government is necessary and sufficient for breaking gridlock—or so goes the conventional wisdom. Referring to the 1992 election and its aftermath, Morris Fiorina aptly summarized this viewpoint:[13]

> When Bill Clinton was elected, advocates of activist government breathed a sigh of relief. With unified government restored, the country could once again expect innovative programs, decisive government action, and efficient institutional performance. Such expectations were not just the exaggerated expectations of naive observers. Experienced congressional leaders convinced President-elect Clinton that he should ignore moderate Republicans and adopt a legislative strategy that relied exclusively on the Democratic majorities of Congress. For his own part, Clinton imprudently announced that he expected his first 100 days to be the most productive period since Franklin Roosevelt. (Fiorina 1996, 159)

We will see in Chapter 3 that, by some recent accounts (Mayhew 1991), the conventional wisdom about unified versus divided government has serious limitations. Nonetheless, it is a viewpoint to be taken seriously if for no other reason than it so clearly defines hypothetical conditions for gridlock. Similarly, as with other party-based schools of thought, the divided government perspective at least suggests (if not predicts) that coalitions in unified government will be majority-party sized and partisan.

Median Voter Theory

A certain degree of stretching is required to move from party theories or schools of thought to their empirical implications. Often, and especially as theories become more explicit and formal, the requisite amount of stretching diminishes. The classic median voter theory of Duncan Black (1958) provides a good example. This theory says that if an odd number of members of a majoritarian voting body (say Congress) can be ordered on an

---

13.   An apt summary of conventional wisdom, however, is not to be equated with endorsement of it. See also the rest of Fiorina's excellent summary of recent literature.

issue space such that their preferences over policies are single-peaked, then the unique equilibrium outcome is that proposal corresponding to the median member's ideal or most-preferred point.

Application of median voter theory to U.S. lawmaking, gridlock, and coalition sizes is straightforward. Elections can be thought of as exogenous determinants of legislators' preferences, which are therefore sometimes called induced preferences. After each election, such preferences may and usually do change. Any time the position of the median legislator changes—as in the case of national partisan tides, for example—the old status quo (the previous-period median legislator's ideal point) is out of equilibrium. A new play of the lawmaking game then occurs, and the new median voter's ideal point is selected via majority rule as the new policy.

According to this theory, gridlock *never* occurs, except in the rare case in which the legislative median is perfectly constant. Similarly, winning coalition sizes are usually small, that is, near minimum-majority size, or $(n + 1)/2$.[14] Finally, the theory is nonpartisan, so winning coalitions will be bipartisan in proportion to the extent that distributions of ideal points of the two parties overlap.

Majoritarian Chaos

Extensions of Black's median voter theory to multidimensional issue spaces led to the generation of several analytic results sharing the rubric of *chaos theorems*. The basic result is that, under a wide range of assumptions about voters' preferences, truthful revelation of such preferences (sincere voting) fails to yield stable policy outcomes. Majority rule, therefore, is utterly unpredictable or chaotic.[15]

If taken seriously as a positive theory of lawmaking (see, e.g., Aldrich 1995), chaos theories seem to predict no gridlock, because under all but exceedingly rare circumstances (Plott 1967) any status quo policy can be defeated by a majority vote.[16] Predictions about coalitions are not easy to

14.   More precisely, they are larger than minimum-majority sized in proportion to the size of the exogenous electoral shock (see Chap. 4).

15.   See Riker 1980 for a classic review essay, and Diermeier 1997 for an excellent update. See also original works by Arrow 1951; Plott 1967; McKelvey 1976; and Schofield 1978.

16.   Some theorists quite reasonably reject the premise of this interpretation, arguing that McKelvey's theory was not intended to be positive (Austen-Smith and Banks 1997). Another defensible objection to my positive interpretation is more subtle and goes something like this: not only is chaos consistent with the theory, but so too is policy stability at a (necessarily) noncore point in the multidimensional space. Under either of these alternative interpretations, the bottom-line assessment here is not affected. Specifically, chaos theories are not good positive theories for U.S. lawmak-

extract because these theories are not explicit about agenda formation. Under reasonable assumptions, such as centrally located status quo policies, though, coalitions are likely to be small and bipartisan: small because with a centrally located status quo policy it is difficult to find a large majority that wishes to change it; bipartisan because, as an empirical matter, party distributions overlap one another, and these theories do not recognize partisanship as a factor shaping voting decisions.

Stability-Inducing Theories

The characteristic inability of chaos theories to yield sharp predictions about collective choice gave rise to another class of formal theories that can be labeled *stability-inducing* theories. One distinguishing feature of these theories is obvious from the label: they are motivated by a perceived need to identify stable outcomes in analytic settings similar to those in which prior theories show that stable outcomes are not likely to exist. In other words, stability-inducing theories by definition take very seriously the problems of preference aggregation illustrated in Arrow's theorem (1951), strict sufficient conditions for a core illustrated in Plott's theorem (1967), and the prospect of endless majority cycling suggested by McKelvey's theorem (1976).

A second distinguishing feature of stability-inducing theories concerns how the so-called chaos problem is solved. Stability-inducing theories generally assume that some players (committees, more often than not) have special procedural rights, such as agenda setting and gatekeeping powers (Ferejohn 1986), restrictive amendment rules (Weingast 1989), or ex post vetoes (Shepsle and Weingast 1987). Intuitively, when exogenous constraints are imposed on some players' actions, collective choice behavior and outcomes tend to become more predictable.

Important works such as these have received a great deal of attention elsewhere, and it is not necessary to rehash the finer points of associated theoretical and empirical arguments.[17] For present purposes the main ques-

---

ing. Either (1) they do not try to be predictive, or (2) they try to be predictive but predict the wrong thing (chaos, not gridlock), or (3) they try to be predictive but predict everything (and therefore explain nothing). Kramer, perhaps, puts it best: "To show that a particular set of premises is inconsistent, or that a certain model does not have an equilibrium (and therefore can't make any clear-cut empirical predictions which could be tested against data) is to show, basically, that the model has problems: these premises can't account for much" (Kramer 1986, 17).

17. See, for example, Cox and McCubbins 1993; and Krehbiel 1991.

tion is: What do these theories as a class say about gridlock and coalition sizes in U.S. lawmaking?

The good news is that stability-inducing theories succeed in their primary objective. They demonstrate the existence of stable outcomes where, in the absence of their superimposed institutional features, preference aggregation would be plagued by various forms of instability. This is very much the flavor of "structure-induced equilibrium" arguments (Shepsle 1979; Shepsle and Weingast 1981), and the corresponding prediction about gridlock in this class of theories is clear. It happens. Indeed, equilibrium outcomes in these models are, by definition, instances of gridlock.[18]

The not-so-good news is that stability-inducing theories as a class are not especially conducive to systematic data analysis. Part of this problem is attributable to the remarkable diversity of such theories and their corresponding differences in conditions for breaking gridlock and the sizes of coalitions that will enact new policies.[19] Most of the problem, however, lies in the multidimensionality of the choice space in these theories—an uncontested feature of realism that nevertheless exacts a high price for empirically inclined researchers. If ultimately we are interested in testing whether these theories identify approximately the right conditions for policy change and predict approximately the sizes and partisanship of coalitions, then a prior theoretical challenge must be confronted. How are these endogenous features (gridlock, coalition sizes) related to the exogenous parameters (preferences and the status quo policy) of any given stability-inducing theory? In multidimensional settings, this is an exceedingly difficult question to answer generally and with testable implications.[20] Conse-

---

18. Somewhat more can be said about gridlock within some specific stabilty-inducing theoretical frameworks. For example, one such theory that brings the president, bicameralism, and committees all into the picture is Thomas Hammond and Gary Miller's (1987) theory of the "Core of the Constitution." Hammond and Miller show that in bicameral settings with a presidential veto and congressional override (i.e., "institutional features"), stable (core) outcomes exist. More specifically, the requirements to pass new laws are increasingly demanding as the number of institutional constraints increases. Thus, a rough prediction that goes beyond "gridlock happens" might be that the number of institutional constraints is positively related to the propensity for gridlock.

19. For reviews, see Shepsle 1986; Shepsle and Weingast 1995; Weingast 1996; and Krehbiel 1988.

20. Technically inclined readers are advised to see for themselves by attacking the following problem, which, relatively speaking, is a simple and tractable theoretical problem of the stability-inducing type. Consider a three-person legislature whose members have Euclidean preferences and ideal points that form an equilateral triangle centered within a unit square (thus a two-dimensional space). Designate any one member as an agenda setter and stipulate that her proposal will be subject to a single majority vote against an exogenous status quo point. In other words, the proposal is not

quently, even under the questionable assumption that preferences and the status quo can be measured effectively over a multidimensional choice space, it remains unclear what the more precise predictions of stability-inducing theories are, and why.[21]

Divide-the-Dollar Games

In a series of influential papers employing noncooperative game theory, David Baron and John Ferejohn are more explicit about the sequence of play in a legislative game than is customary in earlier, stability-inducing theories.[22] The consequence is favorable in terms of clarity of predictions. First, gridlock never occurs (though under some legislative procedures—namely, an open rule—delay may occur). Second, winning coalitions are almost always small and often are minimum-majority sized. Some extensions of these theories have slightly different implications. Susanne Lohmann and Sharyn O'Halloran (1994), for example, develop a divide-the-dollar theory for trade politics that incorporates a president and predicts no gridlock, minimum-majorities, and explicitly bipartisan coalitions.

Reduced-Form Theories

Finally, a set of miscellaneous theories has comparable, but somewhat re-mote, implications for gridlock and coalition sizes. None of these explicitly

---

subject to amendment. Identify the equilibrium outcome for all status quo points in the unit square. For any given status quo, q, is it possible to say not only that the resulting outcome, x^*, is stable (i.e., will not change if the game were replayed) but also what the unique one-stage outcome x^* is? Is the mapping from the two-dimensional status quo, q, into the two-dimensional outcome space, x, smooth? What is the size of the winning coalition for any given q? If this problem was solvable, then repeat the exercise with two minor extensions that capture two major elements of U.S. lawmaking: the president and his veto right. Specifically, form a pentagon with five legislators' ideal points, and add a president whose ideal point is in the center of the pentagon and who has a veto subject to a $2/3$ override of the legislature. Answer the above questions for the pentagonal setup. Is this model testable?

21. As with chaos theories, stability-inducing theories do not exactly predict—but seem to sug-gest—that coalitions will be bipartisan and minimum-majority sized.

22. Baron and Ferejohn's choice space is, in effect, multidimensional in several of their theories, so one might regard these as stability-inducing theories, too. I categorize them separately for two reasons, one of which is quite subjective. First, they seem less motivated by cyclical majorities than in earlier stability-inducing theories. Second, their modeling technology yields sharper and sometimes different predictions than those of earlier theories. See Baron and Ferejohn 1987, 1989; and Baron 1989, 1991, and 1994.

characterizes collective choice (i.e., voting) within government, and most of them opt for a unitary-actor or reduced-form view of lawmaking.

Economic Theories of Regulation

Theories of regulation, proposed mainly by economists, focus on the responsiveness of governmental policy to the various interest group pressures brought to bear on politicians (see, e.g., Stigler 1971; Peltzman 1976; Becker 1983; and Grossman and Helpman 1994). As a general matter, these are neither voting theories of legislatures nor legislative-executive bargaining theories but rather theories that portray government as a unitary optimizing agent, subject to exogenous changes in the economic or political environment. (In the latter case, the economic theories are conceptually much like theories of pluralism in political science, although the methodology is much different.) Comparative statics of these theories almost invariably suggest that, when interest group pressures change, so, too, does the optimal governmental action. In other words, governmental responsiveness, not gridlock, is a central characteristic of these theories. The theories are necessarily silent about coalition sizes because government is not modeled as a collective, voting entity.

Downsian Electoral Party Competition

In another classic economic theory, Anthony Downs (1957) models an electoral process in a way that complements the prior (normative) theory of responsible party government. Parties adopt platforms and compete for votes only for the sake of gaining office, whereupon they implement their platforms. Gridlock rarely occurs, and divided government never occurs. Coalition sizes are presumably majority-party sized and partisan, although here, too, internal governmental processes are not modeled explicitly. In other words, the extracted predictions seem to be the same as from the theory of responsible party government. The chief differences are that Downs's theory is intended to be positive, but it is not intended to be a theory of lawmaking per se.

Balancing Theory

In a similar vein, a series of innovative works by Alberto Alesina, Morris Fiorina, and Howard Rosenthal (1991) and a book by Alesina and Rosenthal (1995) focus on electoral behavior. Nonetheless, these theories, too, have implicit but clear assumptions about the governmental arena. The basic behavioral postulate is that voters in the electorate derive utility from a desired *balance* of governmental officials. Thus, for example, a moderate voter prefers a Republican president and a Democratic Congress to a unified Democratic government, because the divided government arrangement is believed to yield moderate policies compatible with the voter's preferences, while a unified Democratic government would be too liberal. Clearly, the implicit theory of lawmaking in balancing theory is that policies are a weighted average of preferences of the set of officials who make laws—for example, the president and the Congress.

Viewed as such, the balancing theory assumes (implicitly) that gridlock does not occur, because any electorally induced change in the composition of government changes the weighted average. As usual, coalition-size implications are hard to pin down, but for reasons approximating the interpretation of median voter theory, we would expect winning coalitions to be small, except in cases of exceptionally large interelection swings. Finally, like most other formal theories discussed, the balancing theory neither presumes nor derives different behavior by different party members, other than the fact that partisanship and preferences are likely to be correlated. So, coalitions will be bipartisan to the extent that interparty distributions overlap.

THE BASIC NEED

Overall, the theories and schools of thought that have a bearing on lawmaking exhibit a number of desirable properties. The responsible party government viewpoint outlines a vision of democratic government that has considerable normative appeal. The conditional party government theory—offered more as a positive than normative theory—focuses attention on issues of party strength and conditions under which the majority party in Congress can govern effectively. The distinction between divided and unified government brings the president into the picture and, also with a partisan focus, offers a hypothesis about conditions under which important laws are likely to be passed. Formal theories offer additional advantages: they tend to be explicit, they are cumulative in many respects, and often they generate plausible and testable propositions about observable political phenomena. Furthermore, some formal theories have received impressive levels of systematic empirical corroboration.[23]

However, when it comes to the substantive crux of table 1.1—the two

---

23. See especially Alesina and Rosenthal 1995, and the voluminous literature on Downsian electoral competition.

basic facts of U.S. lawmaking—the theories and schools of thought falter, individually and collectively. Most extant theories predict either all gridlock or no gridlock. Only the relatively amorphous perspective about divided versus unified government offers a clear statement about necessary and sufficient conditions under which gridlock is broken, and its expectation, if anything, seems not to be borne out. Similarly, on matters of coalition size, most theories are either silent, require stretched arguments to obtain a prediction, and/or suggest predictions of small and/or partisan coalitions, which also seem inconsistent with the basic facts.

In summary, the basic need is for a new theory of lawmaking in the United States. The theory should predict that gridlock occurs often but not always, and it should identify testable conditions under which gridlock is broken. The theory should predict the regular formation of bipartisan coalitions of greater than simple-majority size, and it should identify testable conditions under which coalition sizes grow or shrink relative to baseline expectations. Last but not least, the theory should expose and clarify the essential constraints faced by lawmakers in a democratic society.

∾· T W O

A THEORY

Who is pivotal in U.S. lawmaking? This is a difficult
question insofar as "the United States has the most intricate lawmaking
system in the world" (Jones 1994, 297). However, based on the hope that
even a simple theoretical answer to a difficult question is better than no
answer at all, this chapter introduces a theory of pivotal politics that is un-
abashedly elementary by contemporary modeling standards. The theory not
only answers the question of who is pivotal in U.S. lawmaking but also
generates a sizable set of empirical implications that will be the focus of
the following four chapters. After a brief overview of the general properties
of good theories—assumptions, results, and interpretations—this chapter
turns to their specific manifestations in the pivotal politics theory.

Assumptions in a formal theory are not intended to be comprehensive
and unequivocally true. If they were comprehensive and unequivocally true
they would simply restate or describe reality as we know it, and they would
be much too complex from which to derive testable propositions about
political behavior. Instead, assumptions are intended to satisfy aims that are
at once more modest descriptively and more constructive analytically. They
should reflect the essence of choice settings with sufficient simplicity that
the model itself remains tractable, because a model that cannot be solved
is not a data-ready model. What, then, are the essential features of U.S.
lawmaking settings? One plausible answer is separation of powers, heterogeneous preferences, and multistage collective choice.[1]

Theoretical results, of course, are derived from assumptions. In light of

---

1.   A noteworthy omission from the model that will surface regularly is parties.

the discussion in Chapter 1, a minimal requirement for an improved theory of lawmaking is that its results comport with two basic facts: gridlock is common but not constant, and coalitions are regularly bipartisan and greater than simple-majority sized. A higher standard for results is that they not only comport with these basic facts of U.S. lawmaking but also yield predictions (or interpretations) regarding occasional variation in these approximate constants. More specifically, an improved theory of lawmaking should identify *conditions* under which gridlock is broken, and it should account for some *variation* in (usually large) coalition sizes.

Interpretations constitute another class of desirable properties of a useful theory. An improved theory of U.S. lawmaking also should help to account for anomalies or puzzles that are not necessarily empirical motivations underlying the necessarily sparse assumptions of the theory. For example, why do we often have gridlock even in unified governments (Mayhew 1991, 1995)? Why do presidents launch fewer policy initiatives the longer they are in office (Light 1991)? Why does presidential popularity diminish over the course of terms (Hinckley 1990)? And why are ideological moderates, of all people, so often frustrated about U.S. lawmaking? To the extent that a new theory can answer questions such as these in addition to providing an explanation for more basic facts, it will have added appeal.

ASSUMPTIONS

Assumptions of the theory cover preferences, players, policies, procedures, and behavior. These can be addressed in varying degrees of mathematical precision and generality. Here I opt for a relatively informal and example-based exposition.[2]

Policy Space

Collective choice occurs via voting over proposals or policies that can be arranged on a line. That is, the *policy space is unidimensional.* It is convenient and intuitive to think of the policy space as a continuum on which liberal policies are located on the left, moderate policies are located in the center, and conservative policies are located on the right. Because the policy space is continuous, it is possible to consider policies at any point between liberal and conservative extremes. Finally, an exogenous *status quo point, q,* reflects

---

2. See Krehbiel 1996a for a formal exposition.

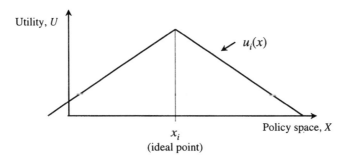

Figure 2.1
Single-peaked utility function for legislator *i*

existing policy and can be interpreted as the outcome from a prior period of decision making.

Players and Preferences

Players in the game are generically referred to as *lawmakers* and include a president and *n* legislators in a unicameral legislature. Each player has an *ideal point* in the policy space, that is, a policy that yields greater benefits to the player than all other policies. Each player's preferences are *single-peaked,* meaning that as policies in a given direction farther and farther from an individual's ideal point are considered, utility for that player never increases. Figure 2.1 shows a simple example of one player with an ideal point x_i and a single-peaked utility function $u_i(x)$. For convenience and spatial intuition, it is helpful further to assume that utility functions are symmetric. Therefore, for any two policies y and z in the policy space, a player always prefers that policy which is closer to his ideal point.

Procedures

In contrast to generic pure-majority-rule voting models, the capacity of politicians to enact policies in this theory is tempered by two *supermajoritarian procedures:* the executive *veto,* and the Senate's *filibuster* procedures. The U.S. Constitution confers to the president the right to veto legislation subject to a ⅔ majority override by the Congress. Similarly, the Senate's Rule 22 confers to each individual the right to engage in *extended debate*

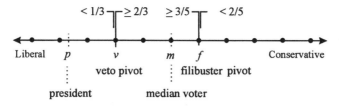

Figure 2.2
Pivotal legislators if the president is liberal

(filibuster) subject to a ³/₅ vote to end debate (invoke cloture). Under configurations of legislative preferences to be specified, the filibuster, too, effectively raises the voting requirement for policy change.

Pivots

Webster's *New World Dictionary* defines a *pivot* as "a person or thing on or around which something turns or depends." This commonsense definition transports well into the pivotal politics modeling framework. The "something" that depends on the pivots in the theory is the collective choice, that is, the law. The focus of the modeling exercise is to discern which of n legislators or the president is pivotal in various lawmaking situations and why.[3]

Among the n legislators (for convenience, n is odd), two players may have unique pivotal status due to supermajoritarian procedures, even though these players possess no unique parliamentary rights. A third player, the median voter, is also singled out for baseline purposes. These are illustrated in figure 2.2 which shows an eleven-person legislature and a liberal president. The key pivots in the most basic version of the pivotal politics theory are the *filibuster pivot* with ideal point f and the *veto pivot* with ideal point v. These are defined with reference to the president, whose ideal point is p.

If, as shown, the president is on the left (liberal) side of the median voter m, then the veto pivot is the legislator for whom his ideal point and all

---

3.   The present use of the term *pivotal* is narrower than that in many game-theoretic models. For example, in coalition theory a player is sometimes said to be pivotal if his or her departure from a winning coalition renders the coalition nonwinning, in which case every member of a minimum winning coalition is necessarily pivotal. The narrower meaning employed here will become clear as the chapter progresses.

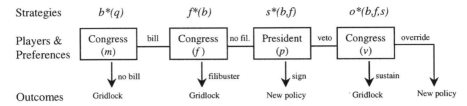

Figure 2.3
The pivotal politics model

ideal points to his right make up exactly or just more than ⅔ of the legislature. The number of ideal points to his left therefore make up no more than ⅓ of the legislature. For the eleven voters in figure 2.2, for example, the veto pivot is the fourth voter from the left. A similar definition can be given for a president on the right (conservative) side of the median voter *m*.

The definition of the filibuster pivot follows a similar fractional algorithm. If the president is on the left (liberal) side of the median voter *m*, then the filibuster pivot is the legislator for whom his ideal point and all ideal points to his left make up exactly or just more than ⅗ of the legislature. The number of ideal points to his right, then, make up no more than ⅖ of the legislature. For the eleven-voter case, this would be the seventh voter from the left, as shown in figure 2.2. If the president were instead on the right (conservative) side of the median voter *m*, then the filibuster pivot will be on the opposite side of the median, likewise splitting ideal points into exact or approximate groups of ⅖ and ⅗.[4]

Sequence of Play

A formal version of the four-stage model is shown in figure 2.3.[5] First, to reflect the strictly accurate procedural fact that it takes only a simple majority to pass a bill in Congress, the median voter of the legislature moves by choosing any bill *b* in the policy space, or by deciding to accept the exogenous status quo point, *q*. Though seemingly dictatorial, this one-player choice is more appropriately interpreted as a strategic simple-majoritarian action by the median voter on behalf of all voters with ideal points to one

4. Operationally these fractions are sometimes ⅓ and ⅔, depending on the era studied. See Chapter 5.

5. The game is finite and noncooperative with complete information.

side of *m*. This is tantamount to assuming that the legislature decides under an *open rule*. That is, no restrictions are placed on amendments or on who can offer them.[6]

Second, if a bill, *b,* is proposed in stage 1, then the filibuster pivot with ideal point *f* as defined above chooses whether to mount a filibuster, which leads to a status quo outcome, or whether to let the game proceed to the next stage. This one-player choice likewise can be interpreted as a ⅖ minority action even though it is modeled as an individual's strategy.

Third, if the filibuster pivot does not filibuster in stage 2, then the president with ideal point *p* decides whether to sign or to veto the bill. (In reality, this stage may be reached when a filibuster is mounted but cloture is subsequently invoked.)

Fourth, if the president vetoes the bill, then the veto pivot with ideal point *v* decides whether to sustain or to override the president's veto. As with stages 1 and 2, this unilateral action represents the behavior of a bloc of voters with identical preferences with regard to the two surviving policies in question—the bill, *b,* and the status quo, *q.* Thus, the model condenses a large number of individual choices into a tractable but plausible simplifying structure.

Behavior

Players in the game are assumed to adopt strategies that maximize their utility, conditional on the expectation that all other players in future stages of the game do likewise. The equilibrium concept is subgame perfect Nash.[7] In more common terms, the behavior captured by this equilibrium concept can be summarized as strategic proposal, voting, and veto behavior by players in a multistage, interbranch supermajoritarian setting. Players know the game, know each others' preferences, understand who is the pivotal voter in any given setting, and adopt optimal strategies accordingly. More formally, an equilibrium is an optimal bill, *b*,* which is a function of the exogenous status quo, *q,* and which is predicated on rational expectations

6. The amendment and voting processes do not have to be modeled explicitly because the median voter, in effect, always represents at least a majority composed of himself and all the legislators with ideal points to one side of *m*. Because of this feature, it is a misnomer to think of the median voter as an individual "gatekeeper" or "monopoly agenda setter" as in previous theories such as those pertaining to committee power (e.g., Denzau and Mackay 1983). Elaboration follows the introduction of additional features of the model.

7. For a lucid discussion of this concept, see Kreps 1990, 421–25.

about future behavior; an optimal filibuster choice $f\star$ which is a function of b and which is predicated on rational expectations about future behavior; an optimal veto choice $v\star$ which is a function of b and f and which is predicated on rational expectations about future behavior; and an optimal override choice, $o\star$, which is a function of b, f, and v.

Equilibrium and Gridlock

One analytic focal point is on the institutional basis for *gridlock*. To capture not only stalemate in government but also the sense of majority disappointment or injustice that sometimes accompanies it, gridlock is defined as the absence of policy change in equilibrium in spite of the existence of a legislative majority that favors change. In figure 2.3, notice that outcomes labeled *gridlock* are those, and only those, in which a pivotal player chooses the status quo over the proposed policy (or, in the case of stage 1, chooses the status quo directly). Unless the status quo policy exactly equals the median voter's ideal point ($q = m$), a gridlock outcome invariably is an equilibrium outcome, in which at least a legislative majority wishes to move the status quo policy in the same direction, yet cannot do so.[8]

Parties

No special assumptions are made about the ability of political parties to shape individual lawmakers' decisions. This, admittedly, is a judgment that is likely to be controversial. The present aim is not to preempt or stifle controversy but rather to clarify the issue so that neutral readers can form independent judgments after a substantial amount of evidence is presented. Three preliminary observations are relevant in this regard.

First, considerable empirical evidence suggests that parties in government are not strong in the United States. In the prewar period, few works are

---

8. Any such baseline could be used. For example, gridlock could be defined as the absence of policy change in equilibrium in spite of the existence of a *president* who favors change. In support of this definition, one could make a case that, as a representative of the nation as a whole, the president makes for a better *normative* benchmark. My preference is to adopt a plausible *positive* baseline instead—the legislative median—because it underscores the puzzle of gridlock proportional to the degree of merit in the baseline model. It seems unlikely that many students of U.S. politics seriously expect lawmaking outcomes to lie at the president's ideal point. In contrast, empirical support for median voter theory in legislative studies is nontrivial.

as comprehensive and convincing as E. E. Schattschneider's, whose summary is worth quoting at length:

> On difficult questions, usually the most important questions, party lines are apt to break badly, and a straight party vote, aligning one party against the other, is the exception rather than the rule. (1942, 130)
>
> . . . when all is said, it remains true that the roll calls themselves demonstrate that *the parties are unable to hold their lines in a controversial public issue when the pressure is on.*[9]

> The condition described in the foregoing paragraph constitutes *the most important single fact concerning the American parties.* He who knows this fact, and knows nothing else, knows more about American parties than he who knows everything except this fact. (1942, 131–32; italics in original)

In the postwar era, research on party strength in government is mixed by comparison and will be taken up again in Chapters 8 and 9.[10] For now, on the whole, and controversy notwithstanding, suffice it to say that there is no shortage of studies that provide at least a partial defense for the nonpartisan approach taken in the pivotal politics theory.

Second, it bears emphasis that the nonpartisan modeling choice is, at this juncture, a theoretical postulate—not an empirical argument. As such, the proper perspective for neutral readers is the following. If the choice to

---

9. Schattschneider's footnote, which reads as follows, is more forceful, still.

The success of the parties in concealing this condition from the public is remarkable. Yet the testimony of competent scholars is unanimous: "[I]n the main the bills which come up do not interest the party as party" (Chamberlain 1936, 155). "[I]t is impossible to speak realistically of party responsibility for legislation in the United States" (Odegard and Helms 1938, 153). "On the majority of issues the party takes no stand" (Herring 1940, 29). See also Lowell 1901, 319–542. Merriam and Gosnell say that "the bulk of legislation is either non-partisan or bipartisan" (1929, chap. 2n.3, 55). Robert Luce, who has had extensive legislative experience, says that "the great bulk of the work confronting Congress and Legislatures is not essentially political. . . . Party platforms are futilities. No thoughtful legislator feels himself bound by the make-weights thrown in to catch a few stray votes" (1922, 504). Luce quotes Mr. James W. Good, for 10 years chairman of the House Committee on Appropriations, as saying of the work of that committee: "I do not recall now a single instance during my work of the Committee on Appropriations when the party lines were drawn." Merriam and Gosnell estimate that the percentage of party votes in four representative state legislatures ranges from 1 per cent to 6 per cent of the total. "The remaining part of the legislation is local, special or non-partisan in character" (1929, chap. 2n.3, 55).

10. On the strong-party side of the ledger, enter Cox and McCubbins 1993; Rohde 1991; Aldrich 1995; Aldrich and Rohde 1995; Dion and Huber 1996; and Sinclair 1992. On the weak-party side (in varying degrees of explicitness and forcefulness), consider Burns 1963; Clausen 1973; Gross 1953; Huntington 1965; Mayhew 1974; Manley 1970. More recent empirical studies include Schickler and Rich 1997; and Krehbiel 1993, 1995, 1997a.

model lawmaking as a nonpartisan game is flawed, then the data are less likely to corroborate the theory. Judgments regarding this assumption (or nonassumption, more precisely) ought therefore to be suspended.

Finally, in spite of the nonpartisan analytic status of the theory, its assumptions and results are amenable to party-related interpretations, and the model eventually can be used to address party-related empirical questions. For example, under the plausible assumption that Democratic presidents are left-of-center on the liberalism-conservatism spectrum, the theoretical pivots in the pivotal politics theory will be as shown in figure 2.2 during Democratic administrations and mirror images of figure 2.2 during Republication administrations. Likewise, we eventually extract hypotheses about divided versus unified government from the theory even though the individual-level behavioral postulates are invariant to party affiliations and regime type.

RESULTS

Formal theories attempt to elucidate behavior by making explicit behavioral postulates, by stipulating a game form or constraints on behavior, and by deriving equilibrium strategies given the above. The pivotal politics theory adopts this methodological approach and shares the aim of elucidating behavior. Unfortunately, for an audience that may be uncomfortable with or wary of this approach, stating theoretical results (theorems, propositions, etc.) up front in their most general form may obscure as much as elucidate the game's behavioral content. This is not an excuse for refusing to derive and present formal, general results. It is only a defense for a relatively inductive or case-based style of presenting what is ultimately a deductive and general result about pivotal players and lawmaking. The answer to the question "Who is pivotal?" is clear in the theory for any given status quo and configuration of preferences. There are several such situations, however, each of which takes on some distinctive properties. The general statement of the equilibrium of the game, then, can be constructed intelligibly from the ground up with reference to recent instances of pivotal politics.

Case 1: The Economic Stimulus Package and the Filibuster Pivot

The war-room mantra for the Clinton-Gore campaign in 1992 was, "It's the economy, stupid!" Democrats campaigned aggressively and effectively on the assertion that the U.S. economy was in bad shape and that, upon the return to unified government, their party could improve it. In the meantime, Democrats alleged that Republicans "just don't get it," which, evidently, is why Democrats added the fourth word to their mantra.

Not surprisingly, an early legislative strategy in the Clinton administration was to try to capitalize on the confluence of unified government, an electoral mandate, momentum, and a honeymoon by proposing an ambitious set of programs that would infuse federal funds into the economy to jump-start a recovery.[11] The economic stimulus package, as it came to be called, consumed a great deal of the administration's time and effort in the early months. The original bill included high-technology purchases for the federal government, summer jobs for youths and unskilled workers, social programs for the poor, and numerous public works projects aimed at creating jobs and spurring economic development. When bundled together in a supplemental appropriations bill, these goodies came with a price tag of $16.3 billion.[12]

After swift and smooth House passage, the ride got rough for the new administration. A divided vote in the Senate Appropriations Committee was a harbinger for the disagreements on the Senate floor. Surprisingly to some, the first obstacles were put up by Democrats, not Republicans. Fiscal conservatives (and overall moderates) such as David Boren of Oklahoma, John Breaux of Louisiana, and Richard Bryan of Nevada wanted to enact spending cuts elsewhere before appropriating money for the stimulus package. As a compromise, they proposed cutting the cost of the bill in half and coming back to the other half after the normal appropriations process had run its course. Eventually, the three B senators dropped their demands after receiving a letter from Clinton, who pledged to propose spending cuts if Congress failed to meet the deficit reduction targets in the congressional budget resolution. But Republicans were not convinced that a stimulus package was needed, or did not view such pledges as credible, or both. Forty-two of the 43 Republicans signed a letter to Minority Leader Bob Dole promising to initiate a filibuster unless major changes to the bill were made. Several Democrats, too, continued to press for changes, including Dennis DeConcini of Arizona, Herb Kohl of Wisconsin, and Bob Graham of Florida. The threatened filibuster occurred, multiple cloture votes were taken, cloture was not invoked, and, to round up cloture votes and

11.   In retrospect (and as Republicans had claimed during the election), the economy was probably well on the way to recovery even before this initiative was launched. Nonetheless, it was launched.

12.   *Congressional Quarterly Almanac* (1993), 706.

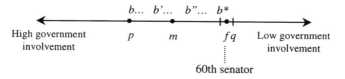

Figure 2.4

f is pivotal on the stimulus package: incremental change

bill support, the bill was eventually diluted nearly beyond recognition. What had been a complex $16 billion omnibus initiative became a simple $4 billion measure to extend unemployment benefits. It passed on a voice vote.

Who was pivotal? The case can be analyzed in the pivotal politics framework to answer this question. As shown on figure 2.4, the standard liberal-conservative spectrum can be given somewhat more precise labels pertaining to the desired level of government involvement in the economy. Liberals tend to favor high involvement (a large cash infusion); conservatives tend to favor low involvement (status quo or lower levels of cash infusion). Notwithstanding his self-proclaimed New Democrat credentials in other spheres, President Clinton clearly lay on the liberal end of this spectrum, and his initial legislative proposal reflected it. Congress, however, does not take-or-leave presidential proposals as offered, and, besides, it quickly became evident that this proposal would have been left behind—not taken—as originally offered. Thus began a long and tortuous process of diluting the bill (*b, b', b''* . . .). The parliamentary device that made such dilution necessary for passage of any package at all was, of course, the filibuster. A credible blocking coalition of 41 or more Republicans and moderate-to-conservative Democrats refused to vote to invoke cloture unless and until the provisions of the bill were sufficiently moderate, relative to the status quo, *q*, that 60 senators preferred the bill to the status quo.[13] In the end, the scope of the package was small. The dramatic "change" that had been promised repeatedly in the election was incremental at best, and the reason it was not larger than incremental is that the supermajoritarian requirement of cloture has the effect of making *f*, the sixtieth percentile senator, pivotal. Given this, the equilibrium legislative proposal is the bill, *b★*, which leaves the filibuster pivot, *f*, indifferent between the status

13. Technically, the sixtieth senator, who is pivotal, needs only to be indifferent between the status quo and the bill.

quo, q, and the bill, $b^\star$. Given such a bill, cloture is invoked (or the filibuster is called off because the obstructionists know their blocking coalition has been eroded), the bill is passed (by a bipartisan supermajority), and the president signs the bill (even though its content is a far cry from the initial proposal and even a substantial cry from what the median voter in the Congress wanted). In short, while this is not a case of gridlock in the sense of complete policy stalemate, it is a case of incremental change and disillusionment by moderates, attributable to supermajoritarian procedures.

Case 2: Family Leave and the Veto Pivot

As early as 1985, Democrats in Congress argued that the United States was alone among industrial nations in its failure to guarantee parents leaves of absence from their jobs in order to care for their newborns. From the mid-1980s and into the 1990s, however, Republican presidents, backed by small-business interests, argued that mandated family leave would undermine companies' competitiveness by disrupting their day-to-day operations. In the early years of this dispute, Congress threatened to act, or did act, on family leave legislation, only to see their efforts fail to come to fruition. In 1986 and 1987, for example, family leave legislation did not make it to the floor, although there was some committee activity. In 1988 and 1989, a wider assortment of committees took favorable action on family leave, but the bill languished in the Senate because of filibusters and Senate Majority Leader George Mitchell's inability to muster the requisite 60 votes to invoke cloture.

By 1990 and 1991, congressional support for the idea of family leave had increased. A key development was that moderate Republicans, such as Labor Secretary Lynn Martin and Representative Marge Roukema of New Jersey, came on board and became more assertive in giving the cause a bipartisan voice. Bipartisanship was also facilitated by the growing affinity of Republicans for family values and by considerable weakening of the family leave bill over the years. As a result, proponents obtained greater than simple-majority support in both chambers in 1991. In the Senate, Republican Kit Bond of Missouri proposed a substitute bill to the Democrats' stronger version; the substitute passed 65–32. The House then passed the bill 253–177. In spite of these seemingly comfortable majority margins, however, the bill languished in conference committee in 1991 because the vote margins were not comfortable *supermajority* margins. President Bush

was clearly opposed even to the weakened legislation, so congressional leaders opted not to force Bush's hand, which had a firm grip on a veto pen.

In 1992 the conferees met and weakened further their version the provisions of the family leave bill.[14] The aims were twofold: obviously, to attract
still broader support; less obviously (perhaps), to embarrass the reelection-
seeking president for being on the minority side of what was widely perceived as a majoritarian cause. So, on the eve of the Republican National
Convention, the Senate passed the conference report on the bill by a voice
vote.[15] Since 65 senators had earlier voted for a stronger bill, a veto-proof
majority seemed within reach. (Three of the senators who missed the earlier
vote had since voiced support for the bill.) In the House, however, support
seemed to be waning by the time the Congress reconvened after the convention. On September 10, the House voted 241–161 to pass the conference report—about 50 votes short of that required to override Bush's certain veto.[16]

The veto occurred on September 22. The resulting preelection rhetoric
was predictably intense, and the Senate, after four years and 32 vetoes from
Bush, finally overrode the president 68–31. House proponents, however,
fared less well, falling 27 votes short of the $2/3$ mark. Thus, the status quo
(and gridlock) prevailed once again.

Who was pivotal? The $2/3$ voter in the House, or veto pivot v, as illustrated in figure 2.5. Similar to the case of the economic stimulus package,
the history is one of fluid proposals, not take-it-or-leave-it agenda setting.
Bill proponents often start with strong proposals to sharpen attention on
the issues, float trial balloons, or mobilize support among more ideological
legislators. Sequential proposals of this sort are not explicitly captured in
the pivotal politics theory. What the theory does say, however, is that given
a status quo point and a profile of preferences such as those in figure 2.5,
the veto-pivotal voter with ideal point v must be made to favor the bill or

14. Exempted now were also the highest-paid 10 percent of companies' work forces. Eligibility
was further restricted to employees who had worked at least 25 hours per week for the previous
12 months. As testimony to the weakness of the bill as well as Democratic frustrations regarding
its dilution, House Speaker Tom Foley said, "This is not a generous bill. It would not require even
one day of paid leave" (*Congressional Quarterly Almanac* [992], 55). (The bill would require only
unpaid leave.)

15. Senator Christopher Dodd of Connecticut had sought a roll call vote, but Republican leaders
objected and threatened delaying tactics that would have resulted in passage only after the convention recess.

16. Still, the bill had attracted 37 GOP supporters, adding credibility to supporters' claims that
it was a bipartisan coalition.

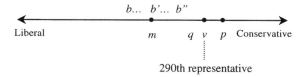

Figure 2.5
v is pivotal on the family leave bill: gridlock

to be indifferent between the bill and the status quo for a new law to be passed. When this is not possible—as was the case in 1992 on the family leave bill and with the status quo, *q*—gridlock occurs.

In brief, the ²/₃ override provision in the Constitution makes lawmaking difficult whenever the president opposes policy changes that congressional majorities favor. In this sense, the pivotal politics theory captures the central tendency to gridlock in U.S. lawmaking.[17]

Case 3: Family Leave and the Filibuster Pivot

Family leave was a salient election issue during the presidential campaign of 1992. On the campaign trail, Al Gore spoke often of his ability to take time off from the Senate to be with his son who was critically ill after being struck by a car. After the election, the new 103d Congress acted quickly on the new family leave bill. HR 1 passed the House 265–163 on February 3, 1993. The next day the Senate passed its own version 71–27, which the House subsequently accepted 247–152.

Although these vote margins were similar to those of the previous Congress, one thing was much different: the new president favored the bill, so a ²/₃ congressional majority was no longer required. Furthermore, although a ³/₅ majority was still required to overcome a possible filibuster in the Senate, this was not a problem insofar as the Senate had crossed that threshold in the previous year. So, on February 5—after approximately eight years of legislative efforts—the family leave bill was signed into law. At last, gridlock was broken.

17. While this may seem to occur due to the presence of divided government (e.g., during the Bush administration), we saw above and will see again below that unified-government gridlock is also common in the theory.

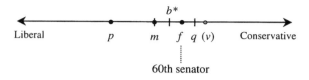

Figure 2.6
f is pivotal on the family leave bill: gridlock is broken

Who was pivotal? The situation is illustrated in figure 2.6. The old veto pivot *v* is unimportant in light of the new president, *p*, who prefers any plausible leftward change in policy. Large leftward changes are still not possible, however, because of the filibuster threat. Therefore the bill, *b**, represents the optimal legislation given the ³⁄₅ senator's pivotal status. It leaves the filibuster pivot, *f*, indifferent between the bill and the right-of-center status quo.[18]

Generalization of Cases: Conditions for Gridlock and Change

The three examples provide hints of hope with regard to the basic needs of a good theory of lawmaking as discussed in Chapter 1. Gridlock happens often but not always. Coalitions are typically bipartisan and significantly larger than simple-majority size. What remains is to illustrate the result of the pivotal politics theory more generally, to explore more precisely the analytic conditions under which gridlock is broken, and to clarify the reasons supermajoritarian coalitions almost always form.

Figure 2.7 graphs equilibrium outcomes and emphasizes that the behavior within the theory is dependent not only on the configuration of pivotal players (*f*, *p*, or *v*) but also on the location of the status quo point, *q*. The horizontal axis fixes players' ideal points: the liberal filibuster pivot, *f*, the median voter, *m*, the veto pivot, *v*, and the conservative president, *p*. We can interpret the situation either as unified Republican government or divided government with a Republican president. The vertical axis represents

18.   In practice, the bill that passed was probably right of *b** as indicated by the 71 votes it attracted in the Senate. An outside-the-model rationalization of this fact is that Democrats did not want to push their luck by proposing a more liberal bill than passed but was vetoed during the 102d Congress. An inside-the-model rationalization is that *f* represents not just a single voter but a faction of 11 or more voters with identical preferences on this issue. In either case, the qualitative features of the model are well illustrated by the case.

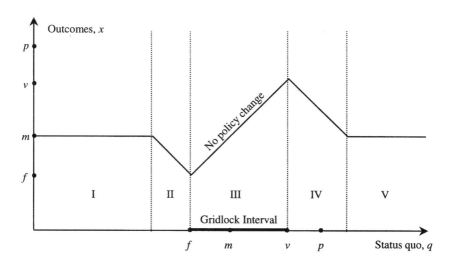

Figure 2.7
Equilibrium policies in the pivotal politics theory

equilibrium outcomes, $x^\star$, that correspond with any permissible status quo point, q, along the horizontal axis.

The primary substantive and analytical concerns are as follows. For any given status quo point, q, what legislative and executive behavior occurs in equilibrium? When equilibrium strategies are played, what is the resulting policy outcome, and why? When and why does gridlock occur? When gridlock does not occur, how large are winning coalitions? Elsewhere the game is presented formally, including a statement of the proposition summarized in figure 2.7 and proofs for this and other propositions (Krehbiel 1996a). The discussion here emphasizes the behavioral intuition captured in the game.

The behavior that generates outcomes is best understood through piecemeal discussion of five intervals in which the status quo may lie prior to governmental decision making. Any of three things may happen: *full convergence* to the legislative median *m*; *partial convergence* toward the legislative median; or *gridlock*—that is, no change in the status quo in spite of the fact that a majority exists that favors change.

Full Convergence
Full convergence occurs only when the status quo is extreme relative to the ideal points of the president and pivotal legislators. For status quo points

in intervals I or V, the median legislator proposes his ideal point, and this policy is accepted. By construction, intervals I and V denote status quo policies that both the first-stage proposer (the legislative median voter) and the pivotal actors (the filibuster pivot, and the president or the veto pivot) all regard as undesirable relative to the legislative median. The filibuster pivot's equilibrium behavior, then, is not to filibuster. The president's equilibrium behavior, likewise, is not to veto. Consequently, the equilibrium outcome for any q in intervals I or V is the legislative median m. Coalition sizes are much greater than simple majorities in these instances: at least $3/5$ for interval I status quo points, and at least $2/3$ for interval V status quo points.

An important caveat accompanies status quo points in intervals I and V. They would seem to be empirically uncommon. If and when they exist, they are artifacts of a prior round of decision making under evidently vastly different circumstances.[19]

Partial Convergence

Partial convergence toward m occurs when the status quo lies in interval II. The behavioral intuition is as follows. The median voter again would like full convergence, but he knows that if he were to propose his ideal point $b = m$, such a policy would be defeated via filibuster. By construction, interval II consists exclusively of policies that the filibuster pivot and everyone to her left prefers to m. An optimizing median legislator, therefore, tempers (in this setting, liberalizes) his proposed bill, b, to make the filibuster pivot indifferent between b and q. Such a proposal has several noteworthy properties. First, it does not elicit a filibuster. Second, neither does it elicit a veto.[20] Third, since it is signed into law it yields a new policy that is closer to the median voter's ideal point than was the status quo, but not as close

19. Various subtleties can be added. First, one exception to this regularity is annual appropriations for discretionary spending, in which case the status quo is indeed extreme (zero $ appropriations) because of the statutorily defined budget process and its provision for annual appropriations. I revisit this situation in detail in Chapter 9. Second, what else might account for extreme status quo points? Either of two things suffices, but it should be noted that both of these are not captured by the theory (hence, the assumption is that the status quo is exogenous). One possibility is that decision makers acquire new and largely unexpected information about the relationship between existing (status quo) policies and their consequences. Upon learning this, they realize that the status quo is not what they formerly thought, so they act to fix it. A second and analytically identical possibility is that they acquire new information about the preferences of their constituents which, likewise, leads them to believe that the consequences of the status quo are not what they thought.

20. A veto threat is not credible because the president and the veto pivot both prefer b to q.

as the median voter would like. Fourth, the winning coalition is greater than simple-majority size. Finally, this is a spatially symmetric scenario to the second family leave case above. All that has changed is that the relevant filibuster pivot, f, is left-of-center here while she was right-of-center on family leave in the 103d Congress.[21]

Partial convergence also occurs when the status quo lies in interval IV. The behavioral dynamics are comparable to those in interval II, except that now the optimal legislative proposal in the first stage is tempered by the preferences of the veto pivot rather than the filibuster pivot. The first-stage proposer knows that the president will veto a bill that is too liberal if such a veto will be sustained by the veto pivot and all legislators to his right. Thus, the optimal proposal is one that makes the veto pivot indifferent between the bill and the status quo. This proposal elicits no veto precisely because such a veto would be overridden. Again, the winning coalition is much larger than a bare majority.

A proper understanding of this theory in comparison with others rests crucially on several technically fine but substantively major distinctions. When partial convergence occurs in this theory, the temptation is substantial to equate its equilibrium behavior with that in Romer and Rosenthal's seminal agenda setting model (1978). Indeed, both models yield similar and nonobvious comparative statics: the worse is the status quo policy from the first-mover's perspective, the better off is the first mover in equilibrium. Accordingly, it may be tempting to interpret the first mover here as empowered by a restrictive procedure such as monopoly agenda–setting authority and a closed rule on the floor, akin to the single take-it-or-leave-it vote by the electorate in Romer and Rosenthal's theory. Comparative statics aside, however, the present model differs significantly from Romer and Rosenthal's. First, the ostensible agenda setter here is the centrally located median voter (in the legislature); the agenda setter in Romer and Rosenthal's theory is a budget-maximizing preference outlier relative to the median voter (in the electorate). Second, the rule here is open in the sense that amendments may be proposed by any legislator; the rule in the setter model is closed in the sense that amendments are prohibited by all voters in the electorate. Thus, third, the institutional arrangements are such that, in this model, the term *agenda setter* is best not used at all. No legislator in the pivotal politics theory enjoys parliamentary rights that exceed those

---

21.   This may be a literal "she." By some accounts and on some issues, the filibuster pivot in the 103d Congress was Senator Nancy Kassebaum, a Republican from Kansas.

of any other legislator. Anyone may propose; anyone may filibuster; anyone may vote to invoke cloture or to override a presidential veto.[22]

Gridlock

Finally, no convergence occurs in the theory for centrally located status quo points, namely, those in interval III. For any left-of-center status quo in this interval, a moderate-to-conservative legislative majority would like to pass a more conservative policy. It cannot do so, however, because such a proposal would be killed by a liberal filibuster. Analogously, for any right-of-center status quo in this interval, a moderate-to-liberal legislative majority would like to pass a more liberal policy. It cannot do so, however, because such a proposal would be vetoed, and the veto would be sustained.[23] The behavioral intuition in these situations is consistent with many popular complaints about gridlock during the Reagan-Bush years. Notwithstanding the existence of Democratic or democratic majorities favoring change, change often failed to occur. Furthermore, when gridlock was alleged, much more often than not the fingers of blame pointed to 1600 Pennsylvania Avenue, where the chief resident had an abundant supply of veto pens. Clearly, this was the case on family leave prior to 1992. Finally, notice that within the gridlock interval *losing* coalitions are typically *larger* than bare-majority sized—a fact that contributes to frustration with, and caustic rhetoric about, gridlock.

Summary

When status quo policies are moderate, cloture and veto procedures prohibit further convergence to centrally located policies. Because superma-

---

22. Similar comparisons can be made between the pivotal politics theory and the class of stability-inducing theories discussed in Chapter 1. There is no question that the pivotal politics theory, like stability-inducing theories, embodies institutional features (senatorial cloture and the presidential veto) and yields stable outcomes. Nor is there any claim that the pivotal politics theory constitutes a bold new step in formal modeling; on the contrary, the theory is elementary by contemporary standards. Nonetheless, there are noteworthy substantive differences between the two types of models that, while subtle, seem not to be mere instances of hair splitting. First, notice that if the filibuster and the veto procedures are taken out of the model, a stable median legislator outcome occurs. Therefore, the institutional features in pivotal politics theory are not needed to induce stability, so it would seem somewhat odd to call such features "stability-inducing." Second, the institutional features in pivotal politics theory do not grant special parliamentary rights to any specific legislators as stability-inducing theories do. If a player is pivotal in pivotal politics theory, her pivotal status is jointly due to the location of the status quo and her position in the ordering of ideal points— not to an ad hoc designation as a gatekeeper or a veto player as is customary in stability-inducing theories.

23. Alternatively, it could be killed by a *president-side filibuster*. This is not modeled presently because the veto pivot or president (the closer to m) is the real constraint. However, president-side filibusters resurface in Chapter 5.

joritarian procedures have antimajoritarian consequences in this fashion, it is hardly surprising that the term *gridlock* is often uttered with disdain. Nor is it surprising that gridlock is often casually associated with divided government. Realize, however, that the proposition on which figure 2.7 is based is invariant to the type of governmental regime. Because legislators in this theory act not as partisan loyalists seeking a larger collective aim but rather as individual utility maximizers, it makes no analytic difference whether government is unified or divided. Gridlock occurs, and occurs often, in either case. And when gridlock does not occur, winning coalitions are large because of the omnipresence of supermajority pivots.[24]

INTERPRETATIONS

Interpreted more broadly, the pivotal politics theory not only meets the bare-necessities standard pertaining to gridlock and coalition sizes, but it also adds some insights into other observations and anomalies prevalent in prior research on lawmaking. These include gridlock in unified government, presidential honeymoons, patterns of policy initiatives, and trends in presidential popularity.

Gridlock in Unified Government

In their rapid reactions to the election of Bill Clinton in 1992, journalists such as Richard Cohen hailed the new regime as a "dramatic shift from a divided government stuck in neutral to one in which a single party was operating the vehicle and had well-defined goals" (Cohen 1994, 2). In their rapid reactions to the first half of Clinton's term, however, editorial assessments even of friendly newspapers were much different. *The New York Times* put it this way: "Bill Clinton and the Democrats have failed to persuade the American people that they *[sic]* can govern as a party . . . even when [the majority party] has the keys to the Capitol and the White House." *The Washington Post* concurred: "It's back to gridlock . . . of a nasty internecine kind that makes the Bush administration seem like a checkers game by comparison." Even the public seemed to agree, with only 19 percent of respondents saying that Congress accomplished more

24. The examples in this chapter have assumed that the president's ideal point is exterior to the interval (f, v). In a more general version, the gridlock interval is defined by $(f, \min[v, p])$ for $p > m$, or by $(\max[v, p], f)$ for $p < m$. A still more complex version can allow for a president whose ideal point is more moderate than the "president-side" filibuster pivot (see n.23), however this complexity seems unneeded for the most part.

than it does in a typical two-year period and 52 percent saying it accomplished less.[25] Should this turnabout be surprising? A closer look of the pivotal politics theory suggests that it should not, and thus helps to explain the puzzle of gridlock in unified government.

The theory clarifies the central role the status quo plays in identifying conditions for policy change in a separation-of-powers system, but it can be criticized for two related reasons. First, the status quo is an exogenous parameter in the theory. Second, the theory is multistage but not repeated, thus it is essentially static.[26] How does the substantive conclusion about the probable pervasiveness of gridlock change in a more dynamic setting? For example, is it empirically possible and analytically demonstrable that when divided government gives way to unified government—or, when regimes abruptly switch as in 1992—the ostensibly rare conditions for breaking gridlock are nevertheless met?

To answer these questions and to try to shed more light on the contemporary political scene, we can conduct a simple experiment in which recent U.S. political history is viewed through the lense of the pivotal politics theory. This approach is quasi-dynamic.[27] Specifically, we begin by considering the Carter administration (unified government, left-of-center president). For reasons that will eventually become clear, we initially place no constraints on the location of status quo policies along the liberal-conservative spectrum. Then, under historically defensible suppositions about how preferences and unified/divided government regimes changed up until the Clinton administration, we identify equilibrium changes in policy over time. In other words, after an unconstrained start, status quo points are generated endogenously by replaying the static game under new parametric assumptions that represent what empirically were dynamic changes. The objective is to obtain a better sense of the real-world likelihood of breaking gridlock by thinking through the prior generation of otherwise exogenous status quo points.

25. This paragraph is extracted from the introduction of Mayhew 1995, whose essay provides a much more systematic set of observations that comport with these summary statements. The remainder of the section is extracted from Krehbiel 1996a which was written prior to Mayhew's essay and, indeed, early in the Clinton administration.

26. See Baron 1994 for a truly dynamic theory with convergence properties very similar to the pivotal politics theory (albeit with restrictive procedures and without supermajoritarian pivots).

27. More precisely, it is a repeated application of a static model, not a fully dynamic model. A behavioral defense for this approach is that legislators have short time horizons. An analytic defense is that dynamic theories are more complex and are plagued by multiplicity of equilibria (see Baron and Ferejohn 1989).

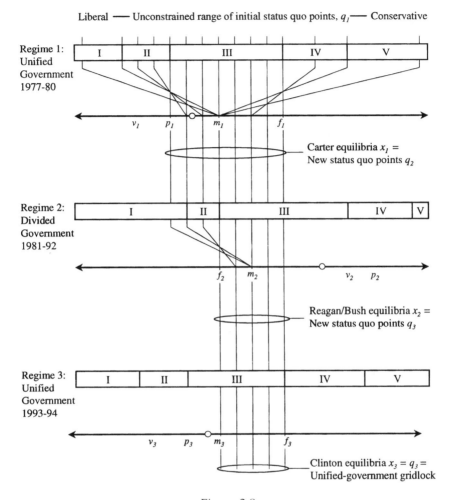

Figure 2.8
Quasi-dynamic properties of the theory

Regime 1

Jimmy Carter was elected in 1976. Along with 292 House Democrats plus enough Senate Democrats to give his party a 61–38 majority in the upper chamber,[28] Carter ushered in the first era of unified government since 1968.

Figure 2.8 represents major regime shifts over the subsequent two de-

28.   Senator Harry Byrd from Virginia was an independent.

cades. The initial question is how much the hypothetical unrestricted initial distribution of status quo points q_1 for regime 1 will converge to more moderate policies after just one play of the game for any possible q. The five-interval equilibrium to the game provides the answer. The vertical lines in figure 2.8 represent policy trajectories that pass through specific intervals which, in effect, embody equilibrium behavior that stipulates whether and how policies change. Thus, all interval I status quo policies ($q < 2p_1 - m_1$) converge to the median m_1. Interval II status quo policies map into outcomes between Carter's ideal point p_1 and the legislative median m_1. Interval III is the gridlock interval where, by definition, policies remain unchanged and thus drop straight down. Interval IV consists of status quo points for which the filibuster constrains convergence to the median. And interval V status quos again converge fully to the legislative median.

Upon the occurrence of these events, all new policies x_1, plus old unchanged policies $q_1 = x_1$, become stable. Indeed, as noted above, gridlock in this theory is an inevitable feature of *any* administration that, with the Congress, has made one pass at the major issues of its term. The exercise also yields refined if not alternative interpretations of so-called presidential honeymoons and presidential success. Depending on starting conditions (more below), an administration may indeed be characterized by a flurry of initial and ostensibly successful legislative activity. The prediction of this theory is that such activity inevitably drops off soon. While the drop-off makes the prior activity appear as if it were a honeymoon, the successful passage of legislation in this model is not generated by those forces identified elsewhere in the literature as central to presidential power: for example, presidential popularity (Rivers and Rose 1985), prestige (Neustadt 1960), going public (Kernell 1986), persuasion (Neustadt 1960), or signaling (Matthews 1989; McCarty 1997). Rather, it is a more straightforward consequence of old policies being out of equilibrium given new preferences. Similarly, so-called presidential success in the present context means only the passage of new policies—not the passage of changes that represent closely the new president's preferences. Often new policies will have diverged widely from the president's ideal point in order to obtain passage, in which case the success is deceptive. For example, in figure 2.8, suppose the status quo is $q_1 = 2p_1 - m_1$ (on the boundary of I and II). Given equilibrium behavior, this "success" moves policy to m_1, and is indeed a case of gridlock being broken. Notice, however, that this "successful" president is indifferent between the old and new policies. In short, ostensible honeymoons in this theory are artifacts of congressional preferences—not instances of congressional deference toward the president.

Regime 2

Shown in the middle of figure 2.8, the Reagan-Bush years marked a change not only to divided government ($p_2 > m_2$) but also to a more conservative Congress ($m_2 > m_1$). Now the theory can be applied to the divided-government Reagan-Bush years.[29] In conjunction with the Carter regime of unified government, the Reagan-Bush regime of divided government yields a prediction about whether, which, and how the policy remnants of the Carter years will change.

Carter equilibria x_1 become Reagan-Bush status quo points q_2. The rightward shift of preferences plus the change to divided government also causes the spatial locations of the behavior-determining intervals to change. Some regime 2 status quo policies ($q_2 = x_1$) are much more liberal than the 1980s median legislator ($q_2 < 2f_2 - m_2 < m_2$) and are thus in interval I. For reasons described above, these status quos converge fully to the new legislative median under divided government. Somewhat less liberal status quos lie in the relatively narrow interval II. Here the left-of-center filibuster pivot (in all likelihood a Democrat) dampens the convergence toward the legislative median. Policy changes, but only incrementally. All remaining endogenously generated status quo policies are in interval III, which is the gridlock interval for divided government. Here the vertical lines drop straight down, signifying no policy change and thus status quos that will be inherited by the next administration. Finally, theoretical behavior for status quo points in IV and V is therefore empirically nonexistent given the brief period of prior history in the exercise.

Regime 3

After a status-quo-unconstrained start and only one regime change, the interval of history-based and theory-consistent status quos has contracted substantially. The funneling effect of liberal policies toward the regime 2 median creates Reagan-Bush outcomes x_2 which serve as status quo points q_3 for Clinton. These are located at or near the 1980s congressional median

29. Insofar as Republicans captured the Senate in 1980, some readers may question use of the term *divided government* through 1986 when the Democrats regained control. Few would question that Reagan was more conservative than the congressional median, though. Analytically $p > m$ is all that matters—not the label for the case in which $p > m$. Similarly, the magnitude of the rightward shift in medians is not important; only the direction is.

m_2. Given the regime shift in preferences as a consequence of the 1992 election (and, in the case of the Senate, the secular loss of seats throughout the 1990s), the new median m_3 becomes more liberal than the old median m_2. Furthermore, we assume that the Clinton-regime filibuster pivot f_3 is the same as that during the Carter-regime f_1.[30]

Piecing these observations and assumptions together, this application of the theory broadly predicts what is appropriately termed *unified-government gridlock*. All history-based status quo points lie in the unified-government gridlock interval III (p_3, f_3), thus no new policies are to be expected.[31]

What actually happened? As always, assessments are somewhat mixed. On the positive/high-productivity side of the argument are researchers who stress that President Clinton received historically high levels of individual-vote-based congressional support and who argue that when the president announced a position on a roll call vote, his position commanded a majority of votes.[32] The methodological limitations of such analyses are significant, though, and, in any event, these assessments are distinctly in the minority. On the negative/low-productivity side of the argument are observers from a broad spectrum of professions and employers. A more typical sample of wrap-ups follows.

> The 103d Congress was going to be different. With one party in control of the Senate, the House, and the White House for the first time in 12 years, and a large freshman class eager to prove that Congress can get things done, it was supposed to be the end of gridlock. But barring a quick burst of activity, it will not be so. (*New York Times* op-ed, "Before Congress Quits," September 20, 1994)

30.   Altering the location of f_3 either strengthens the conclusion to which we are working or leaves it unchanged.

31.   The broad-brush prediction of unified gridlock stands in stark contrast with the empirical implication of the balancing theory, which is approximated by the hollow dots in figure 2.8. The antithesis of gridlock, of course, is immediate and nonincremental change in policy associated with any and all exogenous changes in congressional-median and presidential preferences. This is exactly what Alesina et al.'s balancing theory implicitly assumes: left-of-center policies under Carter, abruptly right-of-center policies under Reagan-Bush, and abruptly left-of-center policies again under Clinton. If anything, this interpretation of the balancing theory is charitable. A more literal interpretation is that policies would change at every election—not just upon switching regimes between divided and unified government. For example, to the extent that Bush was more liberal than Reagan, the balancing theory also predicts a leftward shift in policy within regime 2 in figure 2.8.

32.   See Bond and Fleisher 1995 for a first-year assessment of Clinton and Congress that uses president's position data. See Bond and Fleisher 1993 for a "congressional support" argument in an unusually upbeat essay whose title tells all: "Clinton and Congress: End of Gridlock."

The 103d Congress that began by boasting that it would break gridlock is coming to an end mired in it. (*Wall Street Journal* op-ed, "Glorious Gridlock," October 4, 1994)

With a Democrat in the White House and with Democrats firmly in control
of Congress, government gridlock would end. The executive and legislative
branches would work together, with a minimum of rancor. That was the prediction. That hasn't been reality. (*National Journal* cutline for Richard E. Cohen's
"Some Unity!" September 25, 1993, 2290)

Finally, what about the constitutional and weak-party mechanics underlying the modal assessment of the 103d Congress and unified government?

Clearly, unified government does not provide the administration with the auto-
matic ability to move its initiatives ahead. . . . The administration will appeal
to party loyalty, but lacking the ability to command it, will engage in the pains-
taking process of assembling majorities, issue by issue, in a Congress whose
members remain willing (often eager) to assert their constitutional powers. Mad-
ison lives! (Rieselbach 1993, 10, 11)

In summary, the exercise in dynamics sheds some light on recent events
and provides clear answers to the two broader questions raised at the beginning of the section. How does the earlier conclusion about the probable
pervasiveness of gridlock change in a more dynamic setting? It is strength-
ened. The dynamic application focuses attention on empirically plausible
status quo points, whereas the general results cover all status quo points.
Regardless of whether the government is unified or divided, the model
exhibits weak dynamic convergence. Any given governmental regime, unified or divided, has only so much to do that is politically feasible. Furthermore, when something can be done—that is, when status quo policies are
not in the gridlock interval—that which is feasible is typically incremental.
Is it, then, empirically possible and analytically demonstrable that, when
divided government gives way to unified government, the ostensibly rare
conditions for breaking gridlock are nevertheless met? Of course it is empirically possible for unified government to break gridlock. Indeed, this had
been the hope and expectation of critics of divided government. This empirical expectation, however, has at best a weak analytic basis within the
present framework, and recent events seem to provide at least a weak form
of support for the theory.

Presidential Honeymoons, Initiatives, Popularity, etc.

The funnel-like form in figure 2.8 has additional interpretations that serve to bring the theory a step or two closer to more conventional studies of the presidency, albeit in a rather loose way. In addition to numerous historical accounts of FDR's Hundred Days, research suggests that newly elected presidents consistently try to exploit their honeymoon period by initiating a burst of significant legislation early in their terms. With reference to the pivotal politics theory, it is easy to see that quick and dramatic starts begin with relatively extreme status quo policies. By definition, these are clearly out of equilibrium with respect to congressional and presidential preferences, many of which changed in the recent election.

But after a brief bout of this legislative version of picking sweet ripe cherries, the prospects for further legislative success become sour. Fewer out-of-equilibrium policies remain uncorrected so, other things being equal, the quantity of executive (and legislative) initiatives decreases. Furthermore, those remaining old policies that are out of equilibrium with respect to current preferences are less badly (distantly) out of equilibrium. Thus, second- and third-wave initiatives that are crafted to win take on a much more incrementalist hue or fail quickly to attract large and enthusiastic supporting coalitions. Moderates in government may continue to plug away at the tortuous process of coalition building, but increasingly they will become frustrated. This is because, even if their coalition is successful, the extent of policy convergence is dampened by supermajority pivots. And, of course, often gridlock will prevail because the requisite supermajority coalition cannot be assembled. Finally, if the rough account provided above is approximately accurate, public reactions to governmental action (or the lack thereof) is also predictable. Like moderates in Congress, the public, too, will become increasingly frustrated at slow, incremental, and often unsuccessful legislative efforts.

At the level of stylized facts, these expectations are reasonably well borne out. Paul Light (1991), for example, has quantified domestic policy initiatives of many postwar presidents, and—as will be shown in more detail in the next chapter—they steadily decline throughout presidents' terms. Hinckley (1990, fig. 6.1), among others, has graphed presidential approval ratings over time and found a similarly robust regularity; they begin high and drop off as the term progresses. Finally—though much more difficult to quantify—there seems to be a biennial wave of congressional retirees, prevalent of which are moderates. While craving more time with their families, moderates are also prone to complaining about the decline of comity in Congress, partisan gridlock, and the general frustration of the daily grind of lawmaking.[33]

CONCLUSION

The theory of pivotal politics identifies a single, conceptually tidy, necessary and sufficient condition for breaking gridlock. Policy change requires that the status quo must lie outside the gridlock interval, as defined by the president, filibuster, and veto pivots in theory and illustrated in figures 2.7 and 2.8 as interval III. Chapter 3, accordingly, operationalizes the width of the gridlock interval and tests the hypothesis that this width is negatively related to legislative productivity.

More generally, from the standpoint of the basic facts identified in Chapter 1, the pivotal politics theory seems promising. It implies that gridlock is common but not constant, and it identifies the condition under which it will be broken. Furthermore, when gridlock is broken, it is broken by large, bipartisan coalitions—not by minimal-majority or homogeneous majority-party coalitions.

The theory has some bonus features as well. Loosely applied, it serves as a rationalizing device for one of the biggest recent surprises in U.S. politics: unified government gridlock. Also loosely applied, it provides a sort of lens through which we can better envision other regularities: honeymoons, fast starts, and eventual fizzles within presidential terms; intraterm decreases in the number of presidential initiatives; declining presidential popularity; and frustrations of moderate legislators.

The remaining concern is whether this rather loose set of arguments-via-anecdotes or carefully selected sets of observations can be tightened. That is, can the pivotal politics theory be used fruitfully not just as a rational-

---

33.   It is probably premature to call this a basic fact. Nevertheless, 1996 seemed to have been an exceptionally good year for moderate burnout. As the list of retiring moderates grew longer and longer, journalists more often than not grieved: "Why couldn't it have been Strom Thurmond?" some asked. See, for example, Lloyd Grove, "The So-Long Senators," *Washington Post,* January 26, 1996, who puts Sam Nunn, Bill Bradley, Nancy Kassebaum, Alan Simpson, and Bill Cohen in the category of frustrated moderates. See, also, David Broder, "The Party's Over," *Washington Post,* August 11, 1996, who mentions all of the above plus John Danforth, George Mitchell, Paul Simon, Gary Hart, and Paul Tsongas. Still other recent senatorial retirees include James Exon, Bennett Johnston, Howell Heflin, and Mark Hatfield. A final add-on is Warren Rudman, who hit the circuit to peddle a book in which the themes of gridlock, bitter partisanship, and burnout are salient.

izing device but as a theory that accounts for variation in more systematically collected data? I address this question in the next four chapters. The data and methodological approach in each chapter have distinctive strengths as well as weaknesses. The intention is to be explicit about both strengths and weaknesses so that readers are ultimately well-equipped to form their own judgments. The questions always to keep in mind have been introduced and illustrated above. Who is pivotal in the theory as it applies to the situation? What are the corresponding empirical expectations? Are the expectations borne out in data?

II

EMPIRICAL
TESTS

THREE

GRIDLOCK

A common assertion of political scientists studying U.S. politics throughout the 1980s and into the early 1990s was that, for better or worse (by which was usually meant, for worse), divided government had become a "stylized fact" of contemporary American political life. The main implication was pithy. Get used to gridlock. Coincidentally or not (probably not), the high point for this perspective coincided almost perfectly with George Bush's stratospheric approval ratings in the wake of the Gulf War in 1991, when journalists and political scientists alike proclaimed that Bush was unbeatable but Congress would nevertheless remain Democratic. The subtext was the same. Get used to gridlock.

What happened next is well known. In 1992 Democrats maintained their majorities in the House and Senate while Democrat Bill Clinton was elected president on a campaign of change. The first noteworthy change was in the subtext of common political discourse. Gridlock will be broken.

Political scientists were neither oblivious to the unexpected turn of events nor rendered speechless on the subject. Divided government, after all, had been merely a stylized fact (now with more emphasis on *stylized* than *fact*). Theories of divided and unified government (now with more emphasis on *unified* than *divided*) may well survive the onslaught of recent events. Indeed, a critical empirical test for the conventional view of divided versus unified government was now at hand. Will the newly elected unified government do what its leaders had promised and what most political scientists had predicted? Will gridlock be broken?

The answers to these questions are subjects of ongoing debate, some portions of which are addressed below. A preliminary task, however, is to break away from the composite and arguably oversimplified account of conventional wisdom and turn to some apparently less conventional views of divided and unified government. These come in two potentially complementary forms: empirical and theoretical. The corresponding focal points of this chapter are evidence (beginning with Mayhew's) and theory (beginning with the theory of pivotal politics). The methodological aim is somewhat daunting: to compress a large quantity of keen intuition about, and thick description of, contemporary U.S. government into a single, parsimonious, and measurable theoretical concept introduced in Chapter 2 as the *width of the gridlock interval*. Measurement and analysis of this concept then provides a preliminary comparative assessment of conventional and unconventional accounts of divided and unified government. The chapter first summarizes the origins of Mayhew's revisionist view about divided and unified government—more specifically, that party control does not much matter in U.S. national politics. It continues with a Mayhew-based but significantly modified empirical analysis, the chief property of which is that measures and interpretations of findings are explicitly formal-theory based. Overall, and with several limitations noted, the analysis provides preliminary support for the theory of pivotal politics.

A REVISIONIST VIEW OF DIVIDED GOVERNMENT AND GRIDLOCK

David Mayhew's *Divided We Govern: Party Control, Lawmaking, and Investigations, 1946–1990* was a splash of cold water on the faces of researchers who subscribed uncritically to conventional views about divided and unified government. Summarized most generally, the focal question of Mayhew's book was: What difference does it make whether the government is unified or divided? By observing systematically investigations of executive misbehavior and lawmaking, Mayhew produced the answer: Not much.

The supporting evidence for the lawmaking component of this claim is systematically summarized in a regression equation that captures predictions about the opposite of gridlock—namely, the number of "important legislative enactments"—as a function of unified versus divided control and a handful of other variables identified by others as potential sources of variation. Table 3.1 is a reproduction of Mayhew's table 7.2. The most striking finding is in the first line. Controlling for other variables, unified and divided governments are essentially indistinguishable from one another in

Table 3.1
Mayhew's Findings

Variables	Estimates
Unified control	−0.59
	(−0.53)
Start of term	3.47
	(3.24)
Activist mood	8.52
	(7.61)
Budgetary situation	0.53
	(0.96)
Constant	7.90
	(7.85)
N	22
Adjusted R^2	.756

SOURCE: Mayhew 1991, table 7.2. OLS estimates with *t*-statistics in parentheses.

terms of their propensities for gridlock or, conversely, for producing important legislative enactments. Although unified government seems to *suppress* legislative productivity, the coefficient is not statistically different from zero.[1]

Depending on one's vantage point, this finding can have disturbing properties. From the vantage point of conventional accounts of U.S. government, the finding is disturbing because it fails to support the theory implicit in most schools of thought about divided government and gridlock.[2] From the vantage points of theorizing and hypothesis testing, the finding is disturbing because it is a null finding that, at the time of its discovery, lacked an explicit theoretical foundation. That is, Mayhew did not propose a theory of divided and unified government that accounts for *variation* in legislative productivity or *degrees* of gridlock. Rather, he measured

1.   The appropriate level of statistical significance is subjective. Accordingly, in presenting quantitative findings, I depart from the convention of singling out with stars and daggers coefficients that meet arbitrary standards of significance. I will, however, consistently present *t*-statistics which enable readers to select and apply whatever standard they deem appropriate. Critical *t*s for a one-tail (two-tail) test are as follows for arbitrary levels: for .10 significance, 1.282 (1.645); for .05 significance, 1.645 (1.960); for .01 significance, 2.326 (2.576). Additionally, *p*-values are often reported (for two-tailed tests unless otherwise noted) in text or footnotes, as well as in tables in which specific hypotheses are tested. The *p*-value is the largest probability at which, given the coefficients and their standard errors, one would fail to reject the specified null hypothesis.

2.   See Fiorina 1996, chapter 6, for a concise and balanced review of pre-Mayhew findings and assertions about the differences between divided and unified government.

and analyzed legislative productivity and discovered that whether the government is divided or not fails to account for variation. This observation is not intended to diminish the importance of Mayhew's finding. On the contrary, his finding serves as an essential empirical foundation on which to build a theory.

Before construction commences, a few additional observations about table 3.1 are in order. Apart from the constant term in the equation, only two statistically significant findings are reported: *start of term,* and *activist mood.* Neither of these were integral parts of what I take to be Mayhew's primary argument, which is that unified versus divided control is mostly inconsequential. Rather, Mayhew included these additional variables to inspect hypotheses about "factors that may help to overcome expected differences between unified and divided party control" (Mayhew 1991, table 7.1).[3] In two of the three attempted sources of "alternative variation," significant effects are identified. The tricky issue is how to interpret them. Matters of interpretation are subjective, so the best we can hope for is a clearly defined subjective stance that is conducive to follow-up analysis. The stance I adopt has two components which are taken up below. First, Mayhew's start-of-term variable, while the product of an inductive search in his analysis, is portrayed in a complementary fashion here as an operational measure of an important exogenous component in the theory of pivotal politics. Second, the activist-mood variable is seen not as irrelevant to or inconsistent with the pivotal politics theory but rather as a relatively distant and crude measure of preferences that can be measured more directly than in Mayhew's analysis.

Start of Term

According to Mayhew, "start of term [represents] the idea that more laws are likely to pass during the first half of a four-year presidential term than during the second half" (1991, 176–77). This is intuitive, but it is necessary to flesh out why. Several related possibilities are available from extant presidency research. One interpretation of the variable is that it measures a

---

3.   Of course, Mayhew (1991) should not be criticized for measuring and testing hypotheses about only three of the 18 factors identified in his table 7.1. Most of the factors originated elsewhere. Many are poorly defined (e.g., "norms," "electoral incentives," "events") and thus not immediately measurable. Finally, even if they were well defined and measurable, using 18 such measures to "explain" his 22 data points would be an achievement of dubious merit. The virtues of parsimony and measurability will be a recurring theme here.

honeymoon period for newly elected presidents. Closely related to this idea is that a president has or claims effectively to have a mandate immediately following his election. A third possibility is based on the empirical regularity that public prestige or presidential popularity are greater at the beginning than at the end of terms. Thus presidents can bargain more effectively with the Congress (Neustadt 1960; Rivers and Rose 1985) or go public with greater success (Kernell 1986) earlier than later in their terms.

Authors of these various accounts of presidential success tend to highlight the many subtle differences between them, and I do not dispute these differences. Nevertheless, an alternative approach to dwelling on differences is to identify a common, underemphasized component in these interpretations. Integral to each such argument is a notion of *preferences*. What is a honeymoon? A period of bliss, harmony, or relative agreement about whatever issues are at hand. Political translation: preference homogeneity. What is a mandate? A claim by newly elected officials that they have heard the voters and intend to implement voters' wishes. Translation: a voter-induced shift in elected officials' preferences. When can bargains be struck, whether by direct executive-legislative bargaining or by going public? When major preference shifts have occurred and/or during periods of relative preference homogeneity. For these reasons, start-of-term can be viewed as a rough proxy measure for election-induced shocks, which theoretically should be associated with increases in legislative productivity.

Additionally, these interpretations and observations suggest an alternative measurement strategy compatible with, but potentially more refined than, Mayhew's: to discern more directly interelection changes in preferences and their homogeneity, and to substitute this measure for the start-of-term dummy variable. This strategy, too, is adopted after inspecting the second of Mayhew's significant predictors of legislative productivity.

Activist Mood

Although Mayhew's start-of-term variable is statistically responsible for about 3.5 major bills per Congress in his analysis, the best predictor by a considerable margin is his variable, activist mood. Mayhew interprets this finding as follows.

> Activist mood, coded so as to make Schlesinger's "public purpose" and Huntington's "creedal passion" eras match as well as they could a sequence of whole

> Congresses, which means 1961 through 1976, works extremely well. All else
> equal, the presence of that mood was worth some 8.5 laws per Congress. Moods
> remain elusive, but this quantitative result accords with the discussion in chapter
> 4: In lawmaking, nothing emerges more clearly from a postwar analysis than
> that something special was going on from the early or mid-1960s through the
> mid-1970s (Mayhew 1991, 177)

What is meant by "works extremely well"? If it means accounts statistically
for variation in the number of major enactments, then the claim is solid.
If, however, it means provides a theoretical understanding about such variation, then there is room for improvement. Needed are clearer conceptions
and better measures of "public purpose" and "creedal passion." Mayhew
notes, "A 'mood' seems to be one of those phenomena that drives political
scientists to despair by being at once important and elusive" (1991, 160), and
he proceeds to make progress toward conceptual clarification throughout
chapter 6. As he notes later, however, moods remain elusive. My aim,
therefore, is to push ahead, conceptually and operationally.

Conceptually, Mayhew's mood variable can be viewed as a proxy measure for preferences.[4] If so, then the claim that his analysis supports is that as
public preferences become more amenable to high degrees of governmental
activity, government will become more active. Simple enough. But what
are the mechanics that occur between cause (public mood as preferences)
and effect (governmental productivity of important enactments)? Presumably, the answer lies in elections, which cause changes in the configurations
of preferences of legislators or presidents. Also simple enough. But to the
extent that a refined measure of shifts in preferences caused by elections is
devised along the lines suggested in the discussion of the start-of-term effect,
only the most amorphous part of the concept remains. What is *mood* apart
from preferences? This is not clear.

An additional source of doubt regarding activist mood is the manner
in which it is measured in Mayhew's analysis: a dummy variable is coded
one only for the years 1961–76. If these are years known a priori to be
years of high government productivity, then this variable seems ad hoc
and/or destined to confirm the moods hypothesis. The operational task
taken up below is to devise and employ alternative measures that capture
better the waxing and waning of activist moods over the course of history

---

4. To the extent that activist moods are manifested in activism—that is, high quantities of visible
political participation—there is also, arguably, a preference intensity component.

in order to assess whether they covary predictably with legislative productivity.

Dependent Variables

The dependent variables in the analysis are all forms of Congress-to-Congress *changes in legislative productivity*. Measurement of legislative productivity is a subject of an ongoing controversy about which a neutral stance is adopted here.[5] To facilitate comparisons with Mayhew's study I begin with a straightforward first-difference measure based on his "two-sweep" measure of "important legislative enactments."[6] From his time series, the change in productivity for Congress t is calculated as the number of major enactments by Congress t minus the number of major enactments in Congress $t - 1$.[7] The resulting variable is called *change in important legislative enactments.*

As a robustness check on the findings of the analyses of the Mayhew-based dependent variable, two additional dependent variables are also analyzed. Because some researchers have criticized Mayhew's measure as being too inclusive or not inclusive enough, the lists on which these alternative measures are based are, respectively, less and more inclusive than Mayhew's list. Both measures are adapted from Cameron and Howell (1996). The first alternative measure is *change in landmark enactments,* where the number of such enactments are defined by Mayhew's sweep 1 but not sweep 2 laws. The second measure is *change in ordinary enactments,* a class that includes all bills found in the summary section of the *Congressional Quarterly Weekly Report.*

Descriptive statistics for these and other measures are presented in table 3.2.

---

5.   See, however, Kelly 1993; Mayhew 1993; and Cameron and Howell 1996.

6.   Mayhew's first sweep is based on contemporary assessments such as journalists' end-of-session summaries. His second sweep is based on retrospective judgments of policy experts. See Mayhew 1991, chapter 4 generally and tables 4.1 and 5.1 specifically. See also Mayhew 1995 for an additional data point for, and excellent essay on, the 103d Congress.

7.   In one respect this alteration is trivial: a set of variables x that explain variation of a dependent variable y can be differenced ($x' = x_t - x_{t-1}$) to explain changes in y ($y' = y_t - y_{t-1}$). The practical reason for forming the problem as one of explaining change in productivity is that in the case of one independent variable (change in the size of the gridlock interval), absolute values (width at time t) are not observable but changes are. See below for details.

Table 3.2

Descriptive Statistics of Variables for Legislative Productivity Analyses

Variable	N	Mean	S.D.	Min.	Max.
Change in significant enactments[a]	23	0.435	5.076	−8.00	10.00
Change in landmark enactments[b]	23	0.174	3.881	−5.00	9.00
Change in ordinary enactments[b]	23	−0.348	33.86	−72.00	79.00
Change in gridlock interval	23	1.466	6.182	−13.31	13.29
First two years of term	23	0.522	0.511	0.00	1.00
Change in activist mood[a]	23	0.000	0.302	−1.00	1.00
Change in domestic policy mood[c]	21	0.510	2.843	−4.08	5.98
Change in tax mood[d]	20	0.000	6.314	−14.00	10.00
Change in government regime	23	0.435	0.562	−1.00	1.00

[a] SOURCE: Mayhew 1991.
[b] SOURCE: Cameron and Howell 1996.
[c] SOURCE: *The Political Methodologist* (newsletter), vol. 6, no. 1.
[d] SOURCE: Niemi, Mueller, and Smith 1989.

Independent Variables

The Gridlock Interval

The pivotal politics theory is preference-driven. Preference changes occur most visibly when the composition of the Congress or the occupant of the White House changes. To test the theory, changes in preferences are assumed to be exogenous and thus are treated as components of the independent variable that is most closely related to the theory, *change in the width of the gridlock interval.* Two types of measurement techniques might be employed to approximate this abstract concept. One measure focuses on inter-election swings as proxy measures of changing preferences as manifested in the composition of the Congress and the presidency. Another focuses on revealed preferences of legislators and presidents during roll call voting and announced positions, respectively. The first, interelection swing method, allows for a closer link to Mayhew's study and requires somewhat less stringent assumptions than the latter, so I presently opt for it. The steps in construction of the measure are as follows. (Raw data are given in table 3.3, and illustrations are given in fig. 3.1.)

1. For each chamber, calculate the net percentage of seats that changed party, scoring net Democratic gains as positive and net Republican gains as negative.

2. For each Congress, compute the average of the two chamber-specific

Table 3.3
Measure of Change in Width of the Gridlock Interval

President	Election	Congress	House[a]	Senate[a]	Average	Change	Measure
Truman	1946	80	−12.87	−13.54	−13.21	Expansion	13.21
Truman	1948	81	17.24	9.38	13.31	Contraction	−13.31
Truman	1950	82	−6.44	−5.21	−5.82	Expansion	5.82
Eisenhower	1952	83	−5.06	−1.04	−3.05	Contraction	−3.05
Eisenhower	1954	84	4.37	2.08	3.23	Expansion	3.23
Eisenhower	1956	85	0.46	1.04	0.75	Expansion	0.75
Eisenhower	1958	86	11.26	15.31	13.29	Expansion	13.29
Kennedy	1960	87	−5.06	−2.00	−3.53	Indeterm.	0.00
Johnson	1962	88	−0.23	3.00	1.39	Contraction	−1.39
Johnson	1964	89	8.51	1.00	4.75	Contraction	−4.75
Johnson	1966	90	−10.80	−4.00	−7.40	Expansion	7.40
Nixon	1968	91	−1.15	−6.00	−3.57	Contraction	−3.57
Nixon	1970	92	2.76	−2.00	0.38	Expansion	0.38
Nixon	1972	93	−2.76	2.00	−0.38	Contraction	−0.38
Ford	1974	94	11.26	4.00	7.63	Expansion	7.63
Carter	1976	95	0.23	0.00	0.11	Contraction	−0.11
Carter	1978	96	−3.45	−3.00	−3.22	Expansion	3.22
Reagan	1980	97	−7.82	−12.00	−9.91	Contraction	−9.91
Reagan	1982	98	5.98	−1.00	2.49	Expansion	2.49
Reagan	1984	99	−3.22	2.00	−0.61	Contraction	−0.61
Reagan	1986	100	1.15	8.00	4.57	Expansion	4.57
Bush	1988	101	0.46	0.00	0.23	Expansion	0.23
Bush	1990	102	2.07	1.00	1.53	Expansion	1.53
Clinton	1992	103	−2.03	0.00	−1.15	Indeterm.	0.00
Clinton	1994	104	−11.95	−8.00	−9.98	Expansion	9.98

[a] SOURCES: Ornstein et al. 1994, table 2.3; Barone and Ujifusa 1995.

values given by step 1. This in effect measures average congressional Democratic swing.[8]

3. With reference to the president and whether he was newly elected, determine *contraction* or *expansion* of the gridlock interval as follows. (Fig. 3.1 illustrates the spatial intuition underlying the measure.)

8. Percentages rather than raw Ns were used in step 1 so that this average assigns equal weights to each chamber.

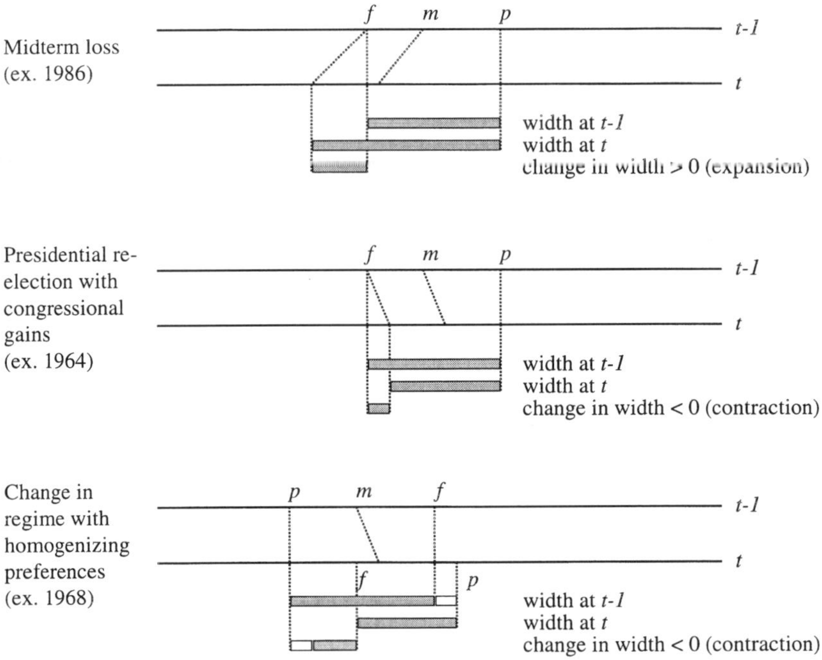

Figure 3.1

Examples of changes in the width of the gridlock interval

a) Midterm elections. By definition, the president does not change, thus a midterm loss for the president implies an expansion of the gridlock interval. The greater is the antipresident congressional swing, the greater is the expansion of the gridlock interval. Spatially, this common scenario is one in which the president's ideal point remains fixed and the congressional median and filibuster pivots' ideal points move away from the president, thus expanding the gridlock interval as shown in the top of figure 3.1.[9]

b) Presidential reelection. The measurement procedure is similar to the

---

9.   Although the theory identifies the more interior of two ideal points (the president's and the veto pivot's) as the boundary of the interval, it is difficult to accommodate this fact into the measure without obscuring the intuition in the stronger assumption that the president is more moderate than the veto pivot (see also n.27 this chap.).

midterm case because again the president's ideal point is presumed to be fixed. Empirically, however, it is common for the president's party to gain congressional seats in such elections. Thus, *contraction* is the usual coding, again proportional to the congressional swing, as shown in the second example.[10]

c) Change in the party of the president. Most elections of presidents from the former out party are also accompanied by congressional gains of the newly elected president's party and are thus homogenizing with respect to politicians' preferences. Accordingly, these are coded as *contractions*.

d) Indeterminacies. The election of Kennedy in 1960 and election of Bill Clinton in 1992 are exceptional in that they coincided with (small) Republican congressional gains. By necessity an ad hoc coding rule is be adopted: to code change in the width of the gridlock interval as zero.[11]

Although the procedure for deriving this measure is not obviously related to prior studies of, or views about, divided and unified government, the measure actually embodies a large component of the multiple interpretations one can give to Mayhew's start-of-term dummy variable. It does so, however, with two noteworthy differences. First, it attempts to capture the magnitude of swings in preferences resulting from presidential and midterm elections. Second, it is closely related to a more parsimonious theory about executive-legislative relations than Mayhew's account. In these respects the measure of change in the width of the gridlock interval is in-

---

10.   Successor presidents—whether elected or not—are treated identically (e.g., Kennedy to Johnson, Nixon to Ford, Reagan to Bush).

11.   The arguments for alternative, contraction codings are as follows. For 1960, a large part of the small swing was undoubtedly a regression-to-the-mean effect attributable to the huge Democratic swing in 1958 which liberalized the Congress considerably. The subsequent election of a Democratic president was probably homogenizing in spite of the small Republican congressional swing, because Kennedy was probably closer to the 1961 median and filibuster pivots than Eisenhower had been to the 1959 pivots. There is no reason, however, why this conjectured contraction should be measured as proportional to the net *Republican* swing. Similarly, in 1992 a homogenizing interpretation can be given to the electoral outcome in spite of small Democratic congressional losses, thereby again rationalizing a contraction coding. Clinton ran as a "New Democrat" which, if true, implies that he was closer to the post-1992 congressional median and filibuster pivots than Bush had been to the pre-1992 pivots. But again, coding a contraction as proportional to the Republican swing seems indefensible. Zero codings are also ad hoc, though, so I ran separate regression analyses for all the tables presented using contraction codings for these two elections. The results were slightly more supportive of the gridlock-interval hypothesis this way, thus the findings reported below are, if anything, conservative with respect to the inferences drawn about the pivotal politics theory.

tended to be a theoretical improvement on, if not an empirical refinement of, Mayhew's start-of-term measure.[12]

Start of Term

As in Mayhew's study, this variable takes on a value of 1 in the first two years following a presidential election and a value of 0 otherwise.

Activist Mood

Following Mayhew, I also estimate the effect of changes in activist moods on legislative productivity. Several measurement strategies are implemented.

The most straightforward measure of *change in activist mood* of the electorate begins with Mayhew's definition (1 for years 1961–76 and 0 otherwise), but postulates that it was not an abrupt and immediately mature mood in 1961 that was constant through 1976, at which point it immediately and utterly died. Instead, the measure assumes an incremental waxing (value of 1) of this mood through the midpoint of the period followed, by a symmetric waning (value of -1) through terminal Congress.

Two additional measurement instruments are based on public opinion data.[13] For much of the World War II postwar period, James Stimson (1991) has assembled survey responses to generate an index called domestic policy mood. It captures at least some of the spirit of Mayhew's discussion of "creedal passion" and "public purpose." The first difference of this variable, that is, *change in domestic policy mood,* is continuous rather than dichotomous and thus may be more closely related to changes in legislative productivity than the dummy-variable moods measure.

Similarly, Niemi, Mueller, and Smith (1989) systematically assemble and present survey data on Americans' attitudes toward taxes. A comparable tax mood variable is constructed in two steps. First, I calculate for each two-year period 100 minus the average percentage of respondents who answered that taxes are too high. The greater is the resulting number, the greater is the fraction of the population that seems not to be strictly opposed

12.   As a validity check on this argument about the close similarity between the two measures, I calculated separate means of the gridlock interval measure for start-of-term and nonstart-of-term Congresses. They were -3.00 and 5.46, respectively. This difference is significant at $p < .001$.

13.   The raw data on which these measures are based were provided by Scott Adler and Charles Cameron.

to a larger tax burden in exchange for more government services.[14] Second, I calculate the first difference of the number, yielding *change in tax mood*.

Governmental Regime

The measure of *change in governmental regime* is the first difference in Mayhew's unified-control dummy variable. It takes on a value of -1 if the government just changed from unified to divided, a value of $+1$ if it changed from divided to unified, and a value of 0 in the case of no change.

HYPOTHESES

The data are used to test three sets of hypotheses:

1. The gridlock-interval hypothesis. Changes in the width of the gridlock interval should be negatively associated with legislative productivity. That is, expansion of the interval impedes legislative productivity while contraction facilitates legislative productivity.
2. Moods hypotheses. (a) Mayhew version: changes in activist moods should be positively related to changes in legislative productivity. (b) Pivotal politics theory version: controlling for width of the gridlock interval, the effect of moods will be negligible.
3. Governmental regime hypotheses. (a) Conventional wisdom version: a change to unified government should facilitate the passage of legislation while divided government should impede it. (b) Pivotal politics theory version: controlling for width of the gridlock interval, the effect of governmental regime on legislative productivity should not be significantly different from zero.

The gridlock-interval hypothesis is of the greatest direct theoretical importance. Not only does it focus attention on the independent variable that is uniquely related to the theory of pivotal politics. It also demands that the theory account for variation in legislative productivity in a predictable way rather than merely rationalize an approximate constant pattern, such as no difference between divided and unified governments (e.g., hypothesis 3b). In this manner, hypothesis 1 sets a higher standard for empirical support than that in studies in which the primary hypothesis is formulated as a null.

The moods hypotheses are of lesser theoretical importance. Although

---

14.   The question allows answers of "too high," "about right," and "too low." At most 2 percent of respondents answered "too low." Thus it seems defensible to portray "about right" respondents as relatively receptive to an increase in taxes, thus governmental activity. Otherwise the variable would exhibit almost no variation.

moods were prominent components of Mayhew's inductive argument, their relationship to existing theories is remote. From the perspective of the pivotal politics theory, moods are not irrelevant but are translated into governmental preferences (exogenous in the theory) via an electoral mechanism. If the concept and measure of the gridlock interval accounts for variation in legislative productivity, it may be traceable to moods external to government, but this is a separate empirical question. Therefore the gridlock interval effect is best seen as proximal and direct, while the mood effect is distal and indirect. Mood measures are nevertheless included in the analysis to check the robustness of Mayhew's finding. One issue is whether moods retain their significance in the presence of the more explicitly theory-based variable, width of the gridlock interval. Another issue is whether the more fine-grained public opinion–based measures explain variation in legislative productivity better than simple dummy variables.

The governmental regime hypothesis, too, is not central to the pivotal politics theory, although it is certainly central to the conventional wisdom surrounding divided and unified government and to Mayhew's revisionist account. Mayhew, of course, found the variable not to be significant in predicting legislative productivity. This is the general expectation of pivotal politics theory, too, provided preferences are adequately measured. I therefore include the change in regime variable to check whether, or the conditions under which, Mayhew's important null finding persists in the presence of the gridlock-interval measure and for alternative dependent variables.

FINDINGS

Changes in legislative productivity of "important enactments" from the 80th through the 103d Congress (1947–94) are plotted in figure 3.2. Considerable variation is evident, including a consistent alternating positive-negative pattern in the first part of the time series. Extreme values of the change in productivity variable provide a useful starting point for the analysis because they comport well with received wisdom. The largest positive change comes in the 87th Congress (1961–62) after the election of John F. Kennedy and a return to unified government. This is consistent with romantic perceptions of Camelot and may be a key source of conventional wisdom regarding unified government and legislative productivity. It also marks the beginning of the "activist mood" period in May-

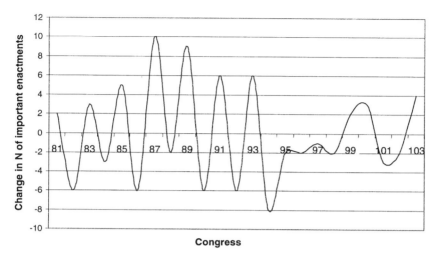

Figure 3.2
The dependent variable

hew's analysis. The largest negative value comes during the Ford years in the 94th Congress (1975–76)—the terminal two years of an eight-year run of divided government. This, too, is broadly consistent with received wisdom.

The main objective is not to generalize from extreme values, however, but rather to identify systematic patterns throughout postwar history. Regression analysis is a convenient method for this search. Table 3.4 begins in the most parsimonious manner possible by looking solely at the effects of the primary variable of pivotal politics theory: change in the width of the gridlock interval. Equation 1 shows that this variable alone accounts for considerable variation in legislative productivity and is statistically significant.[15] As the gridlock interval grows by one unit—which, for example, happens when the president's party loses one Senate seat and 4.35 House

15. The coefficient's p-value is .011, indicating that there is a slightly greater than 1 in 100 chance that the null hypothesis of zero effect is falsely rejected in favor of the gridlock-interval hypothesis. An equation also was estimated using a dummy version of the change variable (one if expansion, zero otherwise), and this effect, too, was negative but of lesser significance ($p = .063$). Together, these findings suggest that not just the direction of change (contraction or expansion) in the gridlock interval matters; so, too, does the magnitude of such change (proportion of congressional seats the president gains or loses).

Table 3.4
Simple Regressions for the Gridlock Hypothesis

	1	2
Change in gridlock interval	−0.466	
	(−2.742)	
First two years of term		7.053
		(4.615)
Constant	0.316	−3.636
	(0.338)	(−3.294)
N observations	23	23
Adjusted R^2	0.229	0.504

NOTE: *t*-statistics in parentheses.

seats—the expectation is that about one-half (.466) fewer major enactments will be adopted in the present Congress than the prior Congress.[16] The substantive significance of this finding can be highlighted quantitatively by asking: What is the expected difference in legislative productivity given the empirical regularities (but not necessities) of homogenizing presidential elections and midterm losses? The sample average change in the width of the gridlock interval for presidential election years is −3.0, while that for midterm years is 5.4. On average, then, a president can expect to produce about four fewer major enactments after the midterm elections than before.[17] This quantified difference is due solely to measured election-based shifts in preferences.

Equation 2 in table 3.4 reports a complementary simple-regression finding: that a start-of-term dummy variable also has a strong effect on changes in legislative productivity. Two somewhat different interpretations can be offered. From a purely empirical perspective, this finding is not at all shocking: this relationship represented by the coefficient is transparent in figure 3.2. Moving toward a more theoretical perspective, however, the finding takes on a potentially deeper meaning. If as (normative) democratic theory tends to suggest (prescribe), quadrennial elections function as regular (and

16.   Regressions using separate House and Senate measures were not conducted because chamber-specific measures of change in width of the gridlock interval are highly collinear (*r* = .81).

17.   The average beginning-of-term productivity gain is −3.0 × −.466 = 1.40 enactments. The average end-of-term productivity loss is −(5.4 × −.466) = 2.52 enactments. These sum to 3.92, or about a four bill end-of-term slump. This is comparable to Mayhew's estimate of a 3.47 bill start-of-term surge.

healthy) shocks to the configurations of induced preferences of elected officials, then this dummy variable inadvertently captures the same set of concerns highlighted by the pivotal politics theory. That is, presidential elections tend empirically to be homogenizing elections (or, arguably, to signify mandates, reregister public attitudes, give rise to honeymoons, etc.); they tend to contract the gridlock interval and thereby lead to predictable increases in legislative productivity.

Perhaps this interpretation of start-of-term imputes too much intelligence onto what is, after all, a dummy variable. Stated differently: Is a deductive/theoretical interpretation of Mayhew's relatively inductive/empirical discovery defensible? That is, does the start-of-term variable fit comfortably under the rubric of preference shocks? I think so, but the issue is subjective. Luckily, some independent evidence can be brought to bear on it. What constitutes evidence of the assertion that preference shocks tend to be greatest at the start of presidential terms? One answer is: presidential initiatives. The connective logic is straightforward. If preference shocks give rise to lawmaking opportunities, if presidents attempt to seize such opportunities by requesting congressional action proportional to preference shocks, and, finally, if start-of-term is a reasonable proxy measure for preference shocks, then we should expect to see a well-defined pattern of presidential requests. Specifically, they should peak early in the term and drop off thereafter.

In a comprehensive study of domestic policy initiatives, Paul Light (1991) has collected the relevant data for a two-decade portion of the postwar period. Though used for entirely different purposes in his study, Light's data are strikingly supportive of the suggested interpretation of start-of-term effects. Figure 3.3 graphs Light's data. Requests are *almost* invariably greatest immediately after a presidential election, and the qualification is an understandable idiosyncrasy. Gerald Ford took over the presidency after a historically unique preference shock, and his proposal behavior reflects his rationally diminished expectations. At the very least, this helps to establish that there might be a relationship between start-of-term and preference shocks, and, thus, a still tighter relationship between Mayhew's analysis and mine. In any event, the start-of-term finding is worth noting if only as a potential link between Mayhew's analysis and the pivotal politics theory.

Table 3.5 reports on a comparable set of simple regressions that isolate the effect of different mood measures on changes in legislative productivity. In equation 1, the Schlesinger/Huntington/Mayhew measure is used, con-

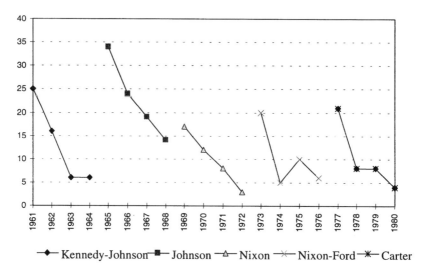

Figure 3.3
Presidents' request behavior

sistent with the notion of cycles of "public purpose"—that is, a waxing and waning of activist mood. Although the coefficient has the predicted sign, it is not significant.[18] In equation 2, Stimson's domestic activist policy mood produces a coefficient that has the wrong sign but is insignificant. In equation 3, the Niemi et al.–based tax mood measure also generates an insignificant result. Overall, the mood hypothesis fails, at least for the time being.[19]

Of course, simple regressions such as these are vulnerable to charges of model misspecification. Table 3.6 therefore presents multivariate regression results that enable the three hypotheses to be tested simultaneously. Three parallel conclusions are evident. First, consistent with prior findings, the gridlock-interval measure consistently yields a statistically significant nega-

18.   An alternative coding of change of mood resulted in a coefficient of greater but still marginal significance ($p = .095$), namely one which, in effect, presumes that the activist mood as defined by Mayhew was switched on in 1961, switched off in 1977, and was constant in the interim. In effect, this is a categorical variable for two Congresses—the 87th which was abnormally productive and the 95th which was average. As such, it seems quite ad hoc.

19.   The reason the activist mood variable was significant in Mayhew's analysis is that he predicted an absolute number of important enactments and coded mood = 1 throughout the bulge of productivity in the middle of the time series.

Table 3.5
Simple Regressions for the Mood Hypothesis

	1	2	3
Change in activist mood	1.680 (0.990)		
Change in domestic policy mood		−0.170 (−0.412)	
Change in tax mood			0.077 (0.387)
Constant	0.117 (0.110)	0.325 (0.279)	0.100 (0.082)
N observations	23	21	21
Adjusted R^2	−0.001	−0.043	−0.047

NOTE: t-statistics in parentheses.

tive coefficient. This reinforces the support for hypothesis 1 and the pivotal politics theory. Second, each of three mood measures revisits Mayhew's argument that "something special was going on" in the 1960s through the mid-1970s. In a key sense this analysis sets a higher standard for his finding that the activist mood variable "works extremely well" (Mayhew 1991, 177). The issue is not whether more major enactments were passed in this period of "public purpose" and "creedal passion" but whether the waxing and waning of these moods correspond with changes in the number of major enactments from Congress to Congress. The answer again seems to be: no. The interpretation, however, should be cautious. The claim is not that normal citizens or even activist citizens' moods (or preferences) do not matter. Rather, it is that they do not matter in an empirically detectable way when more proximal, governmental preferences are taken into account.[20] The findings are thus consistent with the admittedly weak form of the hypothesis (2b) which represents the pivotal politics theory. Third, what is the effect of a change from divided to unified government on legislative productivity? The findings comport perfectly with Mayhew's shockingly unconventional thesis. Whether the government is divided or not fails to make a difference. More precisely, once the gridlock-interval effect

20. Conceptually, a more satisfactory way to explore hypothetical indirect mood effects would be to estimate a structural model in which governmental officials' preferences are endogenous with respect to citizen preferences but then exogenous with respect to legislative productivity. This is beyond the scope of this analysis and, in any event, would require better measures and more than 23 observations.

Table 3.6
Joint Tests of Hypotheses 1–3

	1	2	3
Change in gridlock interval	−0.455	−0.649	−0.456
	(−2.647)	(−3.020)	(−2.438)
Change in activist mood	1.426		
	(0.940)		
Change in domestic policy mood		0.150	
		(0.415)	
Change in tax mood			0.028
			(0.150)
Change in government regime	1.259	2.897	1.002
	(0.731)	(1.542)	(0.479)
Constant	0.317	0.808	0.367
	(0.333)	(0.815)	(0.333)
N observations	23	21	20
Adjusted R^2	0.215	0.262	0.154

NOTE: *t*-statistics in parentheses.

is taken into account, the governmental regime effect is not statistically different from zero. This fails to support hypothesis 3a which represents conventional wisdom, but it is consistent with hypothesis 3b which reflects Mayhew's finding and the pivotal politics theory broadly.

How robust are these findings? Two approaches can be adopted to address this question. One approach is to try to nullify the gridlock-interval finding (or to resuscitate the mood finding or the conventional wisdom about government regime) via indiscriminate expansion of the set of independent variables. Notwithstanding the dubiousness of such exercises, I did some of this and was unable to disconfirm the main findings in tables 3.4–3.6, with one exception. Addition of the start-of-term variable nullifies the gridlock-interval effect, in which case we confront again the puzzle of what the start-of-term effect really means: Honeymoon? Mandate? Proxy for contraction in the gridlock interval? With high multicollinearity between the start-of-term and gridlock-interval variables ($r = .70$), it is not likely that a confident answer can be found.

Another approach is represented in table 3.7 which reestimates the same equations as table 3.6 except using two different dependent variables. As discussed above, a spirited literature has emerged surrounding the issue of what constitutes a major bill. Cameron and Howell (1996) have proposed

Table 3.7
Joint Tests with Alternative Dependent Variables

	Landmark Enactments			Ordinary Enactments		
	1	**2**	**3**	**1**	**2**	**3**
Change in gridlock interval	−0.281	−0.410	−0.279	−2.142	−2.394	−2.101
	(−2.302)	(−2.689)	(−2.170)	(−1.687)	(−1.389)	(−1.560)
Change in activist mood	0.831			6.426		
	(0.769)			(0.573)		
Change in domestic policy mood		0.051			0.725	
		(0.198)			(0.249)	
Change in tax mood			0.093			1.301
			(0.728)			(0.972)
Change in government regime	3.005	4.072	2.717	7.273	10.193	6.827
	(2.448)	(3.053)	(1.894)	(0.571)	(0.676)	(0.454)
Constant	0.244	0.621	0.413	0.869	0.971	1.329
	(0.361)	(0.881)	(0.547)	(0.124)	(0.122)	(0.168)
N observations	23	21	20	23	21	20
Adjusted R^2	0.318	0.361	0.288	0.034	−0.048	0.060

NOTE: Source for dependent variables: Cameron and Howell 1996; *t*-statistics in parentheses.

no fewer than eight alternative measures of enactments, three-fourths of which are major in various ways. In the present context it suffices to employ two of these: their most significant category of "landmark enactments" which is composed of all and only Mayhew's sweep 1 laws,[21] and their second-most inclusive category of "ordinary enactments" which includes all laws mentioned in the *Congressional Quarterly's* summary section. The purpose of equations 1–3 predicting landmark enactments is to provide a robustness check on the pivotal politics theory's ability to account variation in major bills. The purpose of equations 4–6 predicting ordinary enactments is to provide a robustness check on the pivotal politics theory's ability to account for variation in all but trivial legislation.

Again, three sets of findings parallel the three main hypotheses. The gridlock hypothesis continues to be supported, albeit with a qualification. The qualification is that in regressions focusing on ordinary enactments the coefficients, while of the right sign, are insignificant.[22] The strong form of

21. See Kelly (1993) for an argument that this is a better list than Mayhew's "important enactments," and see Mayhew (1993) for an argument that it is not.

22. Their *p*-values range from .113 to .193.

the mood hypothesis continues to be lacking in support no matter what the dependent variable. And most interesting, the conventional wisdom form of the governmental regime hypothesis comes to life in two or three of the six equations.[23] A change from divided to unified government is associated with three or four more landmark enactments, controlling for the gridlock-interval effect. With a mean of about nine such bills over the time series, this effect seems substantively, as well as statistically, significant.[24]

What might account for this breath of life for the conventional wisdom? I am not prepared to say, but I can offer a conjecture for future study. With minor exceptions, the only difference between Mayhew's important enactments and Cameron and Howell's landmark enactments is the inclusion in Mayhew's list of sweep 2 bills, which includes policy experts' retrospective judgments about important bills. (Sweep 2 bills are excluded Cameron and Howell's landmark enactments.) For the sake of argument, suppose there were a government-activism bias in journalists' year-end summaries of major legislation[25] and that such legislation is passed disproportionately during unified Democratic governments in the time series.[26] Suppose further that sweep 2 policy experts' lists counterbalance this bias because, for whatever reasons, they are inclined to see, say, deregulation legislation as equally significant as regulatory legislation. Then, by excluding sweep 2 bills, Cameron and Howell's list will have inflated legislative productivity under unified governments, and the positive effect in table 3.6 is an artifact of activism bias in the press. For immediate purposes, it matters little whether this speculation about measures has merit. Even in the best of circumstances, these data are soft, and the number of observations is small. That any robust findings at all have emerged is somewhat of a surprise.

Overall, the findings are sufficient for drawing three conclusions. First, the pivotal politics theory can consistently account for variation in legislative productivity in classes of important and landmark laws, though it fares somewhat less well within the broader class of ordinary laws. Second, public

---

23. The *p*-value for change in governmental regime in equation (3) is .076.

24. A fourth finding concerns the constant term in all the equations, which is not statistically distinguishable from zero. Although this is a null result, it is of some substantive interest, for it indicates that there is no secular trend in the production of major enactments, for example, due to economic growth, societal complexity, or increasing scope of government.

25. See, for example, Mayhew's discussion on journalists' "scripts" (e.g., Mayhew 1991, 90).

26. The sole case of unified Republican government in the time series was the 83d Congress (under Eisenhower).

moods are at best distant causes of legislative productivity across all classes of laws analyzed. Third, predictable and significant government-regime effects are rare but not nonexistent.

CAVEATS AND CONCLUSIONS

In any empirical analysis of this sort, there are soft spots. Accordingly, with two objectives in mind, known caveats are highlighted at the end of Chapters 3–9 in addition to drawing some suitably qualified conclusions. An immediate objective is to inform readers of weaknesses as well as strengths so that they can reach balanced assessments of the findings. A longer-term objective is to encourage researchers to seek improvements in measures and methods that eventually will lead to more convincing findings.

The most significant limitation of the analysis in this chapter is that, in general, it asks a lot from a small number of observations and a diverse set of measures. Any such measure can be picked to bits. Specifically, on the left-hand side of the equation, the measures of legislative productivity were known to be controversial even prior to undertaking this project. Nothing new has been added to this debate. On the right-hand side, the central and comparably questionable measure is the new variable, width of the gridlock interval. This measure has the main advantage of parsimoniously capturing the essence of pivotal politics theory, but it has several drawbacks as well. First, it implicitly assumes that the party affiliation of a legislator is a proxy for his or her preferences. In isolation, this assumption seems plausible enough. In the application, however, one might question whether a test of a nonpartisan theory should use partisan information in this manner. Second, the measure treats the House and Senate more or less identically even though the Senate but not the House has a supermajority cloture provision. Chamber-specific measures could have been developed, but this would have come at the cost of introducing multicollinearity and losing another degree of freedom in the low-N regressions. Third, the measure does not attempt to measure the president's preferences. This can be rationalized most simply assuming that the president's ideal point is exterior to the legislative pivots, v and f, which, in its most straightforward defense, is what the measure does.[27] But then this assumption, too, can be questioned.

---

27. An alternative but more complex justification for the measure also can be given based on weaker assumptions about the president. It allows the president's ideal point to shift probabilistically between designated intervals of the policy space. Because ultimately it leads to the same destination—the measure as used here—I state only the simpler (but stronger) assumption here.

In short, there are no free lunches, but there are undoubtedly alternative approaches with plausible defenses.[28]

A broad substantive aim of this chapter was to explore the relationship, if any, between divided government and gridlock. As recently as 1990 the *if any* clause would have been viewed as a straw man, propped up only to knock down en route to an obvious alternative hypothesis: that divided government is a leading cause of gridlock. Beginning with Mayhew's seminal book a year later, however, the possibility that there is no relationship between divided government and gridlock has evolved into a straw man to be reckoned with. In Mayhew's book, as here, the central finding is: controlling for other factors, divided and unified governments are usually not significantly different in terms of their ability to produce major legislative enactments. The only exception comes with Cameron and Howell's measure of landmark enactments, which is essentially sweep 1 of Mayhew's important enactments.

The main findings in this chapter, however, are more significant than the frequent inability to reject a null hypothesis. I took a simple formal model of legislative-executive interaction—the pivotal politics theory— extracted alternative hypotheses about the relationship between preference changes and legislative productivity, measured preference attributes in a parsimonious fashion, and found significant positive support for the theoretically derived hypothesis relating the gridlock interval to legislative productivity. The pivotal politics theory, in other words, predicts more than Mayhew's eye-opening finding—that divided versus unified government per se does not affect legislative productivity. It also identifies and makes

28. One measurement strategy that addresses some of these drawbacks but introduces another problem is to use general-ideology measures of legislators' and the president's preferences and to calculate more directly the width of the gridlock interval as defined by the pivotal politics theory (see, e.g., Poole and Rosenthal 1985 and Groseclose, Levitt, and Snyder 1996 for examples of such measures; see Howell, Adler, and Cameron 1997 for a study of legislative productivity that employs Poole and Rosenthal's NOMINATE measures but finds null gridlock-interval results). Such an approach unquestionably imputes both cardinality and intertemporal comparability on the measures. My subjective but strong suspicion is that the measures are somewhat questionable when treated as if cardinal (e.g., a −1 to −.9 change represents the same ideological distance as a 0 to .1 change), and very questionable when treated as intertemporarily comparable (e.g., a .5 conservative in the Eisenhower administration in 1955 has the same overall views as a .5 conservative in the Reagan administration in 1995). Howell et al.'s figure 5 reinforces these a priori suspicions: their NOMINATE-based gridlock-width variable hardly varies. So, for various reasons, I chose not to use such measures in this chapter. Likewise, when Poole and Rosenthal's NOMINATE measures are used in later chapters, they are used only as ordinal data (with the exception of two tables included only for comparative purposes).

a prediction about a probable cause of legislative productivity: roughly, changes in the heterogeneity or homogeneity of elected officials' preferences. Furthermore, when this parsimonious preference-based concept is measured and incorporated into statistical analysis, other apparent causes, such as mood changes, evaporate.

Although these findings are subject to several qualifications, they advance the case for the pivotal politics theory a step beyond anecdotal support which is characteristic of much of the presidency literature and, to be even-handed, Chapter 2. Thus, to the degree that alternative forms of support are found as well, we have the beginnings of not only a basic knowledge of empirical regularities about U.S. government but also, potentially, a deeper understanding of why these regularities occur and what causes variation around central tendencies.

FOUR

COALITION SIZES

Gridlock is common, but it is not absolute. More precisely, although lawmaking is difficult in the presence of supermajority procedures, laws are enacted. By executing a more or less direct test of the pivotal politics theory, Chapter 3 suggests that the degree to which gridlock is broken is not only variable but also can be predicted by the width of the gridlock interval or, roughly, by the degree to which governmental officials' preferences are heterogeneous or homogeneous. This relationship is a straightforward prediction of the pivotal politics theory. A more convincing case for the theory should assess nonobvious predictions as well. Kramer, for example, puts it this way:

> To be meaningful [the system of symbols we call theory] must be precise enough to enable clear-cut empirical implications to be deduced from them, *and to be of much interest, the principles should be some distance from the empirical phenomena they are intended to explain,* and they should also have clear and potentially falsifiable implications in other empirical areas as well, against which they can be tested and validated. (Kramer 1986, 12; italics added)

This chapter attempts to test the pivotal politics theory in a relatively nonobvious venue—or, in Kramer's terms, by using data in which the distance between theory and empirical phenomena is somewhat greater than it was in Chapter 3. More specifically, I derive several unique hypotheses about coalition size from the pivotal politics theory, extract coalition size hypotheses from other theories, and test these with data from postwar U.S. governments.

The study of the composition and size of coalitions is a rich tradition in political science.[1] In light of more recent theories, reexamination of margins of victory on important enactments holds promise for providing new insights not only into coalition sizes but also into the relative merits of the theories themselves. Three models are useful in this regard: a sparse median voter theory of legislative politics, a more-or-less orthodox strong two-party system model, and the theory of pivotal politics. The respective model-specific questions are as follows. First, is there any immediate need to move beyond a simple median voter model of lawmaking? If so, then it should be possible to establish convincingly some deficiencies of the median voter theory that arise when focusing on the margins by which major legislation passes. Second and more constructively, does coalition-size data comport with the expectations of strong two-party government? If so, then we should continue to track this theory's empirical status as we make the transition to individual-level data in Chapters 5 and 6. Third, to the extent that puzzles remain after assessing median-voter and strong-party theories, does the pivotal politics theory help to account for some variation in vote margins across chambers or across various regimes of government? If so, then we will be on more solid footing as we continue to test the theory.

THEORIES AND COALITION SIZES

Extraction and testing of hypotheses about coalition sizes from theories of collective choice is complicated by some underlying needs, about which it is best to be explicit from the outset. The needs can be summarized as auxiliary assumptions or, equivalently, maintained hypotheses. Specifically, much like the analysis of legislative productivity in Chapter 3, the process of hypothesis extraction for the pivotal politics theory rests on an interpretation of a static theory in a dynamic setting. To make this stretch from theory to data, I again employ the construct of *exogenous shocks*. These can take either of two forms: election induced, or status quo induced.

The more conspicuous form is electoral. Elections can bring about abrupt changes in preferences of lawmakers and thus the composition of government. In terms of the pivotal politics theory, such a change can be represented as a movement of the boundaries of the gridlock interval in a manner such that old status quo policies (outcomes from a previous period) come to reside outside the new, electorally adjusted gridlock interval. As

---

1. See Riker 1962 for the seminal study of the size principle; and Weingast 1979 and Collie 1988 on universalism.

such, these newly designated, out-of-equilibrium status quo policies are ripe for policy change. This basic intuition was first illustrated by the quasi-dynamic exercise in figure 2.8 which revealed a theoretical basis for unified gridlock. In this chapter the focus is on the sizes of the majorities that unite behind the newly enacted laws when parameters are such that gridlock is broken.

Another, less conspicuous form of exogenous shock—namely, a shock to the status quo—can play a comparable role when interpreting the static model in dynamic settings. Unlike election-induced preference shocks, status quo shocks may occur at any time, including within periods that are demarcated by elections. A cause might be new information that suddenly becomes available and that alters lawmakers' perceptions about the attributes of outcomes associated with old policies. For example, when the Berlin Wall came down and the Soviet Union disintegrated, a wide range of lawmakers came to perceive the old status quo of defense expenditures as higher in terms of consequences than was perceived prior to the exogenous changes in world conditions.[2] Only rarely is it possible to predict or observe precisely when such changes occur. Given the plausible assumption that such changes do occur, however, it is possible to predict and observe coalition sizes to see whether they comport with theoretical expectations. In other words, substantial leverage in the analysis is obtained from the use of auxiliary hypotheses about these exogenous shocks which, it should be stressed, lie strictly outside the static, complete-information theory.

Extraction of hypotheses from alternative theories requires some stretching, too. In the case of median voter theory, the auxiliary hypotheses are exactly the same as for the pivotal politics theory, so no unique problem is posed in this case. In the case of party theories, however, some special guesswork is required because the implications of such theories for coalition sizes are not abundantly clear. Accordingly, the party analysis is also subject to some additional assumptions that are described below.

Median Voter Theory

A rough prediction about coalition sizes from the median voter theory is *near-minimal majorities*. As illustrated in figure 4.1, equilibrium policies, b^*,

---

2. In some literatures, such phenomena are sometimes called "problems" or "events" to which politicians respond by discussing and sometimes legislating "new ideas." See, for example, Kingdon 1984, chapter 5.

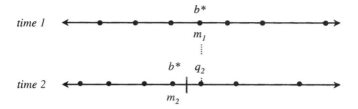

Figure 4.1
Median voter theory and coalition sizes

perfectly track median preferences, m_1 and m_2, in this theory. To the extent that interelection swings in the legislative median's preferences are small, the status quo policy remains close to the median voter's ideal point. The cutpoint between q_2 and m_2 thus separates legislators into almost-equal-sized coalitions of supporters of the equilibrium proposal, $b_2^\star = m_2$, and supporters of the status quo, q_2. This prediction is unaffected by whether the government is unified or divided.[3]

Party Government

While not based on an explicit formal theory such as the median voter model, the conventional party-based view of gridlock offers some clear suggestions about why passage of major legislation would appear to be more difficult under divided than unified government. Consistent with the classical notion of responsible party government, a unified government regime unmistakably assigns responsibility for agenda setting and lawmaking to the governing party which, by definition, occupies the White House and possesses majorities in the House and Senate. Among the supposed advantages of unified government is that bipartisan cooperation ceases to be a necessary condition for enactment of the governing party's agenda. This much seems clear based on standard party-centered arguments. For exam-

3.   A more precise prediction that is not tested is that the average size of coalitions in a Congress is positively correlated with the degree of election-induced change in the median voter's position. That is, for example, a huge election-induced change can leave q far from m, and therefore coalition sizes will be larger than minimum majorities. Nevertheless, it is not being assumed (nor should it be) that smaller shocks occur for median voter theory tests than for pivotal politics theory tests. It can be shown analytically that, for any size of preference shock or q shock, the predicated coalition size for pivotal politics theory is at least as great (and almost always strictly greater) than that for median voter theory.

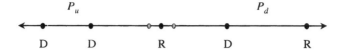

Figure 4.2
Party government theory and coalition sizes

ple: "Common partisan control of executive and legislature does not assure energetic government, but division of party control precludes it" (Key 1964, 688). "To have a productive majority . . . the President and a majority of both houses must be from the same party. Such a condition does not guarantee legislative success but is necessary for it" (Ripley 1969, 168).

If parties are strong in a nontrivial sense, then party leaders are able to command and receive the votes of their backbenchers.[4] What does this conception of strong parties imply about coalition sizes? The answer is not as straightforward as one would like, but at least some weak predictions can be extracted. Suppose as in figure 4.2 that Democrats have a congressional majority in a five-member Congress with ideal points as given. (Ignore the gray dots temporarily.) To govern as in the theory of responsible party government, then, Democrats need the votes of all their party members, and a winning coalition is assembled that includes all Democrats. More generally, this version of the theory seems to predict that coalition sizes will be as large as the size of the majority party. The prediction can be sharpened further if party-specific coalition data are available. Coalitions should be perfectly partisan; that is, all in-party members will vote yes on important legislation, and all out-party members will vote no.[5]

At least two objections to this derivation can be anticipated. Though somewhat diversionary, they are best fleshed out before turning to the data.

Objection 1: Releasing Votes
First, a strong majority party may not need to whip all its members into line to enact a law. Suppose that in figure 4.2 there were five Democrats rather than three (thus a seven-member legislature) and that the added two

4. See Krehbiel 1993 for a more detailed argument and some empirical evidence that parties are not strong in this sense.

5. Exactly this phenomenon has been measured in coutless studies in which the measure is called "partisan voting" and interpreted as evidence of "party strength." See, for example, Rohde 1991; and Cox and McCubbins 1993. For reasons discussed in Krehbiel 1993, I disagreee with this interpretation. This is not to deny, however, that a strict version of strong party government has this implication.

members, as shown by the gray dots, have ideal points near the moderate but left-most Republican. Democratic leaders may then generously release the right-most Democrat to "vote his district" since the majority party does not really need his vote (King and Zeckhauser 1996). This is an instance of majority-party coordination through, for example, whip organizations that may have the long-term party advantage of preserving majority-party status (see, e.g., Sinclair 1992; Cox and McCubbins 1993). If this is the intended theory of strong parties, then the prior derivation of the hypothesis of coalition sizes that are strictly equal to majority-party size is unwarranted. Winning coalitions should instead be *smaller* than majority-party sized.

Objection 2: Weak Minority Party
Second, the derivation of the party hypothesis as stated above can also be muddled by an alternative assumption about behavior on the minority side of the aisle. If, for example, the minority party is weak, then who is to say that the left-most Republican will not defect from her party's right-central tendencies to join Democrats in the winning coalition? If she does (and if Democrats are strong), then coalition sizes may be *larger* than the size of the majority party.

Responses to Objections
Responses to these two anticipated objections are illuminating with regard to the slipperiness of party-based hypothesizing. Using a logical truth table approach, I exhaust three of the four combinations of possible truth values in the two objections[6] and spell out their empirical implications.

First, suppose both objections are warranted. Democrats then release right-leaning Democrats to vote their district while left-leaning Republican votes are picked up essentially for free. The logical consequence of this state of affairs is at once substantively perverse and analytically convenient. It is substantively perverse because now we have straight preference-based voting. Surely this does not warrant the label "strong parties." But it is analytically convenient because, given straight preference-based voting, the coalition-size prediction is exactly that stated above for the median-voter theory. Coalition sizes should be much *smaller* than the majority party's size and somewhat larger than minimum-majority sized only in the case of large exogenous, electoral shocks. Thus, if both objections are true, then we

---

6.   The false-false possibility is omitted because, in the absence of objections, the hypothesis as extracted above stands.

need only to test the median voter theory. (And, if it corroborated, we need also to question seriously where the real strength lies within this notion of so-called strong parties.)

Second, suppose instead that the first objection is warranted, but the second one is not. That is, the majority party strategically releases its outliers, but the minority party is strong and cohesive even when its members have heterogeneous preferences. Then the prediction, again, would be that coalition sizes are *smaller* than the majority party's size. In the limit, they are simple-majority coalitions, because the strong majority party will not waste its resources to obtain unneeded votes. This, too, is testable. Here, unlike the first scenario, corroboration would have some genuine strong-party content. This scenario, however, begs the question of why one party but not the other releases its outliers to vote consistently with their individual preferences.

Third, suppose the second objection is warranted, but the first one is not. That is, the minority party is weak and not cohesive, but the majority party is strong and thus can and does receive the support of *all* its members. In this case, coalition sizes will be *greater* than majority-party sized. However, the puzzle again arises: Why would believers in the salience of the role of partisanship in lawmaking assume, claim, or predict that one party is strong while the other is weak? A coherent theory of party strength, it seems, ought not to portray parties as strong or weak in such an inconsistent fashion.

A more general problem should be apparent now, too. Working within this party framework and depending upon which auxiliary assumptions one is willing to make, one can derive essentially whatever prediction he or she wants: smaller-than-majority-party-sized coalitions, minimum-majority coalitions, or larger-than-majority-party-sized coalitions. Because this is an essentially hopeless setup for a serious empirical test (i.e., a test in which the theory stands a chance of being refuted), I will proceed in what seems to be the most reasonable manner under the circumstances: by assuming that neither of the two objections is valid and that the originally derived hypothesis (which is refutable) stands. This approach necessarily leaves open opportunities for others to make an alternative case for one, both, or other objections and to retest an appropriately reformulated hypothesis.

Pivotal Politics Theory

The pivotal politics theory yields two levels of predictions that are increasingly subtle. The relatively straightforward prediction is illustrated in figure

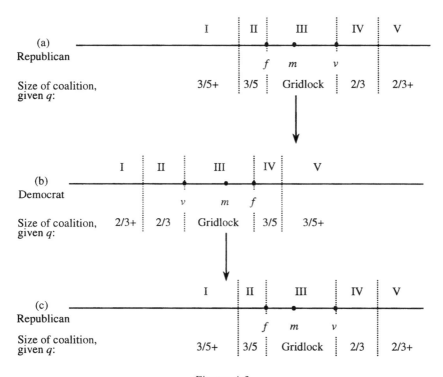

Figure 4.3
Pivotal politics theory and coalition sizes

4.3. In an attempt to accent the nonpartisan nature of the theory (and to break away from a potentially significant shortcoming in the party-based measure of the gridlock interval in Chap. 3), the figure depicts a regime change *not* as a shift from divided to unified government in the conventional sense but rather as a change in the party that occupies the White House. Thus, as history unfolds, different parties occupy the White House and define *presidential regimes*. A change from Kennedy to Johnson or Nixon to Ford, for example, is not a presidential regime shift, but a change from Eisenhower to Kennedy or Ford to Carter is. The necessary analytic criterion for a regime shift is a leapfrogging of the veto pivot, v, over the median voter's ideal point, m. This happens if, and only if, the president's ideal point, p, also leapfrogs over the median voter's ideal point.

We have seen already that a necessary and sufficient condition for policy change in the pivotal politics theory is noncentrist status quo points—more precisely, status quo policies outside the gridlock interval. The focus now is on the size of the coalitions that enact new laws. The figure shows that, given the presence of a nonmedian pivot, such sizes are at least as large as $^3/_5$. Thus, the most straightforward prediction of pivotal politics theory is coalitions that are *greater than minimum-majority size*.[7] Derivation of the more subtle predictions is undertaken after the preliminary findings are presented.

COALITION SIZES ON AVERAGE

To test the predictions about central tendencies, vote totals on final passage are coded for each of Mayhew's important legislative enactments during the 80th through 103d Congresses.[8] For each bill and within each House, the size of the winning coalition was computed as $Y/(Y + N)$, where Y represents the number of yes votes and N the number of no votes. As shown on figure 4.4, with the exception of a large upper tail of near-unanimous votes, the distribution of vote margins is approximately uniform across the 0.5–1.0 interval. It is immediately obvious that one can reject confidently the median voter theory's hypothesis of near-minimum majorities. The average coalition size for all important enactments is .819.[9] Only 12 percent of the observations are within the 0.5–0.6 range, while 43.9 percent are in the 0.9–1.0 range. Clearly, supermajoritarian politics of some form—yet to be discerned—dominates in the enactment of major laws.

The data also fail to support the party-government hypothesis of coalition sizes equal to majority-party size. As Mayhew makes clear in his comprehensive discussion of these data, bipartisanship is the rule, not the exception, in the passage of important legislation. This robust fact is hard to reconcile with the notion of a strong, programmatic, disciplined majority party. Even in unified government regimes in which the theory can be

7.   In an insightful discussion of strategies of coalition leaders, Douglas Arnold (1990, chap. 5) comes to exactly this conclusion for a range of reasons including supermajority procedures. His argument is more detailed than, but consistent with, the formal argument of pivotal politics theory.

8.   David Mayhew generously provided his notes from *Divided We Govern,* from which the data were coded. See Mayhew (1991, chap. 5) for various complexities in coding and interpreting these data. While he considered voice votes unanimous votes (119n.42), I coded these missing. Otherwise my conventions make every effort to stay consistent with his.

9.   This is not a rigorous test because a necessary condition for passage is, of course, a majority of greater than .5. Truncation of the distribution from below necessarily makes it difficult to support the minimum winning coalition hypothesis. Still, coalition sizes are so regularly so much greater than $(n + 1)/2$ that it would take an extremely lax standard to infer support.

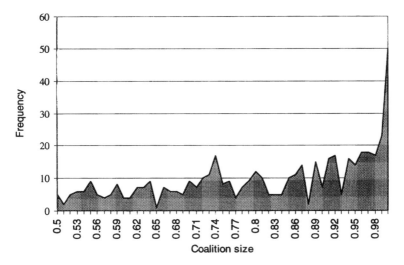

Figure 4.4
Distribution of coalition sizes

expected to have the most relevance, average coalition sizes (.780) are much greater than the average size of the majority party. Nor does the first objection to the derivation of the party-government hypothesis rationalize this discrepancy. For if the strong majority party selectively releases its members to vote independently (e.g., in their districts' interest), then the resulting winning coalition sizes should be *smaller* than the majority-party average size—not greater.

The general finding of large coalition sizes, then, is more consistent with pivotal politics theory than with other theories, because the pivotal politics theory uniquely predicts that coalition sizes are larger than simple-majority sized. However, .819 is much larger than 3/5 or 2/3, so this support is weak. A stronger test can be formulated by moving on to more precise and nonobvious hypotheses about variation in coalition sizes.

VARIATION IN COALITION SIZES
The Coalition-Size Hypothesis

For reasons to be spelled out below, the pivotal politics theory identifies three covariates of average sizes of winning coalitions on major legislation The corresponding predictions are that average sizes of winning coalitions will be:

1. smaller after party of the president changes than during intrapresidential-regime periods (and irrespective of whether government is divided or unified),
2. smaller in the House than in the Senate after such regime shifts, and
3. smaller in the Senate after its cloture reform in 1975 than before such reform.

Return to figure 4.3 in which the key variables are the location of the status quo and the presidential party regime (Republican or Democrat, or, analytically, $m < v$ or $v < m$). The pivotal politics theory identifies the location of the status quo as a determinant of whether change will occur and, more important now, by what margin it will occur. Consider the Republican-president regime in panel (a). If the status quo, q, is left of the filibuster pivot, f, then the theory predicts that a winning bill, b, will command at least a $3/5$ majority over the status quo.[10] However, if the status quo, q, is to the right of the veto pivot, v, then the theoretical expectation is that a winning bill will command at least a $2/3$ majority.[11] Generally, the theory predicts large winning coalitions on final passage votes. Minimum majority coalitions, in contrast, are rarities (but not quite anomalies)[12] within the theory. This general prediction was corroborated above. The average winning coalition size is .819. The theory, however, also makes the three more specific predictions stated above. We take these up in parts.

Part 1: Regime Effects
A necessary and sufficient condition for policy change in the theory is for the status quo to lie outside the gridlock interval. Next we need to consider the *relative* likelihood of a q on the $3/5$ side versus the $2/3$ side of the gridlock interval. In cases of small interelection changes in preferences or intraregime shocks in perceptions about the location of the status quo, there is no reason to expect one type of q to be more likely than another. In instances of large

10.   For q in interval II, the majority is exactly $3/5$. For q in I, the majority grows monotonically from $3/5$ as q moves from right to left.

11.   For q in IV, the majority is exactly $2/3$. For q in V, the majority grows monotonically from $3/5$ as q moves from left to right.

12.   The reason they are not categorically anomalous is that simple-majority coalitions can occur in the House (which has no filibuster rights) when there are cross-chamber differences in the location of pivot points, or in the Senate for certain types of legislation (e.g., budget reconciliation bills). In Mayhew's sample, for instance, only two enactments seem not to have been subject to filibuster and cloture rules in the Senate: the omnibus reconciliation bill in 1981 and a deficit reduction measure in 1987. Special budget-specific rules are discussed and analyzed more specifically in Chapter 9.

interelection swings, however, such as *presidential-party regime changes,* it is clear from figure 4.3 that it is more likely for new-period status quo points to lie on the ⅗ side than on the ⅔ side of the gridlock interval.[13] To better understand the empirical intuitiveness of this prediction, suppose, as in panels (a) and (b), we moved from a Republican (conservative) president and relatively conservative Congress to a Democratic (liberal) president and more liberal Congress. If, contrary to the above assertion, we then saw more status quo points in the new, liberal ⅔ regions (I and II) than in the new, conservative ⅗ regions (IV and V), we would also observe the newly elected liberals adopting policies that are more *conservative* than the old ones. Clearly, the opposite pattern—liberals changing policy in a more liberal direction—is more intuitive and realistic. The same logic holds for changes from Democratic to Republican presidents, as shown in panels (b) and (c).

To summarize somewhat more generally, the prediction rests on two observations. In the absence of a regime change, status quo policies are roughly equally likely to lie on the left side as on the right side of the gridlock interval. After regime changes of the sort displayed in figure 4.3, however, it is much more likely that status quo policies will lie on ⅗ side of the gridlock interval rather than on the ⅔ side of the gridlock interval. Because ⅗ < ⅔, the testable prediction that follows is that presidential-party regime changes should be *negatively* associated with winning coalition sizes. This is part 1 of the refined coalition-size hypothesis.

This otherwise opaque prediction is borne out. Using a dummy variable for new presidential regime governments (Congresses 83, 87, 91, 95, 97, 103) to predict the coalition sizes of bills yields a simple regression coefficient of $-.041$ ($p = .006$), indicating that winning coalitions are about 4 percent smaller during new presidential-party regimes than old regimes.[14] When comparable analysis excludes unanimous and near-unanimous bills (margins of less than .95), this difference increases to over six percentage points.

Part 2: House-Senate Differences
Similar reasoning can be applied to explore House-Senate differences. Both chambers may participate in veto overrides and thus have theoretically sig-

---

13.   The figure magnifies this tendency by moving *m* and *f* in addition to leapfrogging *v*. This is empirically plausible given coattails, national swings, etc., although it is not analytically necessary to generate the prediction.

14.   This is equivalent to a difference-in-means test.

nificant $^2/_3$ pivot points. But only the Senate requires a $^3/_5$ supermajority to invoke cloture; thus the above examples with filibuster pivots arguably reflect Senate coalition sizes more accurately than House ones. Tending to this complication provides another opportunity to push the theory into an unlikely domain for testing. The basic question is: Within the class of regime-change observations, for which chamber is the negative effect of the new regime on vote margins likely to be greater? To the extent that some of the roll calls in the data set are votes on the chamber's first passage (before conference), the answer is the House.[15] The arithmetic reason is that $^2/_3 - ^1/_2 > ^2/_3 - ^3/_5$. The substance behind these numbers is that while new-regime Senate status quos are likely to be external to its $^3/_5$ pivot and thus obtain at least a $^3/_5$ vote for passage, for House status quos this theoretical lower bound on the margin can go as low as $^1/_2$.

One way to test this expectation is simply to calculate and compare means for the various classes of observations: old regime, new-regime Senate, and new-regime House. These are, respectively, .831, .802, and .779. A shorthand way of presenting the finding and of assessing statistical significance is to estimate the regression equation,

$$\text{Vote margin} = \alpha + \beta \, \text{House} \times \text{New regime} + \gamma \, \text{Senate} \times \text{New regime},$$

in which we expect not only negative coefficients for β and γ but also $\beta < \gamma$. Table 4.1 presents three such regressions that sequentially eliminate lopsided votes.[16] The differences are invariably consistent with the hypothesis qualitatively; however, they vary in significance. Take equation (2) for example. The constant term says the average coalition size for old-regime observations is .779—as usual, much greater than simple-majority sized and much greater than the majority-party size. The coefficient for new regime

15.   The reason for the clause "to the extent . . ." is that for votes on final passage (after the conference or on the veto override), the House vote may exceed $^1/_2$ because the bill in its final state has been adjusted to take the Senate filibuster constraint, f, into account.

16.   Although it is more or less conventional to eliminate lopsided votes, this is a convention that should be at least somewhat controversial. While it seems innocuous to omit "hurrah" votes for legislation such as a resolution commemorating mothers and apple pie, omission of lopsided votes on major legislation becomes harder to defend. For instance, the Clean Air Act of 1970 was passed 375–1 in the House. Is this an artificially large majority? Perhaps, since there were many close votes prior to that vote for final passage. How about the Senate's 77–6 vote on the establishment of Social Security in 1935 or the House's 388–19 vote authorizing funds for the National Interstate Highway System in 1956? These are harder calls. The point is that any such truncation rule is arbitrary.

Table 4.1
House- and Senate-Specific Effects of New Regime on Sizes of Winning
Coalitions on Important Enactments

	1	2	3
New regime × House	−0.052	−0.085	−0.076
	(−2.707)	(−4.344)	(−4.165)
New regime × Senate	−0.029	−0.038	−0.027
	(−1.435)	(−1.910)	(−1.429)
Constant	0.831	0.779	0.739
	(105.372)	(99.523)	(96.368)
N observations	492	366	298
Adjusted R^2	.013	.048	.051

NOTE: Regression coefficients with t-statistics in parentheses. Equation (1) includes all of Mayhew's bills. Equation (2) excludes those for which the majority exceeded .95. Equation (3) excludes those for which the majority exceeded .90.

in the House ($-.085$) says the average coalition size in the House after a president of a new party takes office is .085 lower than the baseline given by the estimate of α, or $.779 - .085 = .694$. This effect is consistent with the hypothesis and is significant ($p < .001$). The coefficient for new regime in the Senate ($-.038$) says the average coalition size in the Senate after a president of a new party takes office is .038 lower than the baseline given by the estimate of α, or $.779 - .038 = .741$. This effect is consistent with the hypothesis and fairly significant ($p < .057$). Finally, the House-Senate difference, too, is fairly significant ($p = .064$). Overall, then, the degree of support for the hypothesis is fair to good.

Part 3: Cloture-Rule Effects
The final part of the hypothesis exploits the historical fact that, beginning in the 94th Congress (1975), the Senate operated under a new cloture rule that required votes of $3/5$ of the Senate instead of $2/3$ of those senators present and voting. Applying the same argument used to explicate House-Senate differences, the prediction is that new-regime negative effects on coalition sizes in the Senate should be greater after than before the rules change. To test this hypothesis simultaneously with part 2, we estimate:

$$\text{Vote margin} = \alpha + \beta \text{ House} \times \text{New regime} +$$
$$\gamma \text{ Senate} \times \text{New regime} \times \text{Postreform} +$$
$$\delta \text{ Senate} \times \text{New regime} \times \text{Prereform}.$$

Table 4.2
Pre- and Postreform Effects of New Regime on Sizes of Winning Coalitions
on Important Enactments

	1	2	3
New regime × House	−0.052	−0.085	−0.076
	(−2.720)	(−4.350)	(−4.172)
New regime × Senate after cloture reform	−0.077	−0.063	−0.050
	(−2.715)	(−2.372)	(−2.004)
New regime × Senate before cloture reform	0.010	−0.012	−0.002
	(0.383)	(−0.448)	(−0.088)
Constant	0.831	0.779	0.739
	(105.874)	(99.663)	(96.527)
N observations	492	366	298
Adjusted R^2	.022	.050	.054

NOTE: Regression coefficients with t-statistics in parentheses. Equation (1) includes all of Mayhew's bills. Equation (2) excludes those for which the majority exceeded .95. Equation (3) excludes those for which the majority exceeded .90.

The theory-based expectation is that $\beta < \gamma < \delta = 0$.[17] The findings in table 4.2 tend to corroborate this hypothesis. The qualitative differences are as predicted, except in equation 1 which includes several unanimous votes. Individual coefficients are always significantly different from zero when they are supposed to be. However, it is usually not possible to reject with high confidence the null hypothesis of no differences between pairs of coefficients. In equation 1 the Senate difference before and after cloture reform is significant ($p = .018$), but the House-Senate difference is not ($p = .432$). In equations 2 and 3, neither of these differences is statistically significant.

CAVEATS AND CONCLUSIONS

At least four drawbacks should be underscored to guide future, more persuasive, theory-testing research on coalition sizes.

First, other samples of legislation should be drawn and additional tests should be conducted to confirm that Mayhew's "important enactments"

17. The reason $\delta = 0$ rather than $\delta < 0$ is that the pivot point is at the ²/₃ point whether it is defined by the veto or by the prereform filibuster rule.

are not idiosyncratic. Clearly, the pivotal politics theory should apply to this class of legislation. The significance levels were questionable at times, however, and the theory also should cover legislation of somewhat lesser importance.[18]

Second, a broader range of hypotheses should be derived and tested to make sure that the relatively parsimonious regression analyses here are not biased due to omitted variables. For example, Mayhew (1991, chap. 5) considers "problem solving" and "the logic of aggregating support" as possible clues to the puzzle of large, bipartisan coalitions. No attempt was made to operationalize and test these factors here.[19]

Third, more comprehensive and rigorous attention should be given to strong-party theories and their implications for coalition sizes. Given the diversity of party-centered research, it is almost certain that I have misrepresented some of it and/or objectionably derived my party-based hypothesis of coalition sizes. A welcome response would focus on a more specific party-centered theory, derive a more precise hypothesis of coalition sizes, and retest it jointly with alternative theories.

Finally, there is a somewhat arcane but potentially important qualification to these findings. An implicit assumption in the illustration of how regime changes generate different expectations about coalition size is that the president's ideal point, p, is exterior to the legislative pivot, v, that defines one endpoint of the gridlock interval (see again fig. 4.3). In the construction of the gridlock interval measure in Chapter 3, the opposite assumption was made: that the president is less extreme than the veto pivot, or that p lies inside the interval (f, v) or (v, f). In both instances, these assumptions were operational necessities rather than substantive judgments. The hope is that over an extended period of history, p and v are sufficiently close to one another on average that these assumptions are inconsequential. This, however, cannot be guaranteed.

In conclusion, the coalition-size hypothesis of the pivotal politics theory stretches the theory into a domain in which several previous theories have

18. I am reluctant to expand the scope too far, however. For instance, the theory is not intended to explain commemorative legislation, House and Senate resolutions (that do not require the president's signature), and certain types of budget legislation which skirt the normal supermajority rules (see Chap. 9). But it should account for legislative activity of a more encompassing sort than Mayhew's selective set (see Chaps. 5 and 6).

19. In one respect, this route is not particularly promising. If these hypothetical causal factors are conceived as approximate constants, then they cannot hope to explain variation in coalition sizes. However, they can be more entertained as factors consistent with the basic fact of large, bipartisan coalitions.

broad implications but in which there have been few systematic empirical inquiries—and none, to my knowledge, that identify covariates of coalition size. The covariates suggested by the pivotal politics theory are presidential regime shifts, House versus Senate, and the Senate before versus after cloture reforms. For the most part, the findings are consistent with the predictions. On one hand, this is not a stunning finding in the sense that some coefficients are not highly significant, and some differences between otherwise well-ordered coefficients are not significant. On the other hand, it is not likely that one would observe all of these patterns by chance alone. Furthermore, the predictions seem to reside comfortably within the category of the nonobvious.

Reflecting back on this and the previous chapter, we can recapitulate concisely the macro phase of the empirical analysis. In Chapter 3 we saw modest empirical support for the relatively obvious hypothesis that links the width of the gridlock interval to legislative productivity. In this chapter we saw somewhat weaker empirical support for relatively nonobvious hypotheses that link congressional rules and presidential regimes to coalition sizes. In each case, the data with which the hypotheses were tested are soft. However, in spite of the fact that the data come from a diverse set of bills that represents a huge amount of idiosyncratic political behavior, the pivotal politics theory seems to fare well enough to move on to micro- or individual-level analysis.

FIVE

FILIBUSTER
PIVOTS

If the supermajoritarian institutions that are represented in the pivotal politics theory account for macropolitical phenomena such as gridlock and sizes of winning coalitions, then it should be possible to detect micro- or individual-level behavior consistent with pivotal politics, too. As reviewed in Chapter 2, the theory provides a tractable number of situation-specific answers to the question: Who is pivotal? One such answer—the filibuster pivot—is uniquely senatorial and is taken up in this chapter. Another answer—the veto pivot—plays theoretically identical roles in the House and Senate and is the subject of the next chapter. In both instances, the objective is to spell out in greater detail the implications of the pivotal politics theory and to test these implications with reference to the behavior of individual legislators.

FILIBUSTERS AND CLOTURE: RHETORIC AND REALITY

Since the adoption of its Rule 22 in 1917, the U.S. Senate has had a clearly stipulated parliamentary procedure for terminating *extended debate* (a filibuster) and bringing to a vote the motion at hand.[1] The procedure is called *cloture*. With some minor historical variations, the general theme is simple.

---

1. Stages of the legislative process subject to filibusters under currect rules include the motion to proceed to consideration of a bill, consideration of amendments or of the bill itself, motions to go to conference, and the passage of the conference report.

When a motion susceptible to extended debate is pending before the Senate, any senator may file a cloture petition which, with the signatures of 16 other senators, guarantees that it shall be in order two days later to bring a cloture vote before the full Senate. If the cloture vote receives the requisite supermajority—$^3/_5$ of the Senate currently, $^2/_3$ of senators present and voting prior to 1975—debate cannot continue for more than a stipulated number of hours after cloture is invoked.[2] Therefore, the consequence of cloture being invoked is that the initially pending motion can be brought to a vote over the vocal objections of opponents of the motion. The consequence of cloture not being invoked, in contrast, is that the motion is not brought to a vote unless or until the filibuster is called off or another cloture petition and vote are successful. In other words, a successful filibuster preserves the status quo policy.

As it is portrayed in the pivotal politics theory, these procedures have the practical effect of making the off-center filibuster pivot a locus of—to put it benignly—accommodating activity. That is, although the motion in question (say, to pass a conference report) nominally requires only a simple majority, the prospect of a filibuster and the corresponding parliamentary need for cloture makes the filibuster pivot, not the median voter, pivotal. If the filibuster pivot (f in the model) is not accommodated—more precisely, if she prefers the status quo, q, to the bill, b, that is offered—she and all colleagues with more extreme preferences can mount a filibuster and vote no on cloture, thereby keeping the status quo intact.

Do real-world filibuster pivots exploit their pivotal positions in this manner? To ease into this challenging question it is useful to survey recent rhetoric about the filibuster and facts about cloture votes. Take the 103d Congress, for example. Leaders in the Democratic majority had a well-articulated position on filibusters. Majority Leader George Mitchell made so many speeches on the subject that one partisan observer questioned whether he was speaking against filibusters or illustrating them. The following excerpt highlights his basic arguments:

> When the American people think of the Senate now, the first thing they think of is the filibuster, because it has become such a common tactic [to] use on almost every major bill that we try to consider. It is unfortunate. It is regrettable. It prevents the will of the majority from taking place. Mr. President, the rules are there for everyone to use. I expect that almost every member of the Senate

---

2. The number of postcloture hours of debate, too, has been subject to periodic changes.

has at one time or another used the rules to delay action. That is not the issue here. The question is not when it is used occasionally, but when it is used as a part of a deliberate pattern, an unmistakable pattern, an unmistakable record of filibuster after filibuster after filibuster after filibuster. It is not anymore reserved for issues of great national importance. It is not anymore limited to those matters which do not have anything to do with one party or the other, but, by consensus, affect grave national issues. It is used on virtually every major bill. I repeat: From an average of less than 1 filibuster a year for more than a half century to 48 in the last Congress. It is regrettable. I hope it stops. (*Congressional Record,* May 7, 1993, S5718)

It didn't stop. In the 103d Congress, during which Mitchell gave this and 26 other speeches on the filibuster, the number of cloture votes subsided only somewhat, to 42.[3]

And what about the 104th Congress in which Democrats lost their majority and Senator Tom Daschle of South Dakota took over as Democratic Leader? Rhetorically, Daschle followed in the footsteps of his filibuster-frustrated predecessor, George Mitchell. Daschle campaigned for the position of leader with reference to the filibuster as "one of the most abused parliamentary tools in the Senate."[4] However, although the number of cloture votes had dropped slightly in the 103d Congress, it rose again to 54 in the 104th. Evidently, "abuse" is in the eye of the majority.

In a recent and uniquely comprehensive study of the filibuster, Sarah Binder and Steven Smith (1997) cut through the rhetoric to inspect the reality of filibusters and cloture throughout the history of the Senate.[5] Roughly consistent with the majoritarian words of the Democrats under Mitchell and their subsequent minority actions under Daschle, Binder, and Smith's thesis is that senators' true views on filibusters are predominantly "political," not "principled." They find, for example, that only a few senators vote perfectly consistently for or against cloture, which would be consistent with a pure "principle" hypothesis. Instead, ostensible positions for or against *cloture* are really positions against or for the *legislation* on which cloture is being sought.

Although the labeling of the alternative hypothesis as "political" is somewhat ambiguous, the substance of Binder and Smith's main argument is

---

3.   The number of cloture votes is at best a rough indicator of the number of filibusters, cited here only because it appears to be Mitchell's measure and it has become somewhat conventional.

4.   Adam Clymer, "Two Senators Vie to Lead Minority," *New York Times,* November 25, 1994.

5.   See also Patterson, Caldeira, and Waltenburg 1995.

perfectly consistent with the pivotal politics theory. In the parsimonious spatial model, legislators do not have "principled" views about procedures. In fact, they do not care about procedures at all, apart from their bearing on policy outcomes. So, when cloture procedures make it more difficult to change policies that senators dislike relative to the alternatives, senators such as George Mitchell in the 103d Congress lash out against the filibuster. However, when cloture procedures make it more difficult to change policies that senators like relative to the alternatives, senators such as Tom Daschle in the 104th Congress take the opposite pseudoprocedural stance. In general, a careful look at actions and not just words suggests that the rhetoric about procedures is at best an incidental sideshow to the main event. The main event is policy, and policy is driven by preferences.

Although Binder and Smith's primary substantive argument—politics, not principle—can comfortably coexist with the pivotal politics theory, their analysis should not be construed as a test of this theory. Indeed, the authors are admirably cautious about what they can and cannot test, writing at one point, "Unfortunately, a direct test of the filibuster-as-politics and filibuster-as-principle perspectives is not possible" (Binder and Smith 1997, 94). The approach here is necessarily indirect, too, but it also differs from Binder and Smith's in other important ways.

First, I do not adopt as a premise "the explosive growth in Senate obstructionism" or seek "to explain the explosive growth in filibustering" that drives much of Binder and Smith's analysis (1997, 19, 13). For reasons described painstakingly and clearly by Richard Beth (1995), a cloture vote is neither a necessary nor sufficient indicator that a filibuster has occurred.[6] I therefore remain agnostic about whether the incidence of filibusters (threatened or real) has changed substantially over time.

Second, the focus here is not on correcting empirical myths about filibusters. While this is important, Binder and Smith do an excellent job of it, and replication seems unnecessary. Nor is the focus on the consistency of senators' pro or con positions on cloture votes. Rather, the aim is to develop a technique whereby we can infer something about theories from *variation* in senators' cloture votes. Details, of course, are provided below.

Third, Binder and Smith make a rather passionate normative plea about filibuster reform. I shall not argue that normative debates are unimportant,

---

6. For example, some filibusters do not lead to cloture votes (e.g., when bill supporters clearly number less than $^3/_5$). Conversely, occasionally bill proponents file cloture petitions in order to jump the gun on potential filibusterers who back down. Beth provides examples of these and other instances in which cloture votes means something quite different from what one might first think.

but neither will I engage in them. The more modest aim here is to shed some light on positive theories in which filibuster and cloture procedures play a role. This is viewed as a necessary but not sufficient condition for confident progress in the normative domain.

In summary, the relatively narrow focus of this chapter is on whether real-world filibuster pivots exploit their special spatial status to alter policies relative to what they would be in a strictly simple-majority legislature.[7] Anecdotes of this sort were presented in Chapter 2 with reference to the Republicans in the 103d Congress, and comparable cases exist for Democrats in the 104th. More badly needed than another barrage of anecdotes, however, is a method that permits a test based on systematic data.

SWITCHER ANALYSIS

To assess whether filibusters and the cloture procedures work in practice approximately as depicted in theory, I introduce and implement a novel and indirect technique called switcher analysis. First employed in a study of cosponsorship and waffling in the House of Representatives (Krehbiel 1995), switcher analysis is based on the assumption that changes in behavior are most likely to occur among decision makers who are indifferent, or nearly indifferent, between two policies (a bill and the status quo) in the set of alternatives from which they choose. Two apolitical examples reveal the essential intuition of switcher analysis, while a third example places the technique squarely in the senatorial setting.

Ice Cream

Suppose two girls are regular customers at an old-fashioned small-town ice cream parlor that stocks and sells at most three standard flavors. The merchant notices that one girl invariably selects strawberry, while the other girl randomly chooses chocolate or vanilla with approximately equal probability. The merchant reasonably infers that the first girl has a definite preference for strawberry over both vanilla and chocolate, while the second girl is roughly indifferent between chocolate and vanilla. Therefore, if the merchant were to run out of strawberry, he may lose a sale. If he were to run

---

7. In another chapter, Binder and Smith (1997) inspect the hypothesis that the filibuster is a "moderating" institution and find this claim lacking. This argument, too, is loosely consistent with the pivotal politics theory, which holds that the supermajoritarian cloture requirement tempers or inhibits full convergence (moderation) to the Senate's median voter position.

out of either chocolate or vanilla, however, he would probably just sell a scoop of the flavor that remains and incur no loss. Sales aside, the first point is elementary: the nonswitching behavior of the first girl and the switching behavior of the second girl suggest something about the girls' ice cream preferences. Switching is an observable indicator of approximate indifference, which otherwise is hard to observe.

Autos

Suppose three types of adults exhibit car purchasing behavior similar to the two girls in the ice cream parlor. Type A adults always buys Hondas. Type B adults regularly switch between Hondas and Toyotas. Type C adults always buy Toyotas. A parallel and again reasonable inference of an auto dealer who attempts to track these things systematically (realistically, via *correlates* of switching behavior since actual switching itself may not be observable) is that type A consumers have definite preferences for Hondas over Toyotas; type B consumers are happy with, but roughly indifferent between, both brands; and type C consumers, of course, have strong preferences for Toyotas.

Now a strategic element can be incorporated into the scenario. Suppose a shrewd Toyota salesman has information about customer types that he can use on a case-by-case basis as customers visit the showroom. With which customer types is the seller most likely to want to deal? Clearly, the seller will not *have* to bargain hard to make sales to type C customers. Their behavior is sufficiently predictable in favor of Toyota that no special deals are needed to maintain their loyalty. The sticker price is made for these folks. Similarly, the seller will not *want* to pursue seriously the type A customers. Their behavior is sufficiently predictable in favor of Honda that a Toyota dealer's offer would have to be *too* special (e.g., below cost) to induce Honda loyalists to switch. This leaves the near-indifferent customers—type B—as the likely targets of the seller's attention and efforts. For these potential buyers, a small price break, free floor mats, or a CD option in the stereo system can seal the deal, and the seller's commission is roughly proportional to the degree to which she can cut deals close to type B buyers' indifference points.

Vote Buying

Although they state it somewhat differently, James Snyder and Timothy Groseclose argue convincingly that Senate leaders are like Toyota salesmen.[8] A successful deal for a legislative leader is a winning coalition for a preferred policy. Although leaders are free to negotiate with any of a large number of colleagues who have a wide assortment of preferences, they face constraints: minimal time, finite resources, reluctance to alter significantly the content of bills to avoid alienating initial coalition partners, etc. Leaders therefore must make choices with whom to bargain. These political choices reflect the same incentives and concerns identified in the economic examples. Leaders ought not to waste resources on colleagues whose support is virtually assured, and, for the most part, leaders know who these colleagues are. Similarly, leaders ought not to waste resources on colleagues whose support is expected to be too expensive to obtain because of, say, their consistent track record of opposition to similar legislation, or their reelection constituency which tends to be hostile to such bills. Finally, leaders should (according to Snyder) and do (according to Groseclose) expend resources on colleagues who are nearly indifferent between the proposed legislation and the status quo. Good leaders know who these legislators are on an issue-by-issue basis. Good leaders "buy" (according to Snyder), "trade for" (according to Groseclose), or seek most aggressively (according to the auxiliary hypothesis here) the votes of nearly indifferent legislators because such votes are relatively cheap.

Switchers and Cloture

By piecing together these political and economic intuitions, an empirical test of the pivotal politics theory becomes possible by focusing on switching behavior in cloture situations. In effect, the approach constitutes a joint test of two theories: the pivotal politics theory, and the Snyder-Groseclose vote-buying theory. Given a pair or set of same-bill cloture situations in which individual senators have opportunities to switch their votes, the method assumes that observed switchers are nearly indifferent between the bill in question and the status quo. Switching, then, is interpreted as an instance of vote buying a la Snyder and Groseclose.[9] Leaders are likewise

---

8.   See Snyder 1991; Groseclose 1995; and Groseclose and Snyder 1996.

9.   The figurative currency with which votes are bought can remain ambiguous. Bribery is, of course, illegal, so neither Snyder, Groseclose, nor I have cash transfers in mind. Plausible substitutes include promises to help to move other legislation, assurances regarding conference participation, compromises on the bill itself, or concessions on other pending legislation. Clearly, none of these is observable and measurable in any systematic way, which is why I employ the vote-buying theory as a maintained hypothesis.

assumed to be rational vote buyers in the sense that they target near-indifferent senators in their coalition-building efforts. The operational question, then, centers on the pivotal politics theory. Who is pivotal? Three answers can be imagined, and they are summarized in figure 5.1.

One possibility is that this whole scheme is too far-fetched to uncover anything but gibberish. Cloture situations are highly idiosyncratic, and the issues on which cloture votes are taken are very diverse.[10] If these issues are not nicely reducible to a simple liberal-conservative dimension (or any other measurable dimension), then switching may appear to be—and may, in fact, be—a random, uniformly distributed phenomenon. This possibility is represented by the dotted line in figure 5.1.

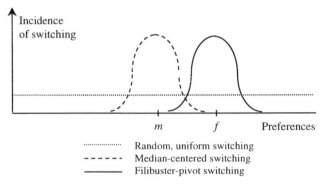

Figure 5.1
Hypotheses about switching on cloture votes

A second possibility is that the essence of vote buying by leaders who target near-indifferent legislators is right, but that the essence of the way the pivotal politics theory portrays filibusters and cloture is wrong. If, for example, filibusters and implicit filibuster threats do not dampen convergence to the median voter's preferred outcome—that is, if the so-called filibuster pivot is not really pivotal—then a simple-majority, median-voter theory would make a better predictive partner for vote-buying theory be-

10. The common perception that most filibusters in history were those launched by Southerners in opposition to civil rights legislation is mythical, in spite of some excellent works on the role Rule 22 played in civil rights lawmaking (Mann 1996). See Binder and Smith 1997, chap. 4, for perspective.

cause switching behavior will be concentrated at and around the Senate's median voter. This possibility is represented by the dashed curve in figure 5.1.

The third possibility is that the vote-buying theory and the pivotal politics theory are both good approximations of voting behavior in the Senate, in which case switching should be most prevalent at or near the filibuster pivot.[11] This possibility is represented by the solid curve in figure 5.1, and it is the main hypothesis to be tested.

DATA

Data are drawn from the universe of cloture votes in the U.S. Senate, commencing with the first such vote on February 2, 1921, and continuing through the 103d Congress which adjourned in 1994. During this period, the Senate held roll calls on motions to invoke cloture on 389 occasions.

Substantial variation is evident within this set of observations. The substance of legislation on which cloture was brought to a vote appears to be a good cross-section of congressional matters: trade and foreign policy (8.3 percent of cloture votes), military and defense policy (5.9), welfare and civil rights (27.8), government and economy (38.1), energy and natural resources (9.5), and other matters (10.3).[12] The number of yes votes on cloture motions ranges from 2 to 98 while the number of no votes ranges from 0 to 93. Within this wide range, the central tendencies are consistent with the thrust of supermajoritarian politics. The average number of yes votes is 59.1, and the average number of no votes is 34.4. In other words, the average percentage of yes votes is 63—about midway between the two historic cloture-invoking thresholds of 60 and 67. In spite of this average proximity of vote totals to the threshold, cloture motions fail more often than not. Table 5.1 provides a simple breakdown for two historical periods: before and after the threshold was changed from $^2/_3$ of senators present and voting to $^3/_5$ of the full Senate. Overall, about 36.5 percent of cloture motions pass.

---

11.   Although it may seem more accurate to center this distribution somewhat to the left of f based on the reasoning that successive cloture votes occur only if fewer than 60 votes (or in earlier periods $^2/_3$ of the Senate) are obtained, this reasoning is based on a false premise. As shown below, cloture can be invoked at one stage but still requested again at another stage, in which case switching to the right of f necessarily occurs.

12.   Such classification schemes are subjective and imprecise, of course. The limited aim is to show that cloture reaches deeply and broadly into legislative affairs. For more evidence consistent with this assertion, see Beth 1995; and Binder and Smith 1997.

Table 5.1
Success of Cloture Motions before and after 1975

	Failed	Passed	TOTAL
Before 1975	78	22	100
	(78.0)	(22.0)	(100.0)
During and after 1975	169	120	289
	(58.5)	(41.5)	(100.0)
TOTAL	**247**	**142**	**389**
	(63.5)	**(36.5)**	**(100.0)**

Passage, however, was almost twice as likely after the threshold was lowered (41.5 percent) than before (22 percent).

Successive ·Cloture Votes

The remaining analysis in this chapter focuses on approximately two-thirds of the universe of cloture votes. More specifically, we restrict attention to instances in which there were at least two cloture votes on the same measure before the same Senate. These and only these vote pairs provide opportunities to observe switching behavior, as discussed above. Eventually, the unit of observation will be a *senator switch opportunity* within a given Congress and for a given bill. Table 5.2 shows the distribution of numbers of votes held for each measure subject to a cloture vote and the corresponding frequency of bills that had the specified number of cloture votes. Although the modal number of votes per measure is one, a large fraction of the bills and nominations subject to cloture votes were subject to more than one such vote. Thus, there is no shortage of senator switch opportunities.

From the 222 − 130 = 92 bills with multiple cloture votes in table 5.2, 167 vote pairs are formed.[13] The distribution of these votes across time is graphed in figure 5.2. As noted in several other sources,[14] cloture votes have become more common in recent history. Recall, however, that this graph

13.   The number of vote pairs is not straightforwardly related to the number of bills because of varying sizes of votes per bill. For example, a set size of two, of course, can make only one pair; a set size of three makes two pairs (A and B, B and C, but not A and C because we analyze only switching on *successive* cloture votes). Generally, a set size of n makes $n - 1$ vote pairs.

14.   See, for example, Beth 1995; Binder and Smith 1997; and Oppenheimer 1985.

Table 5.2
Distribution *N* Cloture Votes for Each Measure

N Cloture Votes	Freq. of Bills	%
1	130	58.56
2	52	23.42
3	23	10.36
4	10	4.50
6	4	1.80
7	2	0.90
8	1	0.45
TOTAL	**222**	**100.00**

is of pairs of successive cloture votes. While the quantity of such pairs in-creased dramatically after the 91st Congress, the likelihood of having succes-sive cloture votes conditional on a first vote seems not to have risen over time. For example, the first quartile in the pairs distribution (fig. 5.2) ends at exactly the same historical point as the first quartile of the all-votes distri-bution (not presented).

What tends to happen when successive cloture votes are taken? Table

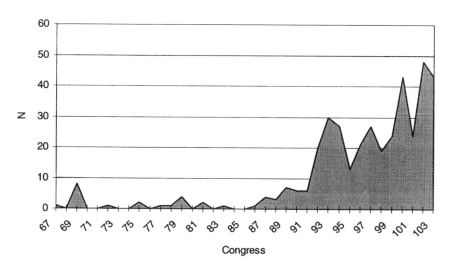

Figure 5.2
Distribution of pairs of successive cloture votes

Table 5.3

Success of Cloture Motions on First and Second Votes in a Pair

	Second Vote		
	Fail	**Pass**	**TOTAL**
First vote			
Fail	110	29	**139**
	(79.1)	(20.9)	**(100.0)**
Pass	11	17	**28**
	(39.3)	(60.7)	**(100.0)**
TOTAL	**121**	**46**	**167**
	(72.5)	**(27.5)**	**(100.0)**

NOTE: Row percentages in parentheses.

5.3 gives a preliminary indication by cross-tabulating successful invoking of cloture on the first vote with success on the second vote of pairs.[15] When the first cloture vote in a pair fails, as happens over four-fifths of the time, the successive vote fails, too, 79 percent of the time. In contrast, passage of the first vote in a pair is followed by failure only 39 percent of the time. This suggestion of a modicum of consistency in vote pairs is underscored by central tendencies in margins of success or failure, relative to the historically variable cloture-invoking threshold. On average, the first vote in a pair falls short of the threshold by five votes, while the second vote falls short only three votes.[16] While this pattern provides a hint of momentum or coalition building, it also accentuates the on-average difficulty of assembling a super-majority to close debate.

Individual-Level Data on Switchers

The vote pairs identified above are the building blocks for the main, individual-level dataset. The dependent variable in the analysis is the presence or absence of a change in a senator's vote from one cloture vote to the next. Of the 15,549 switching opportunities in the dataset, there are 1,281 instances of actual switching. That is, the probability that a randomly selected senator switches on a randomly selected pair of successive cloture

15. Because the same measure can be filibustered at numerous stages in the process, all four pass-fail combinations are possible. For example, cloture may be invoked on the motion to proceed but may fail subsequently on, say, closing debate on the conference report.

16. The respective medians are six and four votes below the threshold.

Table 5.4
Descriptive Statistics

Variable	Mean	S.D.	Min.	Max.
Switch	.083	.276	0	1
f-quartile	.252	.434	0	1
f-adjacent moderates	.248	.432	0	1
f-adjacent extremists	.250	.433	0	1
Nonadjacent extremists	.250	.433	0	1
President-side filibuster	.293	.455	0	1
Divided government	.711	.453	0	1
Democrat	.553	.497	0	1
Distance from *f*	.360	.242	0	1.61

votes is .083. In one respect, this number seems rather high. For instance, recall that on average the vote margins on successive cloture votes move only from -5 to -3. On the other hand, switching can be either of two forms—YN or NY—so the aggregate patterns may hide substantial individual-level variation.[17] The aim of the analysis is to discern whether independent variables identified by the pivotal politics theory or by more casual conjectures can account for a statistically significant amount of such variation. Summary statistics for the dependent variable, *switch,* and various independent variables are presented in table 5.4.

Four dummy variables denote quartiles in senators' ideological predispositions relative to the filibuster pivot. Figure 5.3 illustrates a situation in which the president, *p,* and veto pivot, *v,* are left-of-center (Democratic).

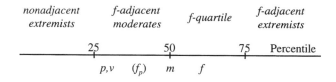

Figure 5.3
Preference quartiles

<hr>

17.   Analysis in Chapters 7 and 8 is sensitive to directional switching; analysis in Chapters 5 and 6 is not.

As in the theory, senators are presumed to be arrayed along a unidimensional line. The dummy variables are accordingly derived from a unidimensional ideology measure.[18] First, cutpoints are identified at the twenty-fifth, fiftieth, and seventy-fifth centiles. Then each senator within each Congress is assigned a 1 for membership in one and only one of the resulting four intervals and a 0 for each remaining quartile. The quartile that includes the filibuster pivot is called the *f-quartile*. In the bordering intervals are *f-adjacent moderates* and *f-adjacent extremists*. On the far side of the *f*-quartile are *nonadjacent extremists*.

An annoying but curable exception to these codings arises in approximately 30 percent of the vote pairs that involve *president-side filibusters:*

> From time to time, the president seems to prefer that a bill be killed by a filibuster rather than having the measure make it to his desk for signature or veto and thus force him to take a stand on the issue. Aware of the president's interests, his Senate supporters filibuster a bill that could more easily be killed by a veto. . . . The effect is to spare the president the political fallout of making a choice. (Binder and Smith 1997, 149)

As developed and discussed in Chapter 2, the pivotal politics theory focuses on only one of two empirically possible filibuster pivots—that which lies on the opposite side of the median voter from the president and the veto pivot. This expository simplification, however, is not intended to deny that senators on the president's side of the median voter also have the right to engage in extended debate. When they exercise these rights, the theoretically relevant pivot is f_p rather than f in figure 5.3. Operationally, these filibusters are identifiable as cloture situations in which at least a majority of the president's party members oppose cloture (and thus seem to be the initiators of, and participants in, the filibuster), and at least a majority of opposite-party members favor cloture. In vote pairs involving president-side filibusters, so defined, the quartile dummy variables must be recoded. The *f*-quartile becomes the f-adjacent moderate quartile and vice versa, and the two extremist-quartile codings are likewise reversed.

The remaining independent variables are straightforward. *Divided govern-*

---

18. Any such measure can be used, such as ratings from the Americans for Democratic Action, the American Conservative Union, Heckman and Snyder's 1996 principal components measure (the first dimension), or Poole and Rosenthal's 1985 nominal three-stage estimations, more commonly known as NOMINATEs. All such measures are highly correlated ($r > .9$ often), suggesting that the specific choice from this class of measures is not crucial. Due to its widespread availability, I use Poole and Rosenthal's NOMINATE measure (first coordinate).

Table 5.5
Switching within Quartiles

	Non–Switchers	Switchers	TOTAL
Nonadjacent extremists	3628	258	3886
	(93.36)	(6.64)	(100)
f-adjacent moderates	3520	333	3853
	(91.36)	(8.64)	(100)
f-quartile	3497	395	3892
	(89.85)	(10.15)	(100)
f-adjacent extremists	3541	295	3836
	(92.31)	(7.69)	(100)
TOTAL	**14178**	**1281**	**15549**
	(91.7)	**(8.3)**	**(100)**

NOTE: Row percentages in parentheses.

ment takes on a value of 1 only if the partisan control of the House, Senate, and White House are not all identical. *Democrat* takes a value of 1 when the senator belongs to, or organizes with, the Democratic party. Although in the chapter on vetoes there are some a priori and arguably theoretical reasons to expect these variables to affect switching, here party and government-type dummies are included solely as atheoretic checks on the robustness of the preference-based findings. Finally, *distance from f* is an alternative, continuous preference measure that is the absolute difference between the senator's and the filibuster pivot's preference measure. Unlike the quartile dummy variables, this measure presumes that the underlying ideology measures are cardinal in nature.[19]

Cross-tabulations of the independent variables with the dependent variable provide preliminary support for the expectation that switching behavior has systematic measurable components. Table 5.5 shows that switching behavior is most prevalent in the filibuster quartile, next most common in adjacent quartiles, and least common among extremists farthest from *f*. Comparable tables not presented confirm lower rates of switching during president-side than opposite-side filibusters, greater rates of switching dur-

19. For reasons discussed in Chapter 3, note 28, I am wary of the cardinal properties of such measures and therefore am more comfortable with the quartile recodings, which, in effect, assume only that the ideology measures are ordinally valid. The distance-from-pivot measures used here and in Chapter 6 are included mainly for readers who more confidently presume that the ideology measures have cardinal validity, or for readers who might otherwise suspect that this methodological judgment has a bearing on the substantive findings.

ing divided than unified government, and lower rates of switching among Democrats than Republicans. Interpretations of these and related findings are taken up in the next section.

MULTIVARIATE TESTS

The multivariate analysis is designed to test two sets of hypotheses. The primary aim is to discern whether systematic preference effects are consistent with the theory of pivotal politics. That is: Are senators at or near the filibuster pivot most likely to switch votes in successive cloture-invoking opportunities? Are senators in adjacent quartiles next most likely to switch, but significantly less likely to switch than those in the *f*-quartile? The secondary aim is to discern whether significant differences in switching behavior occur in the presence of president-side filibusters, in divided versus unified government, or among one party or the other, while controlling for preference effects.

Probit analysis is a useful technique for testing such hypotheses. Like the regression analysis employed in Chapter 3, probit estimations summarize the marginal impact of hypothetical causes on a specified dependent variable. In the switcher analysis, however, the dependent variable takes on only two values: o if a senator's pair of votes are consistent (YY or NN), or 1 if the senator switched (YN or NY). This fact makes probit coefficients somewhat more difficult to interpret than regression coefficients, but the essence of the technique is the same as regression. As a baseline, consider an equation whose estimates of β reflect preference effects on switching as follows:

$$\Pr(switch = 1) = \Phi(\beta_0 + \beta_1 \, f\text{-}quartile + \beta_2 \, moderates + \beta_3 \, extremists). \quad (1)$$

With senators exhaustively classified into one and only one quartile as a function of their ideology measures, the group within which switching is hypothesized to be greatest is that which includes the filibuster pivot, that is, the *f*-quartile. The two neighboring quartiles—*f*-adjacent moderates and *f*-adjacent extremists—should exhibit significantly less switching behavior than the *f*-quartile, but more switching than the quartile composed of extremists not adjacent to *f* (see fig. 5.3 above). Because only three of the four quartile dummy variables can be entered into an estimable equation, the constant term of the equation (β_0) reflects the likelihood of switching by a senator who is in the excluded quartile, namely, that composed of senators on the farther extreme from f.[20] Estimates of the remaining coefficients (β_1, β_2, β_3) reflect deviations from this invariably low baseline.

Hypotheses

Formation of precise statistical hypothesis tests that reflect the substantive propositions is now straightforward.

1. The coefficient for f-quartile should be positive and significantly different from zero, indicating that proximity to f is associated with a higher probability of switching. Formally, the null hypothesis we wish to reject is: $\beta_1 = 0$.

2. The coefficient for f-quartile should be significantly greater than that for f-adjacent moderates. The null synopothesis is: $\beta_1 = \beta_2$.

3. Likewise, the coefficient for f-quartile should be significantly greater than that for f-adjacent extremists. The null hypothesis is: $\beta_1 = \beta_3$.

Findings

Table 5.6 presents the estimates for equation (1).[21] Additionally, the bottom three rows of the table present p-values for the three primary hypotheses.[22]

---

20.   More precisely $\Phi(\beta_0)$ is the probability that such a senator switches, where $\Phi(\cdot)$ is the cumulative normal distribution function.

21.   As noted above, researchers hold divergent views on appropriate standards of statistical significance and on conventions for presenting findings such as these. A new twist that arises here is a view that in an analysis in which the universe of cloture switching is analyzed rather than a sample of cloture switching, any observed differences should be considered significant, that is, not attributable to chance. This perspective seems extreme, but readers are free to adopt it. Additionally, even if there were a consensus that tests of significance are desirable in this setting, previously discussed issues resurface. Should one-tailed or two-tailed tests be conducted (e.g., if the underlying theory provides or does not provide a directional prediction, respectively)? Should we be more concerned with type I or type II errors? What critical value of significance should be adopted? And so on. As noted in note 1 of Chapter 3, rather than stake out and defend a position on such questions (which seem inevitably to be subjective), I prefer to supply the requisite information for readers to apply their own standards. So, for example, I will perform hypothesis tests, often reporting p-values. Similarly, (asymptotic) t-statistics are reported under all coefficients, although I shall refrain from single- double- triple-star and dagger conventions of marking coefficients according to whether they attain arbitrary levels of significance.

22.   The p-value is the largest probability at which, given the coefficients and their standard errors, one would fail to reject the null hypothesis. Thus, the smaller is p, the more confident is the rejection of the null hypothesis as stated in 1–3.

Table 5.6

Probit Estimates of Switchers on Successive Cloture Votes: 69th–103d Congresses

Variable	1	2	3	4	5	6	7
f quartile	0.230	0.250	0.233	0.240	0.303	0.475	0.554
	(5.574)	(5.939)	(5.642)	(5.778)	(7.016)	(8.229)	(8.123)
f-adjacent moderates	0.140	0.147	0.142	0.161	0.183	0.226	0.333
	(3.316)	(3.403)	(3.343)	(3.774)	(4.137)	(3.676)	(4.638)
f-adjacent extremists	0.077	0.085	0.080	0.072	0.133	0.142	0.109
	(1.791)	(1.936)	(1.854)	(1.665)	(2.971)	(2.259)	(1.423)
President-side filibuster		−0.577			−0.677	−0.357	−0.269
		(−14.636)			(−16.440)	(−7.277)	(−4.737)
Divided government			0.119		0.293	0.046	−0.084
			(3.598)		(8.408)	(1.020)	(−1.594)
Democrat				−0.223	−0.228	−0.039	−0.035
				(−7.610)	(−7.550)	(−0.962)	(−0.756)
Constant	−1.503	−1.386	−1.592	−1.395	−1.496	−1.805	−1.815
	(−48.500)	(−43.072)	(−39.876)	(−40.923)	(−34.720)	(−36.695)	(−25.976)
N	15,549	15,549	15,549	15,549	15,549	11,965	9,287
Log likelihood	−4,399	−4,276	−4,293	−4,370	−4,209	−2,245	−1,670
Pseudo-R^2	0.004	0.032	0.0053	0.01	0.047	0.029	0.036
p for $H^0:\beta_1 = 0$	<0.001	<0.001	<0.001	<0.001	<0.001	<0.001	<0.001
p for $H^0:\beta_1 = \beta_2$	0.023	0.011	0.021	0.048	0.003	<0.001	<0.001
p for $H^0:\beta_1 = \beta_3$	<0.001	<0.001	<0.001	<0.001	<0.001	<0.001	<0.001

NOTE: Maximum likelihood estimates with asymptotic t-statistics in parentheses. Equations (1)–(5) are based on all pairs of successive cloture votes from 1927 through 1994. Equation (6) restricts observations to those in which both cloture votes in the pair were within 15 votes of the cloture-invoking threshold. Equation (7) restricts observations to those in which both cloture votes in the pair were within 10 votes of the cloture-invoking threshold.

In equation (1), preference effects on cloture switching are moderately strong, highly significant, and in the predicted direction. Senators in the *f*-quartile are not only more likely to be switchers than the baseline nonadjacent extremists (hypothesis 1), but they are also more likely to switch than their more proximate moderate and extremist colleagues (hypotheses 2 and 3). Consistent with the pivotal politics theory, the locus of bargaining over legislation that elicits cloture attempts seems consistently to be at or near the supermajoritarian filibuster pivot.

Although these findings are derived from within the probit framework, this is essentially the same result presented above in cross-tabular form. A more specific question is whether this basic relationship between preferences and switching holds in the presence of controls for other known correlates of switchers and in subsamples of observations that are arguably more defensible bases for inference.

Equations (2) through (7) suggest that the primary findings about preference proximity to the filibuster pivot are robust. The three primary hypotheses are always supported with high levels of significance even though, within these 15,549 switcher opportunities, an inordinate amount of variation is statistically unaccounted for and is thus best described as idiosyncratic.

Secondary findings in table 5.6 can be discussed in left-to-right fashion. Equation (2) addresses the relatively unusual feature of president-side filibusters as introduced and discussed above. The theoretical interpretation of these situations is that, on balance, they should suppress the amount of switching. In the somewhat improbable but imaginable case of a president-issue combination in which the president is more moderate than the filibuster pivot on his side of the ideological spectrum (e.g., $f_p < p < m < f$), the president-side filibuster pivot constitutes a genuine constraint on policy convergence, so switching should take place in the same fashion and at the same rates as in the more common cases in which the binding filibuster constraint is from the opposite side of the ideological spectrum. However, in instances in which the president is more extreme than the filibuster pivot on his side (e.g., $p < f_p < m < f$), the theory suggests that president-side filibusters are mere grandstanding in advance of the real congressional-executive showdown, which is between a legislative majority as proposer and the president and veto pivot as a credible blocking coalition. As such, heavy bargaining and switching is more likely to occur later in the governmental process than at the cloture stage. (This will be studied in Chap. 6.)

In summary, to the degree that the latter, grandstanding cases are common (and conversely the former, binding-f cases are rare), the effect of the dummy variable, *president-side filibuster,* should be negative.[23] Indeed, the estimated effect is negative whenever the variable is included. The coefficient of $-.557$ in equation (2), for example, can be quantified as follows. Imagine two cloture pairs, a relatively common nonpresident-side filibuster and a relatively rare president-side filibuster. In each case, consider further an f-quartile senator, that is, a senator from the most-likely-to-switch group. In the first, normal case, his switching probability is .129. In the second, president-side case it drops by .083 to .046.[24] In other words, it appears that many or most president-side filibusters fail to attract sufficient, or sufficiently serious, bargaining efforts to yield high rates of switching. A theoretical explanation for this finding is that the real pivotal player in these cases is v, not f_p.

Equations (3) and (4) inspect two hypotheses that may be compatible with conventional wisdom but cannot readily be linked to the pivotal politics theory. First, is switching more likely in divided than unified government, other things equal? The answer is yes, although the magnitude of the divided-government effect is small. Again using the most likely switcher category as our baseline (f-quartile senators), the probabilistic increment associated with divided government is only .025, or one in 40.[25] So, to the extent that switching is a manifestation of bargaining, bargaining with senators near the filibuster pivot is slightly more common in divided than unified government.

Second, do Democrats switch more than Republicans, other things equal? Here the answer is no. In equation (4) the magnitude of the secondary effect is greater than that for divided government in equation (3) The probability that a Democrat in the f-quartile switches is .040 less than that for an f-quartile Republican.

Equation (5) considers all primary and secondary effects simultaneously and improves the overall fit. The qualitative findings are unchanged, but some coefficients increase. The preference effects are uniformly greater and of greater significance in the presence of all three control variables, and this

---

23. This condition is suggested—but cannot be conclusively established—by the fact that president-side filibusters are more likely than other filibusters to be dropped prior to successful invoking of cloture.

24. The calculations are as follows. The probability that a normal filibuster-pivot senator switches is $\Phi(\beta_0 + \beta_1) = .129$. The probability that a president-side filibuster-pivot senator switches is $\Phi(\beta_0 + \beta_1 + \beta_4) = .046$.

25. From equation (3), the calculation is $\Phi(\beta_0 + \beta_1 + \beta_4) - \Phi(\beta_0 + \beta_1) = .025$.

is true of two of the three secondary effects, too—president-side filibuster and divided government. Thus, all variables seem to belong in the equation, even though not all of them are directly identified as important by the pivotal politics theory.

As noted earlier, equations (1) through (5) are based on data that are unfiltered. Many of the thousands of senator-switch-opportunities are likely not to involve serious back scratching, arm twisting, or vote buying. For example, about 10 percent of the vote pairs are of the pass-pass type (cloture being invoked in each vote), suggesting that the second cloture vote may have been superfluous.[26] A few vote pairs involve parliamentarily perverse situations. For example, in 1985, Senator Ted Kennedy (D-Mass.) begged colleagues to vote no on a cloture petition on the conference report for the Anti-Apartheid Action Act, even though Kennedy had initiated the petition. Because Kennedy knew the petition was doomed, he wanted to be able to explain the anticipated failing vote to constituents as strictly procedural.[27] Finally, many pairs involve votes that seem in retrospect not to have been serious at all, based on the outcome. For example, in about 12 percent of the vote pairs, at least one cloture vote margin was at least 20 votes away from the cloture-invoking threshold. Peculiar observations such as these (and undoubtedly other types as well) are likely to inject considerable noise into the analysis. On one hand, this may contribute to the impressiveness of the large-sample findings: systematic and theory-consistent effects can be heard even through the cacophony of seven decades of variegated cloture history. On the other hand, we should also be concerned that the effects in equations (1) through (5) may be misleading artifacts of the inclusion of hundreds if not thousands of bizarre cloture votes.

It is impossible to exclude idiosyncratic observations without being somewhat ad hoc and thus casting doubt on the appropriate settings from which to generalize. Thus, equations (6) and (7) should be viewed as attempts to address but not solve this problem. The general aim is the exclu-

---

26.   Consistent with this conjecture, the quantity of switching in pass-pass vote pairs is less than half of what it is for pairs that involve only one successful cloture motion. Reestimation of equation (5) excluding pass-pass vote pairs yields the same qualitative effects and provides a better overall fit.

27.   According to Kennedy, "Cloture in this situation is redundant and meaningless. It is procedural cloture, not substantive cloture" (*Congressional Record*, September 12, 1985, S11327). The eventual motion on which the vote occurred was, "Is it sense of the Senate that debate on the motion to proceed to the consideration of the conference report on H.R. 1460 be brought to a close?" (ibid., S11328). The "sense of the Senate" language is atypical.

sion of vote pairs that, based on their lack of closeness, seem not to pose serious negotiation opportunities. Therefore, equation (6) drops observations in which one or both votes in the pair were greater than 15 votes from the cloture-invoking threshold.[28] Equation (7) adopts a comparable but more selective selection criterion of 10 votes. The consequence is to filter out approximately one-fifth of the observations in each cut. From a theoretical perspective, the minimum requirement of these filters is that they leave intact the preference effects that are central to the theory and that were identified in equations (1) through (5). A more optimistic expectation is that as the set of observations is better tailored to seemingly significant cloture votes, these primary preference effects will become stronger while the secondary effects weaken, vanish, or are exposed as unstable.

The optimistic expectation is borne out. The crucial *f*-quartile effect increases sharply and retains a high level of statistical significance. Moving from equation (5) to (6) to (7), it appears that as one focuses attention on arguably significant cloture votes the prevalence of the filibuster pivot consistently grows. The preference effect in the *f*-adjacent moderate bloc also increases, as does the level of significance of the differences between the *f*-quartile and its neighbors. In short, switching is strongly and positively correlated with proximity to the filibuster pivot, especially when analyses of switching behavior center on relatively close cloture situations.

The secondary effects also exhibit some noteworthy changes. The switcher-suppressing effect of president-side filibusters remains statistically significant but diminishes when only close vote pairs are considered. For a senator in the *f*-quartile, the marginal probabilistic effect of a president-side filibuster in equation (3) was −.083. In equation (7) it is a much smaller −.036. Although in isolation this finding remains consistent with the theory, it is small in comparison to the increases in preference effects. For instance, the marginal probabilistic effects of being in the *f*-quartile relative to the far-extremist, near-extremist, and adjacent-moderate quartiles, respectively, are .210, .199, and .175.

Meanwhile, the effect of divided government becomes unstable as the sample size is reduced. It becomes much smaller and insignificant in equation (6). In equation (7), its sign changes, and it is not possible to reject confidently the null hypothesis of no effect. Finally, the demise of the Democrat effect is similarly abrupt. Divided government and party effects, there-

---

28. Calculations were different before and after Rule 22 changes, accounting for the earlier threshold of ⅔ of those present and voting versus the latter threshold of ⅗ of the entire Senate.

Table 5.7

Distance-Based Probit Estimates of Switchers: 69th–103d Congresses

Variable/Equation	(1)	(2)	(3)	(4)
Distance from f	−0.145	−0.186	−0.617	−0.852
	(−2.434)	(−2.980)	(−7.047)	(−8.089)
President-side filibuster		−0.656	−0.326	−0.229
		(−16.116)	(−6.697)	(−4.047)
Divided government		0.269	−0.014	−0.177
		(7.711)	(−0.302)	(−3.314)
Democrat		−0.223	−0.069	−0.060
		(−7.280)	(−1.714)	(−1.289)
Constant	−1.335	−1.256	−1.312	−1.181
	(−52.347)	(−29.240)	(−24.326)	(−18.966)
N	15,549	15,549	11,969	9,287
Log likelihood	−4,414	−4,231	−2,259	−1,679
Pseudo-R^2	0.001	0.042	0.023	0.031
p for $H^o:\beta_1 = 0$	0.015	0.003	<0.001	<0.001

NOTE: Maximum likelihood estimates with asymptotic t-statistics in parentheses. Equations (1)–(5) are based on all pairs of successive cloture votes from 1927 through 1994. Equation (4) restricts observations to those in which both cloture votes in the pair were within 15 votes of the cloture-invoking threshold. Equation (5) restricts observations to those in which both cloture votes in the pair were within 10 votes of the cloture-invoking threshold.

fore, seem to be artifacts of the inclusion of a large number of cloture pairs in which at least one vote is lopsided.

Table 5.7 presents a final check on the robustness of the findings. The structure of the analysis parallels that in table 5.6, but there is one change in model specification. Rather than classify senators into quartiles based on their ideological proximity to the filibuster pivot—in effect treating such proximity as a simple ordinal phenomenon—this set of equations treats the measure of ideology as if it were cardinal in nature. Thus, the three preference-based dummy variables in table 5.6 are now represented as a single measure, *distance from f*, which, the theory hypothesizes, is negatively related to switching. Entered into the probit equation by itself and estimated using the unfiltered sample of observations, this variable has the expected negative effect in equation (1). This effect, however, is not strong, and the variable by itself explains almost no variation by the summary R^2 criterion. The size and significance of *distance from f* is enhanced somewhat in equation (2) when the secondary variables are included. These findings are generally consistent with equation (5) in table 5.6. Finally, the filters for closeness of cloture votes are applied in equations (3) and (4) with results comparable to those in equations (6) and (7) in table 5.6. The primary, preference effects are much stronger and more significant in the smaller samples, while the secondary effects are weaker, somewhat unstable, and often insignificant.[29]

CAVEATS AND CONCLUSIONS

Results from the study of vote switchers in cloture situations are generally consistent with the expectations of the pivotal politics theory. Switching is not entirely random, nor is it concentrated mostly around the Senate's median voter. Rather, throughout the history of the Senate under Rule 22, switching tends to be concentrated near the filibuster pivot.

Two quite different schools of thought can be anticipated regarding the perceived significance of these findings. The first one centers on the general view that there are several reasons to have had low expectations for a test of this sort. The nature of the test was such that support required that two highly stylized theories—not just the pivotal politics theory but vote-buying theory, too—are good approximations of much more complex real-world political settings. The test also demands a lot from the data, especially measures of preferences, because it effectively reduces all the action onto one general dimension that may not be a good approximation of the conflict evident in any specific case. The test disregards completely the claim that voting for cloture is a matter of abstract procedural principle—a claim that at least one set of researchers characterizes as "received wisdom" (Binder and Smith 1997, 19).[30] And finally, the test focuses on behavior that, in a very strict sense, is off the equilibrium path with respect to the focal theory. That is, in its pure version, the pivotal politics theory predicts

29.   All equations in tables 5.6 and 5.7 were also reestimated incorporating congress-specific fixed effects. On one hand, this is utterly atheoretic because we have no congress-specific theories. On the other hand, such a specification nevertheless provides a useful robustness check on the more parsimonious equations estimated and presented above. The results do not change any of the main substantive findings and interpretations. Preference-quartile coefficients in fixed-effects specifications are always very close to those reported in table 5.6. Coefficients for *distance from f* in the table 5.7 counterpart equations are much stronger, however ($-.258$, $-.392$, $-.877$, and -1.118 in equations (1)–(4) respectively, and always significant at $p < .001$). President-side filibuster coefficients tend to be somewhat larger (and still negative as predicted), while coefficients for divided government and Democrat (which were not central concerns) are again unstable across samples and specifications. Finally, pseudo R^2s of the fixed-effects equations are understandably much greater than in tables 5.6 and 5.7; however, as noted, there is no theoretical basis for this increment in explained variation.

30.   Binder and Smith (1997) do not agree with the received wisdom, however.

no filibusters. My response was, in effect, to concede that the theory is an imperfect predictor of lawmaking behavior and to examine what can be regarded as noisy situations in which a filibuster probably did occur, and thus cloture votes were taken. Such votes, in turn, place before the Senate the uncertain question of whether a supermajority can proceed to make new laws. In other words, by selecting murky situations in which to test a relatively clear theory, it may be more difficult to find support for the theory.

The second school of thought turns some of these arguments upside down and exposes some legitimate doubts about the methods employed. First, selection bias is a nettlesome concern. I selected clear-cut cases where cloture was *the* motion before the Senate. The outstanding question concerns the direction of the bias this introduces. It may have facilitated corroboration because the parliamentary requirement is clearly a supermajority on cloture votes. In effect, this would seem to force the *expected* vote margin away from the median (50–50) point toward the filibuster-pivot (60–40 or 67–33) point. On the other hand, the nature of bias may have been such that corroboration was impeded, because truncation of larger-than-supermajority situations seems more likely than truncation of smaller-than-supermajority situations. The logic of this conjecture is that bill opponents would rather call off the filibuster than get trounced in a cloture vote, so we are less likely to observe super-supermajority votes *(sic)*. In contrast, bill supporters will not call off a cloture vote in an expected sub-supermajority situation because they like to test the waters and/or show the world that the bill commands at least majority support.

It is beyond the scope of this study to resolve these difficult methodological issues, although they seem to deserve additional attention in future studies. In the meantime, a modest closing claim is offered. Filibuster pivots and their spatially close colleagues often attract disproportionate attention of legislative leaders, making it appear as if the pivotal politics theory captures an important aspect of lawmaking.

·❧· SIX

VETO PIVOTS

Students of lawmaking sometimes protest the myopia of researchers of Congress who, when studying the legislative process narrowly, neglect to give the president a prominent role. "Where is the president?" is a more or less standard query. Similarly and more significantly, presidents occasionally protest the myopia of members of Congress who, when making laws, neglect to give the president a prominent role. "I am relevant!" is how one president recently expressed his feelings of pain after the first midterm election of his presidency. And to demonstrate his relevance, he resorted to his Constitution-granted authority to veto legislation.

The president, of course, was Bill Clinton. The government was divided (to put it mildly). A Republican majority had swept into the Congress in both chambers for the first time in 40 years, and the hyped-up majority simultaneously pursued a number of legislative initiatives that the Democratic president did not like (also to put it mildly). Government shutdowns were threatened. Government shutdowns occurred. Vetoes were threatened. Vetoes occurred. By the time the 104th Congress adjourned, 17 vetoes had been cast, only one had been overridden, and major compromises occurred on nearly every major congressional initiative.

Few students of the Congress and probably no student of the presidency would seriously dispute that the veto enhances the president's relevance in U.S. lawmaking.[1] Even when the veto is not used, legislators are cognizant

---

1. A minor exception is that some students of the presidency question the significance of the veto in the first few decades of the republic (see, e.g., Spitzer 1988).

that it might be used, and they modify their lawmaking behavior accordingly. But it is one thing to assert that the president is relevant and quite another to have a demonstrably good predictive theory that links his relevance to the veto.

The pivotal politics theory is one of several formal models in which the veto plays a prominent role, and the aim in this chapter is to test its veto-pivot implications. In contrast with the previous chapter on the politics of filibusters and cloture, this chapter can draw upon a larger and more diverse literature. Empirical studies have focused on the number of vetoes cast or sustained (Hoff 1991; Light 1991; Rohde and Simon 1985), the causes of vetoes (Copeland 1983; Grier, McDonald, and Tollison 1994), whether the president is "victorious" in terms of the content of legislation (Watson 1988b), or the conditions under which the president is "powerful" relative to the Congress (Kiewiet and McCubbins 1988; McCarty and Poole 1995; Dearden and Hasted 1990). Additionally, several formal models of executive-legislative relations have been proposed (Cameron 1998; Cameron and Elmes 1994; Carter and Schap 1987; Ingberman and Yao 1991; McCarty 1997; Matthews 1989; Schap 1986), and some of these have been tested (Cameron 1998; Kiewiet and McCubbins 1988; McCarty and Poole 1995).

To be sure, this is an admirable research base. Somewhat surprisingly, however, most of it is not *directly* relevant to my immediate and narrower theory-testing aims. First, the causes of vetoes are of minor interest here. It suffices to stipulate only one cause—that the president does not like the bills he vetoes—and to inspect behavior given that clear-cut executive-legislative tension is present. Second, simply counting the number of vetoes, the number of vetoes sustained, the rate of sustaining, etc., is not helpful for testing the theory. In a very strict sense, the pivotal politics theory predicts no vetoes. Therefore, it is again necessary to base the analysis on a less strict, off-the-equilibrium-path argument. As with the filibuster analysis, the overarching question is: Given that one deviation from the theory occurred, is subsequent individual-level behavior nevertheless consistent with the theory? Third, it is premature to attempt to test for the nature and extent of presidential power. To do this, one needs, and preferably needs to make explicit, a corroborated theory of executive-legislative interaction. The immediate task, then, is to seek additional support for the pivotal politics theory. In the next two chapters, we will be better equipped to address more difficult questions such as presidential power and its partisan basis.

ANALYSIS OF VETO SWITCHERS

A major item on the Republican agenda in the 104th Congress was to pass legislation restricting investors' securities-fraud lawsuits which are often alleged to be frivolous. As related legislation worked its way through the legislative process, however, congressional coalitions took on a distinctively bipartisan flavor. For example, one of the bill's chief supporters in the Senate was Christopher Dodd, a Democrat from Connecticut, who also happened to be chairman of the Democratic National Committee. Likewise, some Republicans opposed the bill. Senator Arlen Specter of Pennsylvania, for example, not only opposed it but also urged Clinton to veto it and promised to help him seek Senate votes to sustain his veto.[2]

In the meantime, President Clinton played his cards close to his vest. First, he indicated that he was likely to sign the bill. Later, "at the 11th hour," he chose to veto it, citing clauses that his own party leaders considered "relatively minor."[3] Finally, Clinton urged Congress to modify the bill, promising to sign a new measure if stipulated changes were made.[4]

The winning coalitions on initial passage had been large but not clearly veto proof. In the House the winning margin of 320–102 seemed secure and later proved to be. The House voted 319–100 to override the president. In the Senate, however, the winning vote on the final version of the bill was 65–30. What did this greater-than-simple-majority coalition mean? On one hand, a few Republicans, including presidential candidate Phil Gramm, had announced their support for the bill had missed the vote. These votes could take the number of supporters up to or over the $2/3$ threshold of 67. On the other hand, President Clinton was expected to lobby wavering senators—particularly Democrats—to persuade them to switch their votes and oppose the motion to override the veto.[5] In a preemptive strike, Sena-

2. Jeffrey Taylor, "House Votes to Override Veto of Securities Suit Bill," *New York Times,* December 21, 1995.

3. Both quoted phrases are Senator Dodd's, as reported in the *Wall Street Journal,* "President of Torts" (op. ed.), December 21, 1995.

4. Neil A. Lewis, "Senate Puts Off a Vote on Veto of Securities Bill," *New York Times,* December 22, 1995.

5. With a modicum of reading between the lines, one can find evidence that journalists seem to have anticipated the basic thrust of vote-buying theory as introduced in Chapter 5. In this instance, however, the support uncovered was rather thin. One reporter wrote: "It appeared that Mr. Clinton, occupied with budget and welfare matters, did not much bestir himself today to prevent an override of his veto. A check of several Democratic senators *who would likely be targets of a White House effort to enlist support* showed that few were contacted. A spokesman for Senator Jeff Bingaman, a New Mexico Democrat, said that the president had briefly spoken to Mr. Bingaman today but

tor Dodd came out publicly and harshly against his president and worked
with Republicans to retain the votes of bill supporters on the override attempt. In the end, the bill supporters won. The Senate's motion to override
passed 68–30.

This simple description of a complex instance of veto politics serves to
establish one modest but important fact. Just as the analysis of switchers in
cloture situations was helpful in testing the pivotal politics theory in Chapter 5, analysis of switchers can play the same role here with respect to assessing the primacy of the veto pivot in executive-legislative interactions. The
question is not whether the president wins or loses in these showdowns.
Of course, sometimes he wins and sometimes he loses. Rather, the question
is whether, in these executive-legislative battles, the targeted warriors are
those legislators at or near the veto-pivot's position in the policy spectrum.

DATA

From the beginning of the 80th through the end of the 103d Congresses,
U.S. presidents cast 746 vetoes. Of these, the Congress contested 122 bills
with a formal override attempt in at least one chamber. Although the eventual purpose of the analysis is to test hypotheses about individual-level behavior, an overview of the aggregate data as presented in table 6.1 helps to
set the context. Column 1 shows the breakdown of all vetoes for all postwar
presidents. Columns 2–5 narrow the focus to the 122 bills on which at least
one chamber held an override vote. Of these bills, column 3 gives the
number of instances in which the veto was ultimately sustained,[6] column
4 gives the rate in percentage terms at which challenged vetoes are sustained, and column 5 gives the rank ordering of presidents according to
their sustain rate, conditional on an override challenge. I do not endorse this
scorecard approach to ranking presidents in terms of their putative power,
influence, or success. Nonetheless, I include it for two reasons. First, some
researchers do adopt and endorse it. Second, it serves as a useful baseline
against which to compare an alternative set of rankings based on a different
method that will be presented in Chapter 7.

---

failed to persuade him to change his vote." See Neil Lewis, "Senate Puts Off a Vote on Veto of
Securities Bill," *New York Times,* December 22, 1995 (italics added).

6.   This can be via either of the following: both chambers vote to sustain, or one chamber votes
to override while the other votes to sustain. That is, the unit of analysis is the bill—not a single
chamber's action.

Table 6.1

Vetoes and Their Treatment by Congress: 1947–1993

President		1 N Vetoes	2 N Challenged	3 N Sustained	4 Sustain Rate	5 Rank
Truman	(D)	250	19	7	36.8	7
Eisenhower	(R)	181	11	9	81.8	2
Kennedy	(D)	21	0	.	.	.
Johnson	(D)	30	0	.	.	.
Nixon	(R)	43	21	16	76.2	3
Ford	(R)	66	29	17	58.6	4
Carter	(D)	31	4	2	50.0	6
Reagan	(R)	78	16	7	43.8	5
Bush	(R)	46	22	21	95.5	1
Clinton	(D)	0	0	.	.	.
ALL		746	122	79	64.8	.

NOTE: Column 1 is from Ragsdale, 1996, table 8.13, p. 396 (pocket vetoes included). Column 2 includes all vetoes for which at least one chamber cast at least one override vote. Columns 3–5 are based on the sample in column 2. Clinton's row excludes data from the 104th Congress.

In both absolute and in relative terms, table 6.1 makes it clear that congressional challenges are uncommon when Democrats occupy the White House. Excluding President Clinton, for whom there are no vetoes as of his first Congress, the average rate of challenging a Democratic president's veto is barely 5 percent.[7] For Republicans, in contrast, it is over 27 percent. This asymmetry does not cripple the analysis that follows, but the conclusions that can be drawn are necessarily more solid with respect to eras of divided than unified government. Likewise, figure 6.1 shows another departure from uniformly distributed veto events. There are many more instances of override votes in the second half than the first half of the postwar period.

Vote Pairs

The bill-level observations summarized in figure 6.1 represent literally thousands of opportunities to observe switching behavior similar to that studied in Chapter 5. The only remaining prerequisite is that at least one

7.   The data set analyzed in this chapter goes through the 103d Congress. The divided government politics of the 104th Congress, however, is a focal point in Chapter 9.

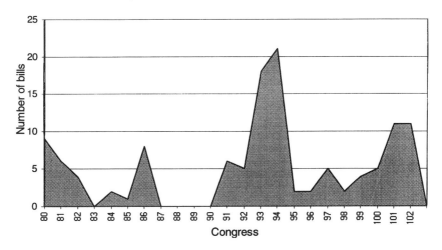

Figure 6.1
Legislation subject to at least one override vote

clean congressional vote on the bill occurred prior to the veto. What is meant by clean? Operationally, a clean vote on a vetoed bill is either (1) a vote by a chamber to pass the bill just prior to sending it to conference or to the other chamber, (2) a final vote on the conference report, or (3) a vote on overriding the president's veto. Thus, three types of vote pairs can occur, all of which are incorporated into the individual-level analysis. These are illustrated in figure 6.2 and described below.

Type I: Precursor Pairs
Some switching opportunities on vetoed bills arise entirely prior to the veto itself and are thus precursors to the more conspicuous legislative-executive

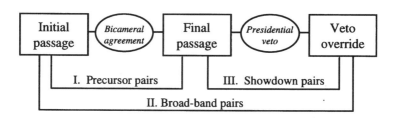

Figure 6.2
Types of veto votes and vote pairs

showdown. These pairs consist of a vote by a chamber to pass the bill just prior to sending it to conference or to the other chamber and a subsequent vote on the conference report. Imagine, for example, a bill that the president opposes but which first passes a chamber with an approximate $2/3$ majority. Pivotal politics and vote-buying theories suggest that legislators at or near v, the $2/3$ pivot, will be pressured by supporters and opponents in anticipation of the veto. Supporters seek a seemingly veto-proof supermajority. Opponents want to expose the softness of the winning coalition to encourage a veto that is seemingly immune from a successful override. The unknown empirical issue is whether pre- and postconference switching behavior is indeed concentrated near the veto pivot.

While these precursor pairs are relatively remote from the final congressional-executive showdown, including them in the analysis makes it possible to corroborate a key rational-expectations component in the theory. Suppose, contrary to the theory, that legislators were myopic or were playing a different game than pivotal politics during these stages.[8] Then switching before and after conference in these immediately majoritarian but eventually supermajoritarian settings may be median centered or perhaps idiosyncratic with respect to the pivotal politics theory. For example, one might expect committee-floor tensions to come to the fore and coalition sizes to shrink to minimum-majority size. Alternatively, suppose legislators are attuned to the larger executive-legislative game of pivotal politics. Then switching behavior in these precursor vote pairs should follow essentially the same patterns as that for vote pairs involving the veto-override attempt itself.

A disadvantage of including these vote pairs, however, is that—as with cloture situations—the votes are not as clean as one would like. We either cannot observe or cannot quantify the substantive changes that occurred in the legislation between the two observed votes. Thus, it is possible that the switching that occurs has less to do with the anticipated big game of executive-legislative bargaining than with the myopic little game of conference politics. Fortunately, we can address these possibilities empirically by discerning whether behavioral dynamics are significantly different across pair types.

---

8. For example, some theorists have portrayed pre- and postconference politics, not as a stage in an executive-legislative battle but rather as the crux of committee power in which the contest pits preference-outlying standing committees against their parent chambers and in which the former win (Shepsle and Weingast 1987).

Table 6.2
Distribution of Senators' Switch Opportunities across Vote-Pair Types

Type of Vote Pair	N Pairs	N Voters[a]	N Switchers	Pct Switchers
I Precursors: preconference passage and postconference passage	40	3,471	359	10.34
II Broad-band: preconference passage and override	53	4,634	651	14.05
III Showdown: postconference passage and override	29	2,526	290	11.48
TOTAL	122	10,631	1,300	12.23

[a] Includes only senators who voted, paired, or announced positions on both votes in the pair.

Type II: Broad-Band Pairs

A second type of switching opportunities includes those that occur between initial (preconference) passage and veto override votes. Like type I precursor vote pairs, type II pairs involve one vote that can be quite distant—temporally and substantively—from the second vote on overriding the president's veto. As a result it may be difficult to find the kind of switching behavior the theory predicts. On the other hand, if it is found it will have been found under difficult circumstances. Thus, inclusion of these observations adds power to the test. An additional, practical advantage of inclusion of broad-band vote pairs is that they are more plentiful than types I and III.

Type III: Showdown Pairs

The least ambiguous switching opportunities occur between the last, pre-presidential, postconference congressional vote and the immediately post-presidential override vote. These are clear-cut legislative-executive showdowns. The main advantage of analyzing showdown vote pairs is that the legislative measures on which the votes are cast are necessarily identical, enrolled bills. Accordingly, switching must be attributable to factors other than the content of the bill at hand. The main disadvantage of this group is that it is the smallest of the three. If we were forced to rely upon these votes alone, some presidents and congresses could not be analyzed.

The upshot of this overview of types of vote shares is twofold. First, we badly need data and thus cast a big net for observations. But second, we also need to be sensitive to the diversity of observations that are dredged.

Table 6.2 summarizes the distribution of types of vote pairs and senatorial

Table 6.3
Descriptive Statistics for Senate Switching Analysis

Variable	N	Mean	S.D.	Min.	Max.
Switch	10,631	.122	.328	0	1
Extreme supporter	11,998	.200	.400	0	1
Supporter	11,998	.199	.399	0	1
Moderate	11,998	.200	.400	0	1
Veto pivot	11,998	.197	.398	0	1
Extreme opponent	11,998	.204	.403	0	1
Distance from v	11,998	.370	.246	0	1.163
Distance from m	11,998	.327	.225	0	1.297
Democrat	12,063	.569	.495	0	1
Divided government	12,063	.974	.159	0	1

switching activity by vote pair. (The House is analyzed separately below.) Vote pairs are reasonably evenly divided across pair types with the chief and unfortunate exception that the cleanest types—showdown pairs—are in shortest supply. Overall, switching is common in veto-related voting. For the 10,631 switching opportunities for senators in the data set, over 12 percent of senators' votes in the second roll call of a pair are different from that in the first roll call. The incidence of switching is somewhat greater among broad-band (type II) pairs. This seems sensible since this type embraces the largest span of legislative activity during which multifaceted forces of coalition building, arm twisting, vote trading, and bill adjusting are at work.

Variables

Table 6.3 presents descriptive statistics for the individual-level data set on which the remainder of the chapter is based.

Switch is a dummy variable equal to 1 if the senator's votes differ across items in the vote pair and equal to 0 otherwise. The necessary exclusion of abstainers accounts for the smaller N for this variable.

As in the cloture analysis, preference effects on veto switching can be estimated in either of two ways: treating the preference data as ordinal or cardinal. The ordinal approach requires fewer heroic assumptions and therefore is the main approach adopted. To make the pivot approximately

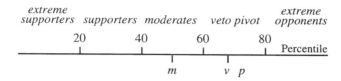

Figure 6.3
Quintiles for veto switcher analyses

central within an arbitrary quantile, legislators are classified into one and only one quintile, as illustrated in figure 6.3: *extreme supporters, moderate supporters, moderates,* senators in the *veto pivot* quintile, and *extreme opponents.* It is important to reiterate that these labels and codings are based on votes over the course of the entire Congress—not specifically or uniquely on the veto-related votes at hand. Thus, an *extreme supporter* is not necessarily a supporter of the bill under consideration but rather is an ideologically extreme senator overall who, based on his or her overall voting record, is merely expected to support the bill. It is also key to bear in mind that the terms *supporter* and *opponent* do not refer to legislators' views of the president. (As a practical matter, they are more likely to mean the opposite.)

Distance from v is the absolute difference between the $\frac{2}{3}$ pivot's ideological score and the senator's ideological score. *Distance from m* is the median-based counterpart. These presumably cardinal measures play only a secondary role in the analysis. Finally, *Democrat* and *divided government* are defined in the obvious manner and are included to test for party- or regime-specific effects.

A DETOUR: DEMOCRATS AND DIVIDED GOVERNMENT

Two sets of hypotheses will be tested in due course: preference-based and party/regime hypotheses. As with the cloture analysis, the preference-based hypotheses can be directly and straightforwardly related to the pivotal politics theory when the vote-buying theory is adopted as an auxiliary or maintained hypothesis. By comparison, party and divided government effects are subject to a wider range of interpretations, some theoretical, some not. The purpose of this detour is to explore inductively the prospects for a credible alternative theory that is perhaps more conventional than the pivotal politics model. The focal dummy variables are *Democrat* and *divided government.*

What should be the effect, if any, of Democratic party affiliation on switching, and why? From a strict, pivotal politics perspective, a hasty answer would be: none, because parties play no role in the theory apart from preferences. From a majority-party power perspective, however, the hasty answer might be: negative, because a strong majority party's leaders are disproportionately effective at persuading or coercing their members to vote the party line and adhere to it, that is, not to switch.[9] A simple cross-tabulation of *Democrat* and *switch* indicates that Democrats are indeed less likely to switch than Republicans. For Democrats the switch rate is 5.1 percent; for Republicans it is over four times greater, 21.6. Should we conclude that Democrats have been a strong party in the postwar era? Not just yet. First, let us make a parallel observation.

What should be the effect, if any, of divided government on switching, and why? From a strict, pivotal politics perspective, a hasty answer again would be: none, because the form of government plays no role in the theory apart from preferences. From a more conventional perspective, however, the hasty answer might be: negative, because split party control forces politicians to dig in their heels, refuse to compromise, to engage in symbolic politics at the expense of gridlock, or to fight, not switch. Likewise, a simple cross-tabulation of *divided government* and *switch* indicates that switching is significantly less common in divided than unified government. In divided government the switch rate is 11.9 percent; in unified government it is over twice as great, 24.2.

Together, these observations seem to bode well for a viable theoretical alternative to the pivotal politics model. The hybrid idea is that an already disciplined congressional majority party is even stronger in divided government. This hypothesis seems consistent with much of the conventional wisdom about divided government. Gridlock happens in divided government precisely because when party control is split, the incentives for give and take (manifested in these data by switching) are negligible. The majority party in Congress is more concerned with recapturing the White House than in colluding with the likes of Ike, Nixon, Ford, Reagan, or Bush. Or so the story goes.

A provocative mathematician once suggested that $2 + 2$ may equal 5 for very large values of 2. In a similar vein, the present excursion is a case

9. Recall that Democrats were the majority party throughout all but two Congresses in the period (80th and 83d). These exceptional Congresses account for only 549 or the 10,631 observations. Chapters 7 and 8 are more explicitly focused on sorting out president's party and majority effects irrespective of whether they are Democrats or Republicans.

of 1 + 1 falling somewhat short of 3. More precisely, the two individual observations—negative relationships between Democrats and switching, and between divided government and switching—do not quite add up to the broader, more coherent, and quite conventional claim that Democrats in Congress and divided government are mutual reinforcers of gridlock in U.S. government. First, this is not true as a matter of logic: it is quite possible that the effects are independent and additive rather than interdependent and multiplicative. Second and more concretely, neither is it true as an empirical matter. To illustrate, it first helps to highlight the substantive question that motivates this detour. Are Democrats as the congressional majority more disciplined than Republicans in terms of resisting switching *because* of something distinctively different about the executive-legislative politics of divided government? Conventional wisdom would seem to say, yes.

To shed light on this plausible conjecture, we can estimate the simple probit equation:

$$\Pr(switch = 1) = \Phi(\beta_0 + \beta_1\ Democrat + \beta_2\ divided + \beta_3\ Democrat \times divided).$$

The evidence presented thus far leads us to expect a negative coefficient for β_1 and β_2, but β_3 cuts to the heart of the claim regarding partisan forces in unified versus divided government. That is, Democrats are hypothesized to switch less especially during, and because of, divided government.[10] The estimate of β_3, accordingly, should be negative and significant. Only one of these holds, however. The estimate is weakly negative (-1.404) but well short of statistical significance ($p = .442$).

What has been discovered in this detour? Quite a lot, actually. Are Democrats more intransigent/principled than Republicans? It seems so. Especially during and because of divided government? It seems not.[11] The key implication of these preliminary findings for the analyses that follow is that the variables *Democrat* and *divided* seem to belong in the equation, even though they are arguably atheoretical and certainly tangential with respect to the pivotal politics theory. Likewise, the variable *Democrat* × *divided* should be included, too, so that when interpreting party and regime effects we resist the temptation to hastily assume, in effect, that 1 + 1 = 3.

10. More graphic interpretations for "switch less" can be offered as a function of one's party affiliations. Suggestions for Democrats: be principled, stand firm, have backbone. . . . Suggestions for Republicans: be stubborn, intransigent, pig-headed. . . . Suggestion for independents: switch less.

11. All such effects are still subject to retesting, controlling for preferences.

VETO SWITCHERS IN THE SENATE

The multivariate analysis of veto switching in the Senate parallels that in Chapter 5 on cloture. The primary aim is to discern whether systematic preference effects are consistent with the theory of pivotal politics. In the cloture chapter we asked two related questions. Are senators at or near the filibuster pivot most likely to switch votes in successive cloture-invoking opportunities? Are senators in adjacent quartiles next most likely to switch, but significantly less likely than those in the *f*-quartile? Here we ask two questions that are veto-pivot counterparts. Are senators at or near the veto pivot most likely to switch votes within pairs of veto-related votes? Are senators in adjacent quintiles next most likely to switch, but significantly less likely than those in the veto-pivot quintile? The secondary aim also pulls a common thread through the two chapters. Here we attempt to discern whether significant differences in switching behavior occur in the divided versus unified government because of party affiliations of senators and while controlling for preference effects.

Hypotheses

With senators exhaustively classified into one and only one quintile as a function of their preference measures (recall fig. 6.3), the group within which switching is hypothesized to be most common is that which includes the *veto pivot*. The two neighboring quintiles—*extreme opponents* and *moderates*—should exhibit significantly less switching behavior than the veto pivot quintile, but more switching than the quintile composed of *supporters*. Because only four of the five quintile dummy variables can be entered into an estimable equation, the constant term of the equation (β_0) reflects the likelihood of switching by a senator who is in the excluded quintile, namely, that composed of senators on the extreme farthest from v.[12] Estimates of the remaining coefficients (β_1, β_2, β_3, β_4) reflect deviations from this low baseline. The basic equation is:

$$\Pr(\textit{switch} = 1) = \Phi(\beta_0 + \beta_1 \textit{ veto pivot} + \beta_2 \textit{ extreme opponent} + \beta_3 \textit{ moderate} + \beta_4 \textit{ supporter}).$$

12.   More precisely $\Phi(\beta_0)$ is the probability that such a senator switches, where $\Phi(\cdot)$ is the cumulative normal distribution function.

Within this framework, formation of primary statistical hypothesis tests is straightforward.[13]

1. The coefficient for veto-pivot quintile should be positive and significantly different from zero, indicating that proximity to v is associated with a greater probability of switching. Formally, the null hypothesis is: $\beta_1 = 0$. The alternative hypothesis is: $\beta_1 > 0$.

2. The coefficient for veto-pivot quintile should be significantly greater than that for extreme opponents. The null hypothesis is: $\beta_1 = \beta_2$. The alternative hypothesis is: $\beta_1 > \beta_2$.

3. The coefficient for veto-pivot quintile should be significantly greater than that for moderates. The null hypothesis is: $\beta_1 = \beta_3$. The alternative hypothesis is: $\beta_1 > \beta_3$.

The secondary hypothesis is a simple follow-up to the concern raised in the previous section. Controlling for preference effects as specified above, does the combination of (supposedly) strong Democrats and divided government produce an individual-level manifestation of gridlock, that is, nonswitching? If so, then we should find support for a fourth hypothesis which, while topical and intuitive, is not implied by the pivotal politics theory.

4. The coefficient for *Democrat* × *divided government* should be significantly less than zero. The null hypothesis is: $\beta_4 = 0$. The alternative hypothesis is: $\beta_4 < 0$.

Findings

Findings are presented for the Senate in two tables.[14] Table 6.4 does not distinguish between veto-pair types, while table 6.5 does. Only preference effects are estimated in equation (1) of table 6.4. Broadly consistent with the pivotal politics theory, switching is clearly most prevalent on the president's end of the spectrum. More precisely, hypotheses 1 and 3 are supported, but hypothesis 2 is not. That is, the veto-pivot coefficient is significant as predicted ($p < .001$), and the difference between senators in the v-quintile and moderate quintile is also significant ($p < .001$). The data,

13.   In light of the refinement of the preference-space from quartiles in the cloture analysis to quintiles here, additional hypotheses of a similar form could be tested. In the interest of brevity, I confine my attention to the veto-pivot side of the preference spectrum.

14.   All of the results reported were run with Congress-specific fixed effects as well. These equations consistently yield R^2s about 50 percent greater than those reported above. Otherwise the estimates with and without fixed effects are not substantively different from one another.

Table 6.4

Predictors of Senators' Switching on Veto-Vote Pairs: 80th–103d Congresses

Variables	1	2	3	4
Veto pivot	1.109	1.009	1.013	1.081
	(17.747)	(13.659)	(11.225)	(8.467)
Extreme opponent	1.163	0.997	0.835	0.685
	(18.726)	(12.978)	(8.812)	(5.064)
Moderate	0.563	0.580	0.537	0.559
	(8.532)	(7.965)	(6.030)	(4.424)
Supporter	0.001	0.046	−0.027	−0.033
	(0.019)	(0.562)	(−0.267)	(−0.231)
Divided government		−1.234	−1.805	−1.978
		(−9.034)	(−10.750)	(−10.979)
Democrat		−1.406	−1.537	−1.515
		(−7.640)	(−6.982)	(−6.665)
Democrat × divided government		1.031	1.291	1.250
		(5.304)	(5.521)	(4.966)
Constant	−1.873	−0.446	0.008	0.005
	(−34.424)	(−3.389)	(0.050)	(0.029)
N observations	10631	10631	7263	4767
Log likelihood	−3520	−3423	−2098	−1122
Adjusted R^2	0.108	0.133	0.125	0.146
p for $H^0: \beta_1 = 0$	<.001	<.001	<.001	<.001
p for $H^0: \beta_1 = \beta_2$	.214	.782	.001	.001
p for $H^0: \beta_1 = \beta_3$	<.001	<.001	<.001	<.001

NOTE: Probit estimates with asymptotic t-statistics in parentheses. Equation (3) excludes vote pairs for which at least one vote total is more than 15 votes under or over the override threshold of 67. Equation (4) excludes vote pairs for which at least one vote total is more than 10 votes under or over the override threshold of 67.

however, cannot differentiate between senators in the fourth (veto-pivot) and fifth (extreme-opponent) quintiles.[15]

Equation (2) in table 6.4 includes government-regime and party measures with the preference-quintile dummy variables. No significant changes occur in the findings of preference effects, but the remaining findings are noteworthy. As in the earlier discussion of bivariate relationships, Democrats are significantly less likely to be switchers than Republicans, and

15.   The inability to differentiate between senators in the extreme two quintiles is also present at the opposite extreme. The coefficient for moderate supporters gives the difference relative to the excluded quintile—extreme supporters—and this coefficient, too, is insignificant.

switching is less prevalent in divided than unified government. However, the hypothesis that links gridlock interactively with defiant Democrats and divided government is not supported. Without the preference measures in the equation, the coefficient (*Democrat* × *divided government*) was negative but not significant. Now it is significant but positive, adding further doubt to the speculation that Democrats switch less in divided government because of something peculiar about divided government politics.

While the weight of evidence favors the pivotal politics theory over the divided-government-and-Democrats conjectures, the inability to observe differences in switching rates across the two president-side quintiles is bothersome. Essentially, the data in equations (1) and (2), for example, suggest that competing vote seekers during a Republican presidency are as likely to lobby, pressure, and persuade Jesse Helms or Phil Gramm (in the extreme quintile) as Bob Packwood, John Chafee, Arlen Specter, or Bill Cohen (in the veto-pivot quintile).[16] This strains credulity but is potentially attributable to the fact that—as in the cloture vote pairs—many of the roll calls in the sample are very lopsided. With the caveat that omission of observations is an inherently arbitrary process, equations (3) and (4) in table 6.4 report on subsamples resulting from filtering out vote pairs that include a lopsided margin of victory or loss. Equation (3) excludes vote pairs for which at least one vote was 15 or more votes away from the threshold of 67, while equation (4) adopts a more stringent cutoff point of 10.[17]

Most results are unchanged when moving from the full data set to the subsamples. The coefficient for *Democrat* × *divided government* remains significant and positive, contrary to hypothesis 4. Individual coefficients as well as tests of hypotheses 1 and 3 are also stable and significant. The only noteworthy difference is that the smaller-sample estimates support hypotheses 2. Not only are senators in the veto-pivot quintile the most common switchers; they are also more likely to switch than *both* neighboring quintiles, extreme opponents as well as moderates. In summary, the prominence of the veto pivot is bolstered.

16.   These examples overstate the problem to the extent that intraquintile variation in preferences is real. Helms and Gramm are at the conservative end of the extremest quintile, while Packwood et al. are at the liberal end of the veto-pivot quintile.

17.   Notice that the truncation is two-sided. That is, I do not omit only lopsidedly positive votes because to do so would virtually guarantee more switching in the extreme opponent quintile. Also omitted are votes where the theoretical spatial cutpoint is in the moderate quintile. For example, in 22 vote pairs (and thus approximately 2,200 observations) the roll call fell more than 10 votes *short* of 67, so these observations were omitted from equation (5).

Table 6.5

Senate Estimates for Different Types of Veto-Vote Pairs:
80th–103d Congresses

Variables	1	2	3
Veto pivot	0.883	1.208	0.821
	(6.503)	(10.473)	(5.779)
Extreme opponent	0.985	1.136	0.794
	(6.986)	(9.435)	(5.414)
Moderate	0.508	0.688	0.490
	(3.945)	(6.012)	(3.418)
Supporter	0.162	−0.071	0.009
	(1.174)	(−0.525)	(0.058)
Divided government	−0.166	−1.251	−2.022
	(−0.518)	(−5.240)	(−8.150)
Democrat	−0.928	−0.951	−2.201
	(−2.103)	(−3.028)	(−6.750)
Democrat × divided government	0.680	0.536	1.754
	(1.487)	(1.639)	(5.056)
Constant	−1.597	−0.445	0.444
	(−5.056)	(−1.913)	(1.843)
N observations	3471	4634	2526
Log likelihood	−1038	−1559	−776.2
Adjusted R^2	0.101	0.171	0.138
p for $H^o:\beta_1 = 0$	<.001	<.001	<.001
p for $H^o:\beta_1 = \beta_2$	.261	.203	.080
p for $H^o:\beta_1 = \beta_3$	<.001	<.001	.002

NOTE: Probit estimates with asymptotic t-statistics in parentheses. Equation (1) includes only vote pairs on first floor passage and postconference passage. Equation (2) includes only vote pairs on first floor passage and veto overrides. Equation (3) includes only vote pairs on postconference passage and veto overrides.

Robustness

Recall that the estimates in table 6.4 employ each of the three types of vote pairs summarized in figure 6.2. To the extent that different kinds of political games are systematically played at different stages of the policy-making process, the findings may be fragile due to pooling of heterogeneous types of observations. To explore this possibility, table 6.5 reports estimates of equations of the same form as equations (2)–(4) in table 6.4, but does so for type-specific vote pairs.

The stability of the type-specific findings is reassuring. Each estimation closely approximates equation (2) in table 6.4. The veto-pivot effect is strong and significant (hypothesis 1). The difference between the veto-pivot effect and the moderate-quintile effect is large and significant (hypothesis 3). But the difference between veto-pivot switching and extreme-opponent switching (hypothesis 2) is either not significant or significant only by a lenient standard ($p = .08$ for showdown types). For several reasons, this lack of across-the-board support for the pivot theory seems tolerable. First, the difference comes closest to significance in the class of vote pairs in which we would most expect it to: those including clean, identical bills in the final passage and postveto stages. Second, we have seen earlier that the probable cause for lack of significance in the difference between v-quintile and extreme-opponent quintile effects is lopsided votes, which are included again in table 6.5. Third, in comparison with the competing hypothesis—unrealized negative interactive effects of divided government and Democrats—the set of hypotheses extracted from the pivotal politics theory fares well.

Finally, all of the findings presented above can be replicated via analogous techniques that make more stringent assumptions about the preference data. Specifically, if one believes that the preference measures have cardinal as well as ordinal content, then the equations in tables 6.4 and 6.5 can be reestimated by substituting a single measure, *distance from the veto pivot,* for the quintile dummy variables. Table 6.6 presents two such sets of estimates that are counterparts of equation (2) in table 6.4.[18] The finding in equation (1) is now familiar: significant preference effects, a negative effect for the separate dummy variables for Democrat and divided government, but a still-puzzling positive interactive effect for Democrats *during* divided government.

Equation (2) adds one new variable—distance from the *median* voter's spatial location. The aim is to confirm that the negative coefficient for distance from v in equation (1) is not simply a median voter result in disguise, attributable to the necessarily high correlation between distance from v and distance from m. These measures are perfectly positively correlated from their lower extremes through m, and from v through their upper extremes. Therefore, significant differences in their coefficients must be attributed to the critical interval of (m, v) in which the measures are perfectly *negatively* correlated. In effect, then, equation (2) makes for a clean test that discrimi-

18.   Counterparts of equations (3) and (4) of table 6.4 were also estimated, with and without Congress-specific fixed effects. The findings are virtually identical.

Table 6.6
Senate Estimates Based on Cardinal Preference Measures

Variables	1	2
Distance from veto pivot	−1.226	−1.502
	(−14.136)	(−14.530)
Distance from median pivot		0.452
		(5.050)
Divided government	−0.895	−0.997
	(−6.859)	(−7.538)
Democrat	−1.229	−1.276
	(−6.774)	(−7.022)
Democrat × divided government	0.534	0.693
	(2.856)	(3.656)
Constant	0.407	0.390
	(3.009)	(2.882)
N observations	10,631	10,631
Log likelihood	−3488	−3475
Adjusted R^2	.118	.120

NOTE: Probit estimates with asymptotic t-statistics in parentheses.

nates between a median-pivot-based theory and a veto-pivot-based theory. If supermajoritarianism is key in veto politics in behavioral as well as in institutional terms, then the negative coefficient for *distance from v* should survive while the coefficient for *distance from m* should be significantly smaller. Clearly, this is what happens in equation (2). The significant and positive coefficient for distance from the median pivot implies that, within the critical interval (*m, v*), switching clearly goes up as one considers senators farther from *m,* which is to say yet again that switching goes up as one considers senators nearer and nearer to the veto pivot. From all indications, then, supermajoritarianism has the behavioral consequences in the Senate that the pivotal politics theory predicts.

VETO SWITCHERS IN THE HOUSE

The pivotal politics theory formally portrays a unicameral legislature. Indeed, based on the analyses thus far, one might reasonably infer that the theory is one not of executive-*legislative* relations but rather of executive-*Senate* relations. In the case of the filibuster pivot and corresponding cloture analysis, this inference is fully appropriate. With no counterpart to cloture,

Table 6.7
Distribution of Representatives' Switch Opportunities
across Vote-Pair Types

Type of Vote Pair	N Pairs	N Voters[a]	N Switchers	% Switchers
I Precursors: preconference passage and postconference passage	42	16,035	1,345	8.39
II Broad-band: preconference passage and override	61	23,653	3,195	13.51
III Showdown: postconference passage and override	51	19,861	1,822	9.17
TOTAL	154	59,549	6,362	10.68

[a] Includes only representatives who voted, paired, or announced positions on both votes in the pair.

the U.S. House of Representatives is for all intents and purposes a majoritarian body in terms of its internal procedures.[19] The focus of this chapter, however, is not on intrachamber rules but rather cross-branch, Constitutional provisions of supermajoritarianism. In this respect, the House is no different from the Senate. Like the Senate, the House can override a presidential veto via a $2/3$ vote. And like the Senate, the House can sustain a presidential veto via a $1/3 + 1$ vote. Theoretically, then, the testable hypotheses in this section are identical to those for the Senate.

Findings

Findings are presented for the House in five tables. Tables 6.7 and 6.8 give an overview of the House data. Descriptive statistics are much the same for the House as for the Senate, most notably in the case of the rate of switching: 10.7 percent for the House, 12.2 percent for the Senate. The distribution of House vote pairs across the three types also closely approximates that for the Senate. Again, the most common type is the broad-band pair, consisting of a preconference vote on passage and the override vote

19. There are, of course, exceptions, chief of which is the House's provision for suspension of the rules to pass a bill as is (no amendments) by a $2/3$ majority. Several facts of House life limit the impact of suspension in the House relative to the impact of cloture in the Senate. For example, no bills in the House must use the suspension procedure, while most bills in the Senate are subject to filibusters. Furthermore, the House's rules on suspension limit both the types of legislation and the days of the Congress during which permissible (and usually minor) measures can be brought up.

Table 6.8
Descriptive Statistics for House Switching Analysis

Variable	N	Mean	S.D.	Min.	Max.
Switch	59,549	.107	.309	0	1
Extreme supporter	67,600	.199	.399	0	1
Supporter	67,600	.201	.400	0	1
Moderate	67,600	.201	.401	0	1
Veto pivot	67,600	.198	.399	0	1
Extreme opponent	67,600	.201	.401	0	1
Distance from v	67,600	.337	.240	0	1.230
Distance from m	67,600	.292	.199	0	1.205
Democrat	68,047	.599	.490	0	1
Divided government	68,047	.941	.235	0	1

itself. Switching is also most prevalent within these vote pairs. This seems reasonable since two kinds of intervening events can occur between these votes: the lobbying and pressure tactics commonly associated with legislative-executive tensions plus changes in the content of legislation on which votes are cast.

Multivariate analyses are reported in tables 6.9 and 6.10. The first table does not distinguish between veto-pair types, while the latter does. Only preference effects are estimated in equation (1) of table 6.9. Consistent with the pivotal politics theory, switching is clearly most prevalent on the president's end of the spectrum. More precisely, hypotheses 1, 2, and 3 are all supported at high levels of significance.[20]

To see whether these patterns hold in the presence of party and divided government effects, equation (2) in table 6.9 includes the same set of dummy variables discovered as significant in the Senate analysis. Practically no change occurs in the findings of preference effects, and the remaining findings again parallel those for the Senate. Democrats are less likely to be switchers than Republicans, and switching is less prevalent in divided than unified government. But again, the hypothesis that links gridlock with defiant Democrats in divided government is not supported.

In the case of Senate analysis, equations (3) and (4) were needed to ad-

20.   In the comparable Senate analysis with unfiltered observations, it was not possible to differentiate statistically between both pairs of upper and lower quintiles. In contrast, in the House analysis we can reject both null (no-difference) hypotheses.

Table 6.9
Predictors of Representatives' Switching on Veto-Vote Pairs:
80th–103d Congresses

Variables	1	2	3	4
Veto pivot	1.063	1.086	1.161	1.322
	(39.298)	(34.295)	(29.943)	(26.518)
Extreme opponent	0.970	0.976	0.908	1.008
	(35.686)	(29.715)	(22.404)	(19.218)
Moderate	0.594	0.666	0.731	0.746
	(20.898)	(21.823)	(19.315)	(15.153)
Supporter	0.171	0.214	0.239	0.226
	(5.474)	(6.528)	(5.789)	(4.129)
Divided government		−0.953	−0.842	−0.513
		(−19.957)	(−11.267)	(−3.640)
Democrat		−0.757	−0.532	−0.526
		(−13.521)	(−6.073)	(−3.183)
Democrat × divided government		0.610	0.466	0.637
		(9.792)	(5.007)	(3.751)
Constant	−1.910	−0.956	−1.169	−1.796
	(−80.950)	(−21.322)	(−16.061)	(−12.800)
N observations	59,528	59,528	40,311	30,501
Log likelihood	−18,671.5	−18,358.4	−11,760.5	−7407.9
Adjusted R^2	0.077	0.092	0.084	0.089
p for H^o:$\beta_1 = 0$	<.001	<.001	<.001	<.001
p for H^o:$\beta_1 = \beta_2$	<.001	<.001	<.001	<.001
p for H^o:$\beta_1 = \beta_3$	<.001	<.001	<.001	<.001

NOTE: Probit estimates with asymptotic *t*-statistics in parentheses. Equation (3) excludes vote pairs for which at least one vote total is more than 15 percent of the chamber size under or over the override threshold of 290. Equation (4) excludes vote pairs for which at least one vote total is more than 10 percent of the chamber size under or over the override threshold of 290.

dress the puzzle of too much switching (relative to the theoretical expectations) at the president's end of the political spectrum. In the case of the House, equations indicate no such problem. Thus, equations (3) and (4) are included here only for Senate-comparison purposes. House-Senate differences are again minor to nonexistent. Two small differences can be noted within the House as vote pairs when large vote margins are omitted. First, there is a somewhat sharpened difference between representatives in the veto-pivot quintile and extreme-opponent quintile. Second, the smaller-sample estimates correspond with a reduced divided-government effect.

Table 6.10
House Estimates for Different Types of Veto-Vote Pairs:
80th–103d Congresses

Variables	1	2	3
Veto pivot	1.296	1.113	0.922
	(19.282)	(23.506)	(16.375)
Extreme opponent	1.260	0.955	0.826
	(18.063)	(19.470)	(14.140)
Moderate	0.740	0.709	0.540
	(11.438)	(15.613)	(9.844)
Supporter	0.270	0.265	0.086
	(3.837)	(5.557)	(1.423)
Divided government	−0.533	−1.022	−0.682
	(−3.699)	(−16.440)	(−6.511)
Democrat	−1.058	−0.844	−0.347
	(−5.727)	(−11.813)	(−2.864)
Democrat × divided government	1.280	0.591	0.083
	(6.614)	(7.165)	(0.632)
Constant	−1.817	−0.730	−1.130
	(−12.746)	(−12.873)	(−11.249)
N observations	16,029	23,644	19,855
Log likelihood	−4225.8	−8377.7	−5,496.7
Adjusted R^2	0.085	0.105	0.096
p for $H^P{:}\beta_1 = 0$	<.001	<.001	<.001
p for $H^P{:}\beta_1 = \beta_2$	.353	<.001	.005
p for $H^P{:}\beta_1 = \beta_3$	<.001	<.001	.002

NOTE: Probit estimates with asymptotic t-statistics in parentheses. Equation (1) includes only vote pairs on first floor passage and postconference passage. Equation (2) includes only vote pairs on first floor passage and veto overrides. Equation (3) includes only vote pairs on postconference passage and veto overrides.

The remaining results are unchanged when moving from the full sample to the subsamples. The coefficient for *Democrat × divided government* remains significant and positive, contrary to hypothesis 4. Individual coefficients as well as tests of hypotheses 1 through 3, however, are also stable and significant.

Robustness

The estimates in table 6.10 employ each of the three types of vote pairs. Again we can assess whether different kinds of political games are played

Table 6.11
House Estimates Based on Cardinal Preference Measures

Variables	1	2
Distance from veto pivot	−1.617	−1.792
	(−38.557)	(−37.483)
Distance from median pivot		0.344
		(7.696)
Divided government	−0.653	−0.715
	(−14.430)	(−15.563)
Democrat	−0.581	−0.598
	(−10.592)	(−10.907)
Democrat × divided government	0.287	0.379
	(4.879)	(6.310)
Constant	−0.026	−0.053
	(−0.569)	(−1.143)
N observations	59,528	59,528
Log likelihood	−18,384.3	−18,354.8
Adjusted R^2	0.091	0.092

NOTE: Probit estimates with asymptotic t-statistics in parentheses.

at different stages of the policymaking process. To explore this possibility, table 6.10 presents estimates of equations of the same form as equations (2)–(4) in table 6.9, but does so for individual vote-pair types.

With only one minor exception, the stability of the type-specific findings is supported. Each type-specific quintile effect closely approximates its counterpart in equation (2) of table 6.9. The veto-pivot effect is strong and significant (hypothesis 1). The difference between veto-pivot switching and extreme-opponent switching is significant in all but precursor vote pairs (hypothesis 2). And the difference between the veto-pivot effect and the moderate-quintile effect is large and significant without exception (hypothesis 3). In contrast, the coefficient for *Democrat × divided government* is no longer distinguishable from zero.

Finally, as was illustrated in the Senate analysis, all of the House findings also can be replicated using cardinal preference data—*distance from v* and *distance from m*—in place of the quintile dummy variables. Table 6.11 presents these estimates. The finding in equation (1) is as expected: a significant preference effect, a negative effect for the separate dummy variables for Democrat and divided government, and the usual positive interactive effect for Democrats *during* divided government. Equation (2) adds *distance from m* to reaffirm that the negative coefficient for *distance from v* in equation (1) is not a disguised median voter result. Just as in the Senate analysis, the significant and *positive* coefficient for distance from the median pivot implies that, within the critical interval (*m, v*), switching clearly goes up as one considers representatives farther and farther from *m,* which is to say yet again that switching goes up as one considers representatives nearer and nearer to the veto pivot. From all indications, then, the primacy of the veto pivot is consistent across chambers.

CAVEATS AND CONCLUSIONS

For reasons comparable to those introduced and discussed in Chapter 5, the findings in this chapter, too, should be interpreted cautiously.

One qualification concerns statistical significance. Except in those equations in which lopsided votes or some types of vote pairs were omitted, the findings arguably are based on the universe of postwar veto-vote-switching situations.[21] Furthermore, even if significance tests were defended as appropriate under the circumstances and were employed in more or less conventional ways, the number of such observations is so large that high levels of significance are easy to obtain.

A closely related caveat concerns the power of the empirical tests as affected by measures of preferences and their underlying assumptions. General measures of legislators' ideology, such as ADA ratings and NOMINATE scores, are constructed, implicitly or explicitly, with the aim of providing summary indices that tend to provide good baseline accounts for, or predictors of, legislators' behavior. And indeed they succeed in this regard.[22] It therefore becomes tempting to infer that these are good measures and to use them without much attentiveness to the matches or mismatches between auxiliary hypotheses (e.g., about NOMINATE measures) and test hypotheses (e.g., those generated by the pivotal politics theory). The specific concern that arises in this application is an outgrowth of several facts. Poole and Rosenthal's NOMINATE procedure—like Groseclose and Snyder's vote-buying theory—embodies a set of well-articulated behav-

---

21. Nor, of course, would it be appropriate to treat any such subsets of observations as a random sample from the all-votes, so-called universe.

22. See, for example, Poole and Rosenthal 1997 on NOMINATE measures; and Krehbiel 1992 on ADA measures.

ioral assumptions about legislators and voting.[23] The pivotal politics theory does, too. So far, there is nothing unusual or bothersome about this. Knowingly or not, most or all individual-level empirical tests of collective choice theories use measures and methods that, at least implicitly, embody behavioral assumptions. Ideally, however, we would like these classes of assumptions—assumptions in the measurement theory, assumptions in the theory to be tested, and any auxiliary assumptions—to be independent from one another: that is, any combination of them could be true or false, logically or empirically. If such independence between classes of assumptions cannot be established—and, as a practical matter, only rarely can it be—then two sorts of problems can occur. Too much overlap between the sets of assumptions can erode the power of the empirical tests, in effect making it too easy to accept the hypotheses of the focal theory or, conversely, almost impossible to reject the theory. Or, contradictions between some of the assumptions of the measurement theory, the focal theory, or the auxiliary hypotheses can undermine the overall logical coherence of the test.

More to the point, Chapters 5 and 6 are instances in which all of these possibilities are illustrated to some extent and with uncertain consequences. At the highest level of abstraction, the pivotal politics theory, the Snyder-Groseclose vote-buying theory, and the Poole-Rosenthal measurement theory are all rational-choice theories, and this fact might be seen as eroding the power of the tests. This seems not to be too worrisome, though, insofar as the family of rational-choice theories is extremely heterogeneous.[24] In particular, these three theories are much different from one another, and it is quite conceivable that any singleton, pair, or trio of them could be (approximately) true or false, thus suggesting that the methodologically desired independence is attained after all, at the level of theories as a whole. However, at a more concrete level—namely, specific assumptions within theories—there are instances of contradictions. For example, two of the theories are unidimensional, while one is multidimensional; one theory postulates probabilistic sincere voting while two derive equilibria in which voting is sometimes not sincere; one theory assumes complete information, one assumes that errors in voting occur, while one comes in complete-information and uncertainty flavors; and so on. In short, indirect tests of

23. See Poole and Rosenthal 1985 for specifics; and Londregan 1996 for a recent and lucid review and critique.

24. As a practical matter, too, the lack-of-power problem seems not to be severe inasmuch as some analyses of veto votes failed to corroborate hypotheses about differences across preference quintiles. In other words, refutation *is* possible.

the sort conducted in Chapters 5 and 6 necessarily entail knitting a complex web of theoretical constructs, and inferences are correspondingly subtle and perhaps tenuous.

Subject to these important but not yet well-worked-out methodological qualifications, the substantive bottom line of this chapter complements and reinforces that in the chapter on cloture. Supermajoritarian choice mechanisms—whether embodied in Senate's Rule 22 or in the U.S. Constitution's Article 1, Section 7—have a deep and fundamental bearing on executive and legislative strategies of lawmaking. The theory of pivotal politics tells us in a simplified and pristine fashion who is pivotal in situations involving significant legislative-executive conflict of interest. The data on presidential vetoes and attempts to override them tell us in a relatively complex and messy fashion that real-world politicians tend to target, lobby, persuade, and influence precisely those legislators who the theory predicts should be targeted, lobbied, persuaded, and influenced: legislators at or near the veto pivot.

III

APPLICATIONS

PRESIDENTIAL POWER?

This chapter marks a major shift in perspective yet without abandoning the theory and methods used in previous chapters. Previous empirical tests have amassed diverse forms of support for the theory of pivotal politics. The question now is: What does this buy us? Two answers can be envisioned.

One answer is that the theory and methods of previous chapters have produced a reasonably parsimonious understanding of a substantial portion of U.S. lawmaking. To recapitulate, the theory generates hypotheses. The hypotheses are tested. The findings are mostly supportive of the hypotheses. Therefore, the theory helps us to understand observable events in the world of politics. To reach such a theory-based understanding—as distinct from mere empiricism in the absence of a theory—has been the primary objective of the book.

A second answer is certainly less grandiose, probably more subtle, but, to some readers and researchers perhaps, ultimately more interesting and useful. To the extent that the theoretical and empirical arguments in previous chapters have been convincing, the pivotal politics theory can serve not only as an abstract instrument for understanding U.S. lawmaking but also as a concrete tool for identifying other, extratheoretic regularities in the U.S. political process. Although the pivotal politics theory is about executive-legislative interaction in supermajoritarian settings, it is a very simple theory about a very complex topic. Acknowledging this, I adopt a unique methodological perspective in this and the next chapter. I take it on faith (albeit a faith now reinforced by considerable evidence) that the pivotal politics theory provides an accurate partial account of executive-legislative lawmaking activity, and I proceed to employ the theory as a *measurement model* whose product will be data on presidential power and, in Chapter 8, its partisan basis. The methodological shift, then, is summarized by the following parallelism. In Chapters 2–6, the pivotal politics theory was a generator of hypotheses subject to refutation or corroboration via data. In Chapters 7 and 8, the corroborated theory is a generator of data that other researchers may use as they see fit to corroborate or refute hypotheses from alternative theories. Because the general substantive focus is on measurable indicators of presidents' strategic success—a long-time interest of students of the presidency—the possibilities for future research seem substantial.

A MEASUREMENT MODEL

In his classic book on the U.S. presidents, Richard Neustadt (1960) argues convincingly that presidential power is the power to persuade. Numerous studies followed Neustadt's in which researchers attempted to flesh out various mechanics of this argument.[1] Nevertheless, three questions still cry out for answers. First, is Neustadt's suggestion sustainable as a stylized fact of the U.S. presidency? That is, are presidents regularly and significantly persuasive, hence powerful? Second, can power-as-persuasion be quantified? Third, if so, how do presidents differ measurably in terms of their power to persuade?

Clearly, answering these questions requires a novel measurement device. My proposed method for measuring presidential power builds on the previous analysis as follows. We restrict attention to evidently nontrivial cases of legislative-executive conflict (first, veto situations; later cloture situations) in which there are two or more votes on substantively similar or identical legislative enactments (vote pairs). In the case of vetoes, the Constitution informs us that these are $2/3$ majority situations. In the case of cloture, Rule 22 of the Senate informs us that they are $2/3$ or $3/5$ situations, depending on the historical period. Furthermore, the data analysis in the previous two chapters affirms that the veto pivot and filibuster pivot are useful empirical as well as theoretical constructs. Consider, then, the second vote of any such vote pair as a *two-sided* opportunity for persuasion or,

---

1. See Cameron 1998 for a comprehensive review of this literature and an excellent extension.

Table 7.1

Dependent Variables for Veto-Based Power Analyses

Variable	N Eligible	N Successes	Pct Switchers	Success Rate
Attraction	56,856	5,813	10.22	.102
Retention	16,292	14,543	10.74	.893

alternatively, "vote-buying" (Groseclose and Snyder 1996). For example, imagine a scenario of dueling Georges on a bill supported by Senate Majority Leader George Mitchell but opposed by President George Bush in the 101st or 102d Congress. From one end of the spectrum, George Mitchell struggles to build and hold together a ⅔ supermajority coalition for a Democratic initiative. This entails not only retaining the votes of supporters but also attracting the support of initial opponents. Meanwhile, from the other end of the spectrum, George Bush mounts an effort to thwart this initiative by keeping bill opponents in his blocking coalition and by persuading former bill supporters to defect from Mitchell's coalition. Theoretically and empirically, the putative persuaders channel their energies at or near the veto pivot v. Therefore, the method, too, should be veto–pivot centered.

Two equations are estimated, each of which represents a strategic problem for the president as a hopeful persuader.

First, an attraction equation is estimated only for legislators who, in the first roll call of the vote pair, voted against the president. The objective of the president is to successfully persuade legislators to switch from proponents to opponents of the bill—that is, to vote for the president (against the bill) on the second roll call of the pair. (Conversely, the strategic aim of the opposing legislative leader is to retain these legislators as supporters of the bill, mirroring the president's problem discussed below.) The dependent variable is called *attraction* and is defined as switching to the president's position in the second vote of a vote pair, conditional on having voted against the president (for the bill) in the first vote of the pair. Table 7.1 presents summary information for this variable based on pooled House-Senate data.[2]

---

2. House-Senate comparisons in Chapter 6 suggest that differences between chambers in veto-pivotal politics are minor. To test more rigorously whether pooling House and Senate observations is defensible, the House and Senate data sets were combined. Equation (2) in table 6.4 was considered the constrained model, while the unconstrained model adds Senate-specific interactive terms for the preference variables x: $\Pr(\text{switch}=1) = \Phi(\alpha + \beta' x + \gamma' \text{ Senate } x \ldots)$. The null hypothesis that the γ coefficients are jointly equal to zero cannot be rejected. The substantive interpretation of this finding is that there are no significant Senate-specific effects. The practical implication is that we can proceed with a larger data set in which House and Senate observations are combined.

Of the nearly 57,000 eligible attractees in postwar veto situations, nearly 6,000 (10.22 percent) were in fact attracted, yielding an average probability of presidential success of .102.

Second, a retention equation is estimated only for legislators who, in the first roll call of the vote pair, voted for the president. The strategic aim for the president in these situations is to retain the support of many or all of his first-vote coalition members. (Conversely, the strategic aim of the opposing legislative leader is to attract these legislators, mirroring the president's problem discussed above.) The dependent variable is called *retention* and is defined as not switching away from the president's position in the second vote of a vote pair, conditional on having voted for the president (against the bill) in the first vote of the pair. The second row of table 7.1 summarizes this variable. While the percentage of switchers (10.74) is approximately the same as that for the attraction variable, it is clearly easier for a president to retain former supporters than to attract new ones. The success rate of .893 reflects this.

The structure of the corresponding equations is similar to the probits reported in Chapters 5 and 6. Attention, however, is now confined to preference effects. Recall that the variable names *opponent* and *supporter* refer to preference-based expectations regarding the bill that was vetoed—not opponents and supporters of the president who vetoed the bill. The equations are:

$$\Pr(Attract = 1) = \Phi(\beta_0 + \beta_1 \text{ } extreme \text{ } opponent + \beta_2 \text{ } veto\text{-}pivot \qquad (1)$$
$$+ \beta_3 \text{ } moderate + \beta_4 \text{ } supporter),$$

and

$$\Pr(Retain = 1) = \Phi(\beta_0 + \beta_1 \text{ } extreme \text{ } opponent + \beta_2 \text{ } veto\text{-}pivot \qquad (2)$$
$$+ \beta_3 \text{ } moderate + \beta_4 \text{ } supporter).$$

With these specifications, the parameter β_0 represents the probability of switching within the omitted group, extreme supporters, while the remaining parameters represent deviations from that baseline. Because of the coding of the dependent variables—a 1 is a presidential success in both equations—the expected relationships between coefficients and within equations are identical and a straightforward function of proximity to the president. Specifically, we expect $\beta_1 > \beta_2 > \beta_3 > \beta_4 > 0$.

Table 7.2 bears out this expectation convincingly. Extreme opponents, who are by definition those legislators who, across all votes, tend to be

Table 7.2
Presidential Attraction and Retention on Veto Votes

	1 Attraction	2 Retention
Extreme opponent	1.903	1.507
	(54.760)	(24.820)
Veto pivot	1.555	1.164
	(46.417)	(18.806)
Moderate	0.858	0.774
	(24.886)	(11.635)
Supporter	0.293	0.368
	(7.652)	(4.885)
Constant	−2.290	0.089
	(−75.196)	(1.579)
N observations	56,840	16,248
Log likelihood	−15,037.3	−5032.9
Adjusted R^2	.198	.094

NOTE: Probit estimates with asymptotic *t*-statistics in parentheses.

ideologically predisposed to the president's position, are most likely to be attracted to the president's stance (equation 1) given prior opposition, and most likely to be retained as presidential opponents (equation 2) given their prior siding with the president. On both of these counts, legislators in the veto-pivot quintile are next-most likely to be attracted/retained, followed by moderates, and then moderate supporters.

Along with these expected relative magnitudes, the high levels of significance of the estimated coefficients provide additional confidence in basing measures of presidential power on these estimates. The procedure is straightforward. Given the estimates, three substantively rich probability numbers are calculated which answer precisely the following questions:

1. What is the probability that a veto-pivot-quintile original yes voter switches to support the president?[3] This is the pivot attraction probability.

2. What is the probability that a veto-pivot-quintile original no voter does not switch to oppose the president?[4] This is the pivot retention probability.

---

3. The calculation is $\Phi(\beta_0 + \beta_2)$ where the β_i are estimates from equation (1).
4. The calculation is $1 - \Phi(\beta_0 + \beta_2)$ where the β_i are estimates from equation (2).

3. What is the net probability that the president is persuasive within the veto-pivot quintile? That is, what is the difference between the probability in question 1 and one minus the probability in question 2? This is the measure of presidential power.

The chief desirable feature of the technique is that it provides an individual-level, empirically based, theoretically justified quantitative assessment of presidential power-as-persuasion in contentious legislative-executive battles. At least two questionable features of the technique should also be stressed at the outset. First, the method is arbitrary in its calculation of the power measure based on switching behavior only in the veto-pivot quintile. Although this seems defensible based on prior empirical findings, other such (comparably arbitrary) judgments could be made. Second, the method implicitly assumes that all first votes within veto-vote pairs form, for lack of a better term, strategically equivalent baselines. To illustrate, suppose that presidents A and B are equally powerful in some objective but unmeasurable sense. One thing that can result in their receiving different power measures, however, is that, say, A consistently and successfully invests more persuasive capital than B in the earlier of two votes in the vote pair. This strategic difference sets a higher baseline standard for A than B against which A's switching-based power measure is calculated. Unfortunately, in light of the difficulties associated with observing and measuring early starting presidents versus late starting presidents (or, even more taxing, trying to measure bill-specific variations of this form), the strategic-equivalence assumption seems to be a practical necessity here and in Chapter 8.

PRESIDENTIAL POWER IN VETO SITUATIONS

Table 7.3 summarizes the findings. The last row uses all available data and summarizes presidential power as persuasion for all postwar presidents who were involved in veto override attempts. The entry of .231 in column 1 answers question 1 above. This is the probability that a president attracts a former bill supporter in the veto-pivot quintile to bill opposition. In other words, the presidential success rate in terms of attraction is about one in four.

Although a one in four success rate seems substantial, this is only half of the story. While the president courts potential converts from bill support to bill opposition, his legislative opponents—often opposite-party leaders in Congress—likewise seek to convert pivotal legislators from bill opposition to bill support. The retention equation, which is the basis for column

Table 7.3
Veto-Pivot Power by Postwar Presidents

Presidents	1 Attraction		2 Retention		3 Power	4 Persuasion Rank	5 Sustain Rank
Truman	.105	(4,465)	.698	(1,211)	−.196	7	7
Eisenhower	.369	(2,909)	.983†	(1,265)	.352†	1	2
Nixon	.408	(8,838)	.926	(1,688)	.334	2	3
Ford	.199	(17,528)	.861	(3,918)	.059	5	4
Carter	.242	(1,963)	.891	(490)	.133	3	6
Reagan	.199	(7,188)	.849	(1,921)	.047	6	5
Bush	.189	(13,949)	.930	(5,791)	.119	4	1
ALL	**.231**	**(56,840)**	**.895**	**(16,284)**	**.126**	—	—

NOTE: Columns 1 and 2 are based on probit estimates evaluated for the average representative in the veto-pivot quintile. The N for the probit estimates on which the cell entry is based is given in parentheses. Column 3 is the difference between the value in column 1 and one minus the value in column 2. Column 4 is the rank of column 3. Column 5 is the rank based on aggregate (bill-level) sustain rates. A † signifies that the calculation is based on a coefficient not significant at the .01 level.

2, tells the other half of the story, also from the president's perspective. The entry of .895 answers question 2 above. This is the probability that an initial opponent of the bill is retained in the president's opposition camp, or, alternatively, the probability that the president's legislative opponents fail to siphon off the president's supporters within the veto-pivot quintile. Almost nine times out of ten, postwar presidents retain the support of these key legislators.

Finally, the entry of .126 in column 3 combines columns 1 and 2 to reflect net presidential power over veto-pivotal legislators. Addressing question 3, this is the amount by which attraction exceeds one minus retention, or, alternatively, the amount by which presidential gains exceed losses in this two-sided bidding war for pivotal votes. The substantive interpretation of this number is that, within the critical cluster of pivotal or near-pivotal legislators, a postwar president can expect a *net* swing of one in eight legislators to his position.

In summary, if presidential power is the power to persuade and the technique employed is regarded as plausible, then Neustadt's qualitative notion of presidential power is now quantifiable. Are U.S. presidents powerful? Yes, somewhat. More precisely, on a theoretical scale of −1 to +1 in which zero means no net power, presidential power as the power to persuade in veto situations is .126. While reactions to this number are likely to be mixed, one interpretation is that this is modest support for the sometimes-doubted stylized fact of presidential power as persuasion.

Power of Individual Presidents

A long-standing tradition in U.S. politics is to evaluate and compare presidents in terms of their success with (or against) the Congress. For example, Peterson (1990, table 16.1) interprets veto sustain rates as indicators of "effectiveness" of the president, Bond and Fleisher (1986, 1995) define as success whether the president's position received a majority in the Congress, Shields and Huang (1995) study the number of vetoes cast, and Hill and Plumlee (1982) evaluate presidents' success using a novel budget ratio.

As a basis for comparison across vastly different methodologies, table 7.3 also gives attraction, retention, and net power measures for individual presidents. In all columns, variation is substantial. Nixon leads the power pack in the attraction column with a rate of .408, followed closely by Eisenhower, who presided in both unified and divided government regimes. Eisenhower and Nixon were also top retainers along with George Bush, each with retention probabilities exceeding .9. Ike's retention rate is sufficiently high to boost him to the top of the heap of postwar presidents, and this finding reinforces more qualitative arguments about the historically underappreciated strength of Eisenhower's "hidden-hand presidency" (Greenstein 1982). However, it comes with a caveat: it is the only instance in which the coefficient on which the calculation is based fails to meet a .01 standard of significance. The attraction veto-pivot coefficient for Eisenhower is significant, but the retention counterpart is not.

When all eligible presidents[5] are rank-ordered according to this measure of power and the measure is compared with other evaluation schemes, several additional findings emerge. Column 5, for instance, gives rankings based on veto-sustaining scorecards as presented in table 6.1. The rankings are close to one another, with two interesting exceptions. First, George Bush is significantly overrated by the veto-scorecard method and relative to the measurement method proposed here. In spite of his impressive 21 of 22 sustain rate, Bush exhibits a middle-of-the-pack performance ac-

---

5.   None of Kennedy's or Johnson's vetoes were subjected to an override vote, so these presidents are excluded from the analysis. Clinton cast no vetoes in the 103d Congress, and data for the 104th are not included.

Table 7.4
Veto-Based Power by Categories

Sample	1 Attraction	2 Retention	3 Power
President wins	.394	.950	.344
President loses	.117	.756	−.138
Precursor pairs	.150	.858	.008
Broad-band pairs	.300	.902	.201
Showdown pairs	.210	.921	.131
House only	.225	.892	.116
Senate only	.269	.913	.182
Prereform	.264	.889	.153
Postreform	.210	.897	.107

NOTE: Columns 1 and 2 are based on probit estimates evaluated for the average representative in the veto-pivot quintile. Column 3 is the difference between the value in column 1 and 1 − the value in column 2.

cording to this measure of power. He is somewhat below average in terms of attraction, and somewhat above average in retention, but an outlier in neither. Second, Jimmy Carter seems to be underrated by the more conventional sustain-based measure. Only Harry Truman keeps Carter out of the cellar in the sustain-scorecard scheme. Yet, Carter performs slightly above average according to the veto-persuasion-based measure of power.

Validity Checks

How reasonable is this method of measurement? The question has no definitive answer, but subsample analyses in table 7.4 shed some additional light on the plausibility of the measure.

First, it is often surmised that good presidents know when and when not to fight. Choosing one's battles carefully is one of the first marks of an effective politician. In the context of veto politics and conditional on a veto having been cast, this skill is facilitated by head counts on Capitol Hill. If, as nearly every observer of U.S. politics believes, a president has finite resources, then he will not squander resources on lost causes but rather will ration them and bring them to bear more forcefully when winning is regarded as an attainable outcome. It follows that if the pivot-based measurement scheme is reasonable, measured presidential power should be greater when presidents win than when presidents lose the legislative vote.[6] The first two rows in table 7.4 confirm this expectation and thus help to validate the arguably audacious decision to use the term *power* for the measured phenomenon.

Second, we can ask and assess the question of when in the legislative process a strategic president is most likely to exert his influence. A basic intuition here is that the president will be more active later than earlier in the process, in which case the phenomenon we measure and call power should be smaller on precursor pairs than in subsequent pairs—the latter of which include the decisive postveto vote and the former of which do not. The next three rows of table 7.4 are consistent with this expectation. For precursor pairs, the presidential attraction rate is less than half of that for broad-band pairs, and the difference between attraction and nonretention in the preveto stage is barely distinguishable from zero (.008). Measured power is greatest for broad-band pairs and about average for showdown pairs.[7]

Under the assumption that switching is electorally costly and that the electorate tends to forget, if not forgive, switchers over time, an expected difference between presidential power in the Senate versus House can be extracted. Senators have longer terms and thus, according to this reasoning, should be easier for the president to persuade than House members. The third comparison in table 7.4 reveals this difference as well.

The last comparison in the table is not grounded in any prior expectation but rather is included only to see whether there are differences across historical eras. Again, a difference exists. Presidential power seems to be approximately 50 percent greater before the congressional reforms of 1974 than after.[8]

---

6. Recall that because of the three different vote-pair types, winning and losing does not always refer to the final outcome in this context, nor does it mean pass by a majority. Specifically, for precursor pairs, winning means that the vote on the conference report fell short of ⅔. For broadband and showdown pairs, winning means the vote to override failed. Thus, this expectation of power differences across winning and losing votes is not guaranteed by the method.

7. On first consideration one might expect a steady increase across types I–III given a rough expectation of increasing presidential involvement over bill histories. Recall, however, that broadband and showdown types employ the same second-vote and differ only in terms of the first vote. Thus, the broad-band pair affords maximum temporal opportunities for presidential influence in which case the pattern of differences that emerges indeed might be expected.

8. Two interpretations for this difference have been suggested. Each is best taken with some skepticism. The first interpretation is that the apparent diminution of presidential power may have been triggered by Nixon's resignation and the ill-will it brought upon the presidency as an institu-

In summary, the measure seems to tap what it is intended to tap: presidential success with the Congress on issues that the president deems sufficiently important to contest publicly by exercising the veto, and that the Congress, in turn, deems sufficiently important to subject to an override vote.

Power in Divided versus Unified Governments

The somewhat validated power measure is also illuminating when used to revisit differences between unified and divided government. The question is simply: Are presidents more powerful in divided government, unified government, or neither? Each answer is plausible even though collectively they are, of course, incompatible.

The expectation that presidents are more powerful in unified government is perhaps most intuitive in light of conventional wisdom. If unified government facilitates the passage of legislation (disregard Mayhew's thesis and most of the Chapter 3 findings for the moment) and the responsiveness of government more generally, then a key component of this mix may be that presidents are more persuasive when their party commands majorities on Capitol Hill.

The opposite expectation—that presidents are more powerful in divided government—is perhaps less intuitive but nevertheless imaginable. When a president lacks a partisan majority in Congress, two sides of a coin can be inspected: legislative productivity, and blocking legislation. In terms of legislative productivity, a premium is placed on bipartisan coalition building. This is likely to be more difficult under divided than unified government. The veto-based measure of power does not address productivity, however, so this argument is not relevant at present. In contrast, in terms of blocking legislation, presidents may have an advantage in divided government due to the mix of supermajoritarianism and the loyal opposition (the minority party) in Congress which tends to support the president.

Of course, both of the above conjectures are implicitly party based, as is the focal question itself. Therefore, depending on the nature and degree of party strength in American national government—a topic to be under-

---

tion. The second is based on Kernell's version of "going public," which may be construed as suggesting that going public is less costly for technological reasons with the passage of time, but that it causes legislators to be more obstinate and thus harder to attract. See Kernell 1986; and Canes 1997.

Table 7.5

Differences in Veto-Pivot Power across Governmental Regimes

Dependent Variables	Divided Government		Unified Government	
	Attraction	Retention	Attraction	Retention
Extreme opponent	2.008	1.198	1.011	2.616
	(52.587)	(16.399)	(10.422)	(12.084)
Veto pivot	1.649	0.862★	0.729	1.907★
	(44.736)	(11.635)	(7.683)	(8.236)
Moderate	0.903	0.539	0.637	0.680
	(23.819)	(6.838)	(6.580)	(4.083)
Moderate supporter	0.298	0.266	0.321	0.162
	(7.039)	(2.963)	(3.126)	(0.978)
Constant	−2.370	0.391	−1.630	−0.617
	(−69.947)	(5.609)	(−20.595)	(−5.608)
N observations	53,353	15,633	8,775	2,310
Log likelihood	−13,512	−4668.5	−2394.4	−640.5
Adjusted R^2	.216	.057	.263	.150
Power probabilities	.235	.895	.184	.901
Net presidential power		.130		.085

★ When observations are pooled in the retention equation, the difference between the veto-pivot coefficients across regimes is not significant.

taken in more detail in the next chapter—a third outcome is also imaginable: that presidents are approximately equally powerful across regimes.[9]

With such a diverse set of more-or-less plausible but largely atheoretic expectations about regime differences, we turn now to the data in hopes of identifying a pattern and thus raising some questions to be addressed later. Table 7.5 presents two pairs of estimates—an attraction and a retention equation for both divided and unified government. The bottom of the table presents power probabilities and measures corresponding to those in tables 7.3 and 7.4. The bottom line of table 7.5 goes to the heart of the question posed. Presidents in divided government have a net power measure of .130, while presidents in unified government have a net power measure of .085.

Several subtleties and qualifications should be stressed. First, although these probability numbers are small, it seems prudent not to dismiss the

9. This finding would not rule out the possibility of strong parties, but it would suggest that, if strong, they are approximately equally strong.

difference as insignificant. As a statistical matter, the differences are highly significant.[10] As a substantive matter, the difference in net presidential power across regimes is large in percentage terms. An implication of the probabilities is that divided government presidents are 53 percent more powerful than unified government presidents.[11]

Second, it seems inappropriate to attribute the relative powerlessness of unified government presidents to the presence of supposedly weak Democratic presidents in the sample (Truman and Carter) and to the exclusion of possibly strong ones (Kennedy and Johnson). One problem with this reasoning is that Carter is somewhat stronger than average. A deeper problem is that such reasoning confuses cause with effect. Clearly, presidential type (weak, strong, etc.) does not cause government to be unified or divided. Rather, it is the opposite hypothesis that the data invite us to entertain: that government type facilitates or impedes presidential strength in a counterintuitive way. Finally, a more subtle reason that the observed difference is not just a Truman-Carter artifact is that one of the Truman Congresses in the data set (the 80th) was a Republican Congress, thereby making these observations divided government observations.[12] In sum, this is not simply a comparison of Truman and Carter versus others.

Having suggested how not to interpret this difference, the natural follow-up question is: What, then, does the difference signify? My answer is regrettably but necessarily tentative. There seems to be a real and potentially significant party phenomenon that has a measurable bearing on when presidents are powerful and that, by implication, may eventually provide insights into why they are powerful. We therefore resume this line of inquiry in the next chapter, which addresses the partisan bases of presidential power.

---

10. In addition to splitting the samples and presenting results separately as in table 7.5, I also pooled the observations and estimated constrained and unconstrained models for attraction and retention. The former equation has the form of that in table 7.5, and the latter adds regime-specific interaction terms (*divided* × *extreme opponent, divided* × *veto-pivot* . . .). For each pair of equations, likelihood ratio tests reject the null hypothesis of no difference between constrained and unconstrained models at $p < .001$. In one instance, however, the regime difference within a quartile was not significant. Specifically, the insignificance of the *divided* × *veto-pivot* coefficient in the unconstrained retention model suggests that cross-regime differences in retention in the neighborhood of the veto pivot are zero. Thus, the real significance of the net power difference in table 7.5 is predominantly attraction based, not retention based. This is true arithmetically, too, since $.895 \approx .901$ (the retention probabilities at v) and $.235 >> .184$ (the attraction probabilities).

11. The calculation is: $100 \times [(.130-.085)/.085]$.

12. Similarly, one of the Eisenhower Congresses (the 83d) was Republican, making this a unified government regime. However, there are no such observations in the data set.

Table 7.6
Dependent Variables for Cloture-Based Power Analyses

Variable	N Eligible	N Successes	% Switchers	Success Rate
Attraction	6447	518	8.03	.080
Retention	8349	560	6.70	.933

First, however, we turn to a second application of the pivotal politics theory for measuring power.

PRESIDENTIAL POWER IN CLOTURE SITUATIONS

With a minor obstacle and a theoretically interesting caveat, measures of presidential power can also be derived using data on cloture switching.

The obstacle is that in cloture situations it is not possible a priori to identify the president's position on the cloture vote. I address this by coding the dependent variables—again *attract* and *retain*—as a function of whether the filibuster is a president-side filibuster or a normal filibuster.[13] The resulting dependent variables are summarized in table 7.6. Switching rates and presidential success rates are lower in cloture situations than in veto situations.

The caveat is that, for several reasons, we should not expect the findings to be as strong in this analysis. One reason was just alluded to: president's positions, while often more-or-less discernible after the fact, are nevertheless somewhat ambiguous. Another reason is that many unobservable and/or unmeasurable bill changes occur between successive cloture votes. The president may like these, he may dislike them, or he may not know about them. Observed switching, therefore, cannot be as closely tied to presidential influence as in the case of vetoes. Another set of reasons for lower expectations is theoretical. On president-side filibusters for which the president's ideal point is more extreme than the filibuster pivot's, there is no strict pivotal-politics-based reason for the bill-opposing president to become involved in cloture politics. Since he wields the veto pen, and its effectiveness can be guaranteed by as few as $1/3 + 1$ legislators, any bill he can block at the cloture stage can also be blocked later at the veto stage.[14]

---

13.   These types of filibusters are explained and operationalized in Chapter 5.

14.   The remaining case—when *p* lies on the other side of the president-side filibuster pivot—would seem to be uncommon. To the extent that it happens, however, this, too, would dilute the estimate of presidential power using filibuster switching data.

Table 7.7
Presidential Attraction and Retention on Cloture Votes

Dependent Variables	1 Attraction	2 Retention
First quartile	1.257	0.699
	(16.566)	(10.770)
Second quartile	0.926	0.418
	(13.100)	(6.751)
Third quartile	0.480	0.197
	(7.163)	(3.005)
Constant	−1.969	1.117
	(−37.413)	(22.965)
N observations	6,447	8,349
Log likelihood	−1625.8	−1985.6
Adjusted R^2	.098	.033

NOTE: Probit estimates with asymptotic t-statistics in parentheses.

The caveats can be translated into expectations as follows. First, measured presidential power is likely to be lower in cloture than in veto situations. If this were not the case, then there would seem to be reason to question the validity of the measure. Conversely, if it is the case, some additional validity may be claimed. Second, and similarly, a further claim to validity can be staked on a finding of greater measured presidential power on normal filibusters than on president-side filibusters. In the former case, the president has a clear theoretical reason to try to influence senators at the cloture stage. In the latter case, he has no formal reason within the pivotal politics framework to act soon because he can always cast a veto later. Finally, but with no theoretical or empirical conjectures, we can and will again examine divided versus unified government effects.

Table 7.7 presents the basic probit estimates on attraction and retention and reaffirms, consistent with all prior analyses, the predictable preference effects on switching. Presidents attract support most easily from the first quartile (that on the extreme end of the president's side of the spectrum), next most easily from the second quartile, and more easily from the third than from the excluded fourth quartile. The same qualitative differences hold for retention, although considerably less variation is explained in the cloture equations than in the veto equations.

Table 7.8 addresses more directly the three expectations stated above. First, there is some positive presidential power in cloture situations, but

Table 7.8
Filibuster-Based Power by Categories

Samples	1 Attraction	2 Retention	3 Net gain
President-side filibusters	.047 (2,614)	.925 (1,968)	−.029
Normal filibusters	.122 (3,833)	.922 (6,381)	.045
Divided government	.101 (4,640)	.901 (5,898)	.010
Unified government	.109 (1,807)	.935 (2,451)	.044
ALL	**.090 (6,447)**	**.916 (8,349)**	**.007**

NOTE: Columns 1 and 2 are based on probit estimates evaluated for the average representative in the filibuster-pivot quintile. The N for the probit estimates on which the cell entry is based is given in parentheses. Column 3 is the difference between the value in column 1 and 1 − the value in column 2.

the amount, .007, is negligible. Second, the difference in measured power between president-side and normal filibusters is as expected. Presidents experience small net losses (−.029) when legislators from the president's party are the likely initiators of extended debate. One interpretation of this finding is theoretical. As indicated above, it may be that this number is negative because presidents choose not to get into the legislative game actively at this early stage. In contrast, when the opposition party is the probable obstacle to the progress of legislation, presidents exhibit positive power (.045), albeit at a level that is still small by veto standards. Finally, the table revisits the divided versus unified government puzzle. In the case of vetoes, the finding was greater presidential power in divided than unified government. For cloture voting the difference is the opposite. Unified government presidents have small net gains of .044, while divided government presidents come out ahead by a minuscule .010.

CAVEATS AND CONCLUSIONS

The most significant substantive question addressed in this chapter has been of long-standing interest to students of American national government. Are U.S. presidents powerful? Historically, this issue has been addressed by richly detailed accounts of presidential behavior in and out of the legislative arena. Quantification of presidential power is not unheard of, but qualitative assessments are far more common. This chapter has attempted to advance the study of presidential power in the legislative arena in a unique way: by using the theory of pivotal politics as a measurement model that quantifies presidential power and thereby enables the identification of empirical regularities that warrant further study. The main finding is that postwar presidents do seem to exert positive influence over individual legislators in the veto arena. More precisely, the expected net gain of presidents over pivotal voters in veto situations is about one vote of every eight.

By no means should this measure be construed as the final word on presidential power. Any such measure is based on a method. Any such method rests on assumptions. Any such assumption may be challenged. The best we can hope for, then, is full disclosure with respect to methods and assumptions so that we can put the measures to good use. Following is a list of considerations in this vein.

First, selection bias is a concern for this analysis and, more generally, for the analyses in Chapters 5 and 6 as well. It is possible, for instance, that presidents strategically choose bills to veto on which they ultimately can prevail. Indeed, the sustain-rate scorecard method seems to bear this out: presidents usually do prevail in the end. Unfortunately, however, we have no theories or even empirical conjectures about how or why presidents vary in their strategic veto traits. Lacking this, the least ad hoc form of analysis seems to be one that treats all presidents—and their associated vetoes—identically. By default, this has been the governing philosophy here.

Second, this operationalization of power as persuasion shares some but not all of Neustadt's overall impression of presidential power. On one hand, Neustadt downplayed the significance of "command and control" power, and so too does this measure. Clearly, there is no hidden assumption that presidents can dictate votes on Capitol Hill. On the other hand, it must be emphasized that the persuasive powers substantiated here are not only powers of persuasion via rhetoric or lobbying. They have an unequivocal structural grounding as well—in no less than the U.S. Constitution. The right to veto legislation is a necessary (but not sufficient) condition for presidential power as observed and quantified here.

Third, however defensible the measure may be in the abstract, a practical limitation in its widespread use is that often the necessary data for its computation do not exist in all unified government regimes. Short of using cloture data, which is questionable for reasons already discussed, a necessary condition for application of the method is the existence of both vetoes and override attempts. In two instances—Kennedy and Johnson—this condition was not met. Along with vetoes and override attempts, a sufficient condition is for these to be in ample enough supply for there to be enough switching of both sorts to obtain significant estimates.

On balance, and for the time being, it seems prudent to view this measure of power-as-persuasion as a sometimes calculable and potentially useful dependent variable for future study. A vast literature exists on comparative power of presidents and conditions which are conducive to its exercise. Much of the literature begs for quantification—for transcending case studies. In a best-case scenario, this measure may ignite an interest in quantitative studies that attempt to account statistically for power. But, if so, the dependent variable as measured here is best viewed as a variable that includes error of an unknown and, for the time being, unknowable sort.

EIGHT

PARTY
GOVERNMENT?

The theory of pivotal politics as developed, tested, and applied in the preceding chapters is nonpartisan. While this much is unquestionable, several additional questions about parties also arise. Why is the theory nonpartisan? Isn't this unrealistic? Aren't parties important in U.S. politics? Haven't legislative scholars argued that partisanship in Congress is on the rise? Weren't some party effects identified in empirical analyses in this book? Doesn't partisanship lie at the very core of the definition of divided and unified government? On the surface, these questions have easy answers. (The answers are, respectively: for simplicity, yes, yes, yes, yes, and yes.) Beneath the surface, they present opportunities to address several misunderstandings that have arisen in recent studies, and to clarify the nature in which political parties might affect U.S. national policy making.

THE PARTY PROBLEM

Consider the following brash but tenable assertion. The single, most significant problem in the modern study of the role of parties in lawmaking is the absence of a well-articulated (preferably formal) theory about the consequences of intralegislative party activity on collective choices of legislatures.

To be sure, there is no shortage of research on, and arguments about, these phenomena. Nonetheless, when it comes to knowing precisely the conditions under which party activity occurs and knowing precisely the consequences of party activity on lawmaking, we remain largely in the dark, in spite of what one researcher calls "the remarkable resurgence of party" in recent Congresses (Rohde 1991). Parties are said to be important, and one criterion of importance is, of course, the influence of parties on laws. But what are the exact assumptions from which such influence can be logically derived? What are the exact predictions of the informal argument? What is an appropriate test—that is, one that provides an opportunity not just for support but also for refutation? The more carefully these questions are inspected, the more daunting they become.

As summarized in Chapter 1, the traditional normative theory of responsible party government holds that parties adopt well-defined and differentiated platforms, a unified government is elected, majority party members in government act cohesively to enact and implement the platform, policy outcomes are realized, and this process repeats (Schattschneider 1942; American Political Science Association 1950). The history of U.S. politics in the postwar period, however, underscores the failure of the normative theory as a positive or predictive device, and the APSA committee was the first (or possibly the second) to admit it.[1] More recently, Charles O. Jones writes, "The party responsibility model provides little or no aid either for describing a significant portion of the politics since 1945 or for predicting policy developments in the period. An alternative perspective is needed" (Jones 1994, 17).

The lack of a persuasive fit between normative political theories and U.S. political realities eventually stimulated an alternative perspective on party government. The new theory centers not on *responsible* party government in the earlier sense but rather on "*conditional* party government" as articulated by researchers such as David Rohde and John Aldrich (e.g., Rohde 1991; Aldrich 1995, chap. 7). Summarizing this important development, Samuel Patterson writes:

> Despite the difficulties that attend to party leadership in Congress, especially in the individualistic Senate, the congressional parties have become markedly more cohesive in the last two decades (see Baumer 1992; Patterson 1989; Patterson and Caldeira 1988; and Sinclair 1994) . . . [By] coordinating the talents and abilities of their diverse memberships, the congressional parties have been able to present a more united, active, and organized policy front than at any time

---

1. Schattschneider (1942) admitted it, but Schattschneider was the chairman of the APSA committee.

in recent history. As one scholar has cogently said, we now have "conditional party government" in Congress (Rohde 1991, 31). (Patterson 1995, 18, 21–22)

Inasmuch as Patterson's concise statement reflects a scholarly consensus on political parties in U.S. national government, it is essential to ask: What is the condition in conditional party government theory? That is, if not always, then under what set of circumstances does the legislative majority party act cohesively to implement policies that, in the absence of its strength, would not be implemented? Rohde (1991) points to intraparty preference homogeneity and interparty preference heterogeneity as key conditions. Aldrich and Rohde (1995) reiterate, sharpen, and extend this claim by highlighting not only the condition but also its key consequence.

> The [conditional party government] theory makes predictions that depend upon the distribution of policy views in the full House and between affiliates of the two parties. Thus, the clearer there is a *majority party viewpoint,* or the more homogeneous the beliefs of the majority party (and the more *distinct* they are from the minority), the more there should be a party effect. . . . In addition, most partisan theories would yield the expectation that the majority party would have sufficient influence, and especially so under its use of rules, to *skew outcomes away from the center* of the whole floor and toward the policy center of the [majority] party members. (Aldrich and Rohde 1995, 7; italics added)

This excerpt becomes even more illuminating when it is formalized and compared with a baseline, nonpartisan theory.

Figure 8.1 illustrates a simple five-person legislature. For concreteness, suppose it is the House. Legislators have single-peaked preferences, and collective choices are made by simple majority rule. The baseline median voter equilibrium, $M^\star = H_m$, is obvious. Also, the Aldrich-Rohde condition of conditional party government is clearly met in figure 8.1a: Ds which represent Democrats (the majority party) and Rs which represent Republicans can be cleanly split into two distinct, preference-defined entities. Let us assume that the "majority party's viewpoint" (Aldrich and Rohde's term) is adequately represented by its intraparty median, D_m. Finally, an intuitive and tractable notion of interparty preference heterogeneity is the degree to which interparty distributions overlap. In figure 8.1a there is no such overlap, so party views are "distinct" from one another, consistent with Aldrich and Rohde's passage.

What does conditional party government theory predict when, as in figure 8.1a, its condition is met? Aldrich and Rohde give the answer, and

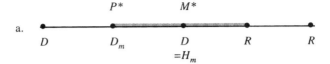

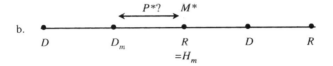

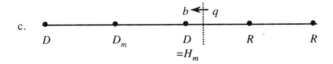

Figure 8.1
The condition and ambiguity of party government theory

figure 8.1a illustrates it. The majority party settles on its position, D_m, and implements this policy via some largely unspecified form of party discipline.[2] This strong-party equilibrium is shown as $P^\star$. Clearly, the median voter in the legislature, $D = H_m$, has to join the coalition for the party prediction to be borne out. Notice also that for any status quo in the moderate, shaded interval, the House median voter must join the majority coalition in spite of her preference for the status quo over her party's proposal.

As such, this simple formalized version of conditional party government theory has significant empirical content at two levels. At the level of outcomes, it predicts that adopted policies are "skewed away from the center," or, more specifically, are noncentrist with respect to the House but centrist with respect to the majority party (operationally, D_m, not H_m). At the level

2. Most party theories are either silent or informal and verbal at this point, thus making it difficult or impossible to know exactly why or whether the prediction follows from the assumptions. An important exception to this rule is Dion and Huber 1997 in which the key mechanical feature is that the Rules Committee can dictate a closed rule even (and always) contrary to chamber-majority wishes.

of behavior, it predicts cohesive party behavior generally (operationally, "party votes"), and it predicts that the House's pivotal voters who are in the majority party will deviate from their individual preferences to support their party's position. These theoretical expectations are reconsidered in the context of tests later, but first a complementary illustration is needed.

What does conditional party government theory predict when, as in figure 8.1b, the condition is *not* met? The verbal theory here is less precise and thus less helpful.

> Conditional party government depends on intra-party homogeneity (especially in the majority party) and on inter-party differences. If there is *much* diversity in preferences within a party, a *substantial* portion of the members will be *reluctant* to grant strong powers to the leadership, or to *resist* the vigorous exercise of existing powers, because of the realistic fear that they *may be* used to produce outcomes unsatisfactory to the members in question. (Aldrich and Rohde 1995, 18; italics added)

In figure 8.1b, one of three undesirable states occurs, depending on the many plausible interpretations of the highly qualified passage. Perhaps the conditional party government theory makes no prediction at all, in which case the theory is not helpful in understanding two-party politics where intraparty distributions have high variance and where the distributions of the two dominant parties overlap. (By most measures, these conditions cover a large portion of U.S. political history.) Or, perhaps the prediction of the theory when the condition is not met is the simple median-voter outcome, in which case the conditional party government theory is super-fluous with respect to the more parsimonious, nonpartisan theory proposed by Duncan Black (1958). Or, perhaps the prediction is simply "something between D_m and H_m," in which case we do not know exactly what the equilibrium policy is or how and why rational legislators choose it. In summary, a well-defined party government theory seems not to exist when the Aldrich-Rohde condition for party government is not met.

While the formal illustrations in figure 8.1 are elementary, their practical research implications are deep. As the preceding chapters attempted to illustrate, two desirable properties of theory are to have a broad domain of applicability and to yield unique and testable predictions. Likewise, we would like to be able to inspect predictions of conditional party government theory under a wide range of conditions to see whether it predicts better than the nonpartisan pivotal politics theory. Unfortunately, four obstacles to this desirable situation arise.

First, as noted above, the domain in which conditional party government theory yields clear and unique predictions seems to be restricted. How common is it to have a single, clear cutting line between ideal points of two sets of partisans? Represented in figure 8.1a, this condition is analytically very strong and empirically very rare. The flip side of this coin concerns predictions in the domain in which the condition is not met, represented in figure 8.1b. Here predictions are either nonexistent, nonunique, or vague. Yet, by casual as well as more systematic inspection, these are the more realistic states of legislative affairs in U.S. government situations in which some Republicans (e.g., northeasterners) are left of some Democrats (e.g., southerners), and the majority party is heterogeneous.

Second, in the rare state in which the theory's key condition is met and genuine theoretical clash is evident, the theory is difficult to refute as a practical matter. The ideal form of support for conditional party government theory would be to map policy outcomes onto a preference space and to see whether realized outcomes are more like the majority party median (D_m) than like the chamber median (H_m). Few researchers do this because, alas, it is hard to do.[3] Instead, conditional party government researchers have moved from the level of policy outcomes to the level of roll-call voting behavior. At first this move is intuitive, but, upon closer inspection, it invites tautological reasoning. Specifically, researchers calculate congress-specific measures of *party voting*—the percentage of times during which at least 90 percent of Democrats vote contrary to at least 90 percent of Republicans—and interpret these as measures of majority *party strength*.[4] Within the context of conditional party government theory, circularity then surfaces. When do preferences meet the condition of conditional party government theory? When rates of party voting is high. When the condition is met, what should we observe? Strong parties. Measured how? By high rates of party voting.

Third, figure 8.1c indicates yet another reason why the inference of party strength from party votes is tenuous in the absence of information about the locations of bills relative to preferences. Suppose that the status quo, *q,* is just to the right of the median voter—say, a remnant of a somewhat more conservative Congress—and an incremental proposal, *b,* is offered to

---

3. See Krehbiel and Rivers 1988 for an exception in which the minimum wage outcome is about three cents from the chamber—not the party—median's estimated ideal point.

4. Examples are common. For recent ones, see Patterson (1995, 18–20); and Oppenheimer (1995, 1–4).

move it leftward just to the House median, H_m. Under the strong-party model a so-called party vote indeed arises: all Democrats vote yes while all Republicans vote no. But suppose instead that these same voters ignored their party labels and the pleas of their party leaders. The resulting vote pattern would be identical under either of two significantly different behavioral postulates: in the utter absence of party strength, and in the maximum presence of party strength. So again, an inference of party strength in the presence of party voting, as conventionally defined, is tenuous if not inappropriate.[5] To make matters worse, it is most tenuous in exactly the domain in which the conditional party government theory offers clear and unique outcome-based predictions.

Fourth, when researchers who claim support for conditional party government theory have looked beyond votes for support, another problem arises: observing frenetic party *activity* and inferring significant party *influence*. This shortcoming is based on qualitative rather than quantitative data and thus is more difficult to illustrate rigorously. Aldrich and Rohde, however, provide a clear and instructive example, with an observation and a question about the 104th Congress.[6] "The Republican majority and/or its leader chose to invest considerable resources in altering rules and procedures. If these were ineffective in helping them achieve desired outcomes, why expend such resources?" (1995, 15). The answer is simple: to help keep the opposition party from assembling a moderate bipartisan coalition to enact less desired outcomes. In other words, the point is not that majority-party organizations and their deployment of resources are inconsequential. Rather, it is to suggest that competing party organizations bidding for pivotal votes may roughly counterbalance one another, so final outcomes are not much different from what a simpler but completely specified nonpartisan theory predicts. Whether this alternative view is correct is, of course, an empirical question. This present discussion is intended only to show that a convincing empirical answer cannot be found by looking at levels of *activity* within the majority party. To claim otherwise is analogous to asserting that a duck that tries furiously to swim up a swift stream is effective whenever he paddles fast.[7]

---

5. Much to their credit, Aldrich and Rohde (1995, 16) also note this.

6. See also Cox and McCubbins 1993; Sinclair 1992, 1994; Patterson 1995; Rohde 1994; and others.

7. Nor does it follow that if the duck were to fail to progress upstream rapidly, he should stop paddling, let the current overwhelm him, and go tumbling over a waterfall. More generally, countervailing political activity is an equilibrium phenomenon (see, e.g., Austen-Smith and Wright 1994) akin to deadweight losses in economics.

In summary, the dominant, most clearly articulated, outcome-consequential, party-government theory to date is problematic for two classes of reasons: theoretical and empirical. As a theoretical matter, the theory either has a severely restricted domain of applicability, or it generates predictions that are vague or not unique. As an empirical matter, the situation is, if anything, worse. The clearest domain of applicability seems empirically uncommon. Within it, the most straightforward test conceptually—namely, comparing outcomes—is usually not feasible. Finally, alternative tests based on party voting or levels of party activity entail major inferential leaps.

Where do we go from here? Either of two responses seems essential. One response is for theorists of party government to be more explicit (e.g., formal) about the conditions for such government.[8] Otherwise, confusion is likely to persist. A second response—and the one taken in this chapter—is simply to table the theoretical ambiguities about conditions under which legislative majority parties successfully implement noncentrist outcomes and to ask a more fundamental empirical question. Is there evidence—even if indirect—that parties are strong in a nontrivial sense? In other words, the analysis that follows is not a direct test of extant party government theories but rather is a more basic and inductive study designed to shed light on the degree to which students of U.S. lawmaking really need a theory of party government in which noncentrist laws are regularly enacted. Like Chapter 7, this is an application of the pivotal politics theory—not a test of it. The primary substantive aim is to estimate the degree to which presidential power, as measured in Chapter 7, has a basis in partisanship.

PARTY EFFECTS IN VETO VOTING

Table 8.1 presents the party-specific effects on veto switching from the president's perspective. As in Chapter 7, the dependent variables—*attraction* and *retention*—represent the president's aims. The independent variables are the usual preference quintiles, plus preference quintiles interacted with a president's-party dummy variable. To pursue substantive questions about partisanship with reasonable confidence, the basic preference effects should

---

8. The model in Dion and Huber 1996 is exceptional in terms of explicitness and consequential outcomes. This is a positive sign in spite of ongoing disagreements about the fit of data to the model (see Krehbiel 1997a, 1997b; Dion and Huber 1997).

Table 8.1
Party Effects on Attraction and Retention on Veto Votes

	1 **Attraction**	2 **Retention**
Extreme opponent	1.667	1.327
	(21.913)	(12.698)
Veto pivot	1.358	0.908
	(30.638)	(11.333)
Moderate	0.663	0.643
	(17.557)	(9.195)
Supporter	0.261	0.370
	(6.592)	(4.814)
President's party × extreme opponent	0.267	0.163
	(3.736)	(1.812)
President's party × veto pivot	0.267	0.283
	(7.554)	(4.526)
President's party × moderate	0.595	0.426
	(17.589)	(5.059)
President's party × supporter	0.629	−0.564
	(7.885)	(−2.480)
President's party × extreme supporter	0.808	−1.136
	(4.228)	(−2.666)
Constant	−2.304	0.116
	(−74.301)	(2.012)
N	56,840	16,284
Log likelihood	−14,814	−5000.7
Adjusted R^2	.209	.099

NOTE: Probit coefficients with asymptotic t-statistics in parentheses.

not be radically different from those observed in previous chapters. (If they were much different, then this would be evidence that the omission of party interactions in previous chapters constituted a major misspecification problem.)

Overall the equations provide a solid foundation on which to build. In each equation the nonpartisan preference effects in the first four rows are significant and perfectly ordered. That is, extreme bill opponents are most likely to be attracted (if initial proponents) or retained (if initial opponents), veto-pivot-quintile legislators are next-most likely to be attracted or retained, followed in magnitude by moderates, supporters, and finally extreme supporters (the omitted category). Not only are these individual coefficients significant and different from zero, but also it is possible to reject at high levels of significance various null hypotheses that coefficients for adjacent quintiles are the same.

In Chapter 7 we used estimates such as those in the top half of table 8.1 to measure presidential power. Now we inquire into whether there is a *partisan basis* for presidential power. If there is, then we should find positive and significant coefficients for the partisan or president's-party-interacted dummy variables, for these indicate that presidents successfully attract or retain their own party members with greater success than opposite-party members. For the most part, this is the finding in the bottom half of table 8.1. In the attraction equation, all five partisan variables are positive and significant. In the retention equation, three of five are positive with two of these significant, including that for the veto-pivot quintile.[9]

Quantification of Party Effects

In addition to the general answer that, yes, there seems to be a partisan basis for presidential power, at least within the critical veto-pivot quintile, it is also possible to quantify these president's party effects. This is done in two stages: graphic and numerical. Figure 8.2 is the graphic approach. The five preference quintiles are ordered such that the first quintile represents legislators farthest from the president (extreme supporters of the bill), the second quintile represents legislators next farthest from the president (supporters), and so on up to the fifth quintile, which represents legislators closest to the president (extreme bill opponents). For each of the quintiles, the three bars represent probabilities of attraction, conditional on initial opposition to the President's antibill position. The left bar of each set of three represents the probability that prior bill supporters from the president's party switch to the president's position of bill opposition. The middle bar, which is always somewhat shorter, represents the analogous probability for opposition-party members. The right bar, then, represents the *net partisan advantage* within the quintile, that is, the difference between the first two probabilities or bars.

Due to the well-ordered coefficients in table 8.1, the probabilities of attraction increase steadily and significantly from left to right in the figure, or as one considers legislators far, nearer, and nearest to the president's

9. The two estimates that represent president's-party members farthest from the president in the ideological space are both negative; however, these represent a small fraction of potential retainees. Only 33 observations are both president's-party and expected-bill-supporters, while only 13 members are both president's-party and expected extreme-bill-supporters. These coefficients play no role in the calculations that follow.

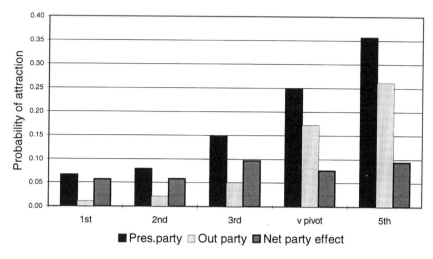

Figure 8.2
Net president's-party effects in attraction by quintiles

antibill position. This pattern holds for members both in and out of the president's party. The net partisan advantage bars, however, lie within a much narrower range: about .06 for the first two quintiles, a peak at .097 for moderates (the third quintile), and a slight drop-off thereafter. Thus, the president's partisan advantage seems to span the ideological spectrum, and the value within the veto-pivot quintile is moderate within this range.

Table 8.2 provides more precise quantitative information that culminates in an answer to the question: How great is the partisan basis of presidential power? The first row of entries is based on the attraction equation in figure 8.1 and, more specifically, its veto-pivot-quintile coefficients. The presi-

Table 8.2
Net Partisan Advantage in Attraction and Retention

		Success Rates		
	N	**President's Party**	**Opposition Party**	**Net Partisan Advantage**
Attraction	56,840	.248	.172	.076
Retention	16,284	.904	.847	.057
Average				.067
Weighted average				.072

dent's-party value of .248 says, in effect, that of every four legislators in the veto-pivot quintile who are members of the president's party and who initially supported the bill, one of these will switch to bill opposition on the second vote of the vote pair. The opposition-party value of .172 has exactly the same substantive interpretation except, of course, the switching probability is somewhat lower: approximately one in six. The net partisan advantage of .076 is the difference in these two values.

The second row presents similar calculations for the retention equation. Success rates in retention are naturally much greater than those for attraction. Because the retention subsample is composed of legislators already on record as favoring the president's position, all the president must do is guard against their defection. Presidents do this effectively about nine times out of ten (.904) within their own party, and slightly less frequently (.847) within the opposition party. The net partisan advantage based on retention, then, is .057.

Finally, the bottom of table 8.2 presents two averages of net partisan advantage. The first of these is simply the arithmetic average between the attraction and retention numbers, $(.076 + .057)/2 = .067$. The second average and last number in the table weights the net partisan advantage numbers by the number of observations on which the calculations are based. Although it does not make much difference in the end, this weighting is defensible because, for instance, a given attraction-based net partisan advantage generates a greater gain in votes for the president than the same retention-based net partisan advantage because the pool of potential attractees is always greater than the pool of potential retainees. The weighted average net partisan advantage of postwar presidents is .072, or, in fractional terms, about one-fourteenth.[10]

Interpretations

Is a net partisan advantage of .072 large? It is not immediately obvious, so three interpretations are offered.

57 Percent

One way to answer the question is to query further: large relative to what? A readily available answer was derived and described in Chapter 7: relative

---

10.   A necessarily identical number can also be calculated by first working down the party-specific columns of table 8.2, weighting the resulting party-specific averages (as in Chapter 7), and then subtracting the opposition-party weighted average (.100) from the president's-party weighted average (.172).

to presidential power overall. In this case the requisite baseline is .126, which has the interpretation that, within the critical cluster of pivotal legislators, a postwar president can expect a *net* swing of one in eight legislators to his position. Building on this overall measure of power, the net partisan component of .072 calculated in table 8.2 is about 57 percent of the overall power measure of .126. Thus, 57 percent of presidential power is partisan. This seems like a hefty partisan kick.

A Vote and a Half
Another way to answer the question is in terms of gaining pivotal (or near-pivotal) votes. For concreteness, consider a veto showdown in the Senate in which, à la the pivotal politics theory, the decisive senators lie at or near the veto pivot. The pool of relevant voters in the Senate, then, is composed of the 20 senators in the veto-pivot quintile. The derived measure of presidential power (.126) says that the president can expect to net one in eight or 2.5 of these pivotal senators. The further refined measure of the partisan basis of this presidential power says that 57 percent of this success is due to the president's asymmetric ability to attract and retain members of his own party. Multiplying 2.5 by .57 gives 1.425. Thus, the quantified *partisan* basis for presidential power in this concrete decisionmaking setting is about a vote and a half.[11] This seems like a less-than-hefty partisan kick.

A Graphic Approach
Finally, figure 8.3 provides a graphic view on the magnitude of party-based presidential power. Within all vote pairs or switching opportunities, represented by the large square, approximately one-tenth are switchers. These make up the first and tallest stick. Switchers are either attractees or retainees, with the former outnumbering the latter. From there, the net gains or presidential power stick is calculated. Presidential power, in turn, has two components: in-party and out-party. The difference between these represents net partisan gains and is shown by the small gray box. Thus, relative to, say, the presidential-power stick, net partisan gains seem significant. Relative to all vote pairs or switching opportunities, however, they are a small part of the big picture.

In summary, how great is the president's net partisan advantage? In per-

---

11.   For the House (in which the veto-pivot quintile has 87 members) the corresponding number of votes is just under 11.

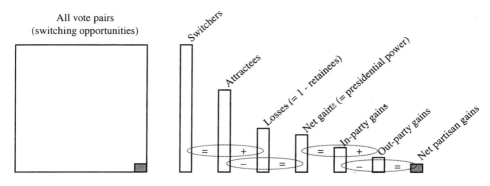

Figure 8.3
Perspective on the partisan basis for presidential power

centage terms: big, or perhaps, really big. In more practical terms: small at the level of votes.

As stressed in Chapter 7, any such method can be questioned. The method implemented above should be questioned, too, in light of the considerable gymnastics required to extract substance from the measure of net partisan advantage. The aim of this section is not to attempt to respond to all imaginable objections but rather to provide a few checks on validity that may help to defend the method or, alternatively, may help to inform critics. The logic of the exercise approximates that for the validity checks in Chapter 7.

One limitation of the calculations has already been noted but bears repeating. The method implicitly treats all bills and all strategic situations identically. Although it is hard to imagine what other assumption one would make that could be implemented, it is a questionable assumption to the extent that presidents pick and choose their battles and undertake legislative lobbying efforts carefully. Nevertheless, if the measure of partisan-based presidential power truly taps partisan-based presidential power, then we would expect it to take on a greater value in vote pairs in which the president wins the vote than in which the president loses. This expectation is borne out in table 8.3.

By similar reasoning, we would expect party-based presidential power to be greater in end-game situations—that is, operationally, when the last

Table 8.3

Group-Specific Measures of Party-Based Power

	Attraction		Retention		Average	
Observations	**Net Partisan Advantage**	**N**	**Net Partisan Advantage**	**N**	**Unweighted**	**Weighted**
President loses	.053	29,659	.067	5,462	.060	.055
President wins	.128	26,886	.043	10,806	.086	.104
Precursor pairs	−.002†	15,873	.026†	4,807	.000†	.000†
Broad-band pairs	.101	21,102	.053	6,225	.077	.090
Showdown pairs	.106	17,865	.091	5,249	.099	.103
House	.091	48,065	.119	13,974	.105	.097
Senate	.075	8,775	.046	2,309	.061	.069
Prereform	.081	21,455	−.053	4,326	.014	.059
Postreform	.072	35,352	.106	11,958	.089	.081
ALL	**.076**	**56,840**	**.057**	**16,284**	**.067**	**.072**

† Probability or calculation based on an insignificant party × pivot coefficient, so average partisan advantage assumed to be zero.

vote in the vote pair is the override vote itself. Here, too, table 8.3 is consistent with the expectation. In precursor pairs there is no significant net partisan advantage. In broad-band and showdown pairs, the partisan basis for presidential power is relatively large.

Finally, table 8.3 also includes two additional breakdowns of observations to satisfy some substantive curiosities or to invite speculation rather than to check validity of the measure. First, is the party basis for presidential power greater in the House or in the Senate? Answer: House. Second, because many legislative researchers have commented on the resurgence of partisanship in the postreform Congress, it is also interesting to ask: In which period is the party basis for presidential power greater? Answer: In the postreform Congress.

PARTY EFFECTS IN PERSPECTIVE

The incidence of party effects—especially if interpreted as large—activates concerns that some of the inferences and interpretations offered in previous chapters may be unduly nonpartisan. In some respects this possibility brings us full circle. That is, we began with an overview of research on lawmaking in the United States, noting that the very existence of the terms *unified* and *divided government* is at least a tacit endorsement of the thesis that partisanship is a significant phenomenon in U.S. politics and policy making. We then took a seemingly curious turn in Chapter 2 to present and illustrate a theory of lawmaking that is essentially nonpartisan in tenor.[12] Subsequent chapters inspected the theory in a variety of empirical ways, many or most of which were supportive of the implications of the theory and few or none of which were consistent with a single party-based theory. With all that said and done, however, a puzzle now emerges: a positive president's-party effect that occurs regularly in salient and outcome-significant veto situations. Is this the Achilles heel of the pivotal politics theory, the knight on a white horse for party government theories, both, or neither? To answer this question, we need to reconsider arguments about strong parties and conduct one additional test—a test for which these data are uniquely suited.

First, what is the finding? It is that for all veto pairs in the postwar period—and for various subsets thereof—presidents overall derive a comparative advantage in attracting and retaining senators and representatives of their own party, especially within the critical veto-pivot range of the ideological spectrum.

Second, how should this finding be interpreted with respect to the pivotal politics theory? This is subtle but important. Recall that a sharp methodological break was made at the beginning of Chapter 7, moving from the mode of testing theory to the mode of applying theory. The empirical findings in this chapter, then, do not constitute support for the pivotal politics theory, because the pivotal politics theory is assumed to be valid in the process that leads to these empirical discoveries. That is, in testing for the existence of president's-party effects in the neighborhood of the veto pivot, the method assumes that—not tests whether—presidents and other influence seekers direct their primary attention and efforts to those legislators whom the theory identifies as pivotal. The only unknown or unassumed component in this experiment is whether cross-party differences in such attraction and retention success rates exist. The finding is that they do. The pivotal politics theory does not predict that they should. So the finding must be viewed as an anomaly with respect to the theory.

Third, how much weight should be given to such anomalies? Reason-

---

12. To reiterate a passage from Chapter 2, the theory is nonpartisan in the sense of its failure to make assumptions that partisanship is a determinant of behavior. It is not nonpartisan in the sense of denying a correlation between party affiliations and preferences.

able people will disagree. Heavy weighters, for instance, may call for rejection of the pivotal politics theory in light of the finding. Light weighters (e.g., me) consider this unduly harsh for a variety of reasons. To repeat, this search is not intended as a test of the pivotal politics theory per se. Rather, the theory is used (and needed) to make the discovery and was chosen as a defensible methodological tool only after and because the theory marshaled empirical support in other contexts. Furthermore, the substantive significance of the finding is questionable. Last but not least, for a social scientist to abandon a theory in light of an anomaly is rather like a middle-class child running away from home after losing an argument with his parents. A regular supply of food, clothing, and shelter, even in the presence of losing an occasional argument, has a lot going for it compared with life on the streets. By analogy, a social scientist confronted with an anomaly should consider the supply of alternative theories before running away from a moderately successful one.

Fourth, what is the supply of alternative theories and how can they be used to help understand the anomaly? Clearly, the candidates must fit comfortably under the rubric of party theories. But, as we have seen, the more clearly articulated of these are not theories of partisanship as a source of *presidential* strength but rather theories of parties—and more specifically of the majority party—within the *legislature*. On first pass this state of affairs seems to impose a severe constraint upon directly answering the question: How do alternative theories help to clarify the anomaly? After further consideration, however, it creates an opportunity to answer the question indirectly.

To see how, note the *two* distinct ways in which partisan forces may give rise to significant marginal effects in these veto situations. First, a *president* as the titular head of his party can draw upon party resources and/or make party-based appeals to attract and retain the support of his party's legislators. Second, *majority party leaders in Congress* can similarly deploy party resources to make party-based appeals. To the extent that these are effective—that is, to the extent that recent theories of majority-party strength have empirical merit—these forces, too, can give rise to the pattern of findings reported in tables 8.1 and 8.2. The ostensible problem, which turns out to be a blessing in disguise, is that these two sets of forces are sometimes coincident in the data set. That is, when Democrats hold majorities in the Congress and a Democrat occupies the White House—or contrariwise for Republicans, which was the case only in the 83d Congress—the discovered party effects have as many as three viable interpretations: (1) party-based presidential power, or a form of *party in government;* (2) majority-party congressional power, or a form of *party in legislatures;* or (3) both. Needed is a way of disentangling these possibilities. The blessing in disguise rests on a familiar distinction: that between divided and unified government.

In unified government regimes, the presidential party and congressional majority party tend to share common goals. As such, it is possible to misinterpret the net partisan advantage in table 8.2 as a presidential phenomenon when it may instead be a congressional majority-party phenomenon. Convincing evidence of such a misinterpretation would be for differences between president's-party and opposition-party attraction and retention rates to be especially large in unified government and considerably smaller or negative in divided government. The issue is simply whether the alignment of party forces in unified government results in stronger party effects.

In divided government regimes, conversely, the presidential party and congressional majority party tend to be in opposition with one another. As such, there is relatively little ambiguity about the interpretation of the net partisan advantage. It cannot be misconstrued as a congressional majority-party advantage because positive differences between president's-party and opposition-party attraction and retention rates are inconsistent with a hypothesis of congressional majority-party strength. Convincing evidence of a genuine president's-party-based advantage, therefore, rests on the survival of a positive net partisan advantage within a subsample composed of only divided-government observations. This finding would not only corroborate the hypothesis of president's-party-based power but also refute the hypothesis of congressional majority-party strength.

Findings

The findings summarized in table 8.4 disentangle the sometimes-compatible but sometimes-competing congressional majority-party and president's-party influences. The focus is again on comparative probabilities of attraction and retention within the veto-pivot quintile.[13] The last row of table 8.4 summarizes the first two rows in table 8.2 and provides a baseline against which the crucial regime-specific results can be compared.

---

13. Probit estimates are omitted because they do not reveal anything fundamentally different from what has already been presented. Table 8.4 more simply reports probabilities based on cross-tabulation of specific preference-party categories by attraction or retention.

Table 8.4
Party-Specific Effects within the Veto-Pivot Quintile
by Government Regime

Regimes	Attraction			Retention		
	President's Party	Opposition Party	Net Partisan Advantage	President's Party	Opposition Party	Net Partisan Advantage
Unified	0.166	0.727	−0.561	0.891	0.875	0.016
	(686)	(11)		(55)	(8)	
Divided	0.256	0.169	0.087	0.904	0.847	0.058
	(6,951)	(2,176)		(3,778)	(737)	
ALL	**0.248**	**0.172**	**0.076**	**0.904**	**0.847**	**0.057**
	(7,637)	**(2,187)**		**(3,833)**	**(745)**	

NOTE: Numbers in parentheses are cell-specific denominators for the probability calculation. For example, in the lower-left cell, there were 7,637 potential attractees across all regime types, within the president's party and within the veto-pivot quintile. Of these, the rate of successful attraction was .248.

Unified Government

Upon first consideration, the unified government findings are positively baffling. The attraction data reveal a huge net *negative* partisan advantage—that is, a partisan disadvantage. Specifically, the number −.561 suggests that a unified government president and/or congressional majority party leaders have a much higher success rate in obtaining vote conversions from opposition party legislators than from within their own party. The retention data, in contrast, reveal essentially no party effect (.016). These summary findings should be questioned, however, because in each instance small numbers lie beneath them. One source of the problem is that a relatively few unified-government vetoes occur. Another source of the problem is that when unified-government vetoes do occur, there is a relatively small base of potential opposition-party legislators from whom the president can seek new votes or retain old votes. (Spatially, these minority-party legislators are located in the approximate center of the majority-party distribution.) It just so happens that among these select few outliers within their party, unified-government presidents do exceptionally well—eight of eleven in the case of attraction, seven of eight in the case of retention. These probable idiosyncrasies weigh heavily when calculating the net partisan advantage measures, which are therefore probably best ignored.

It is harder to make a case that the unified-government findings within the president's party should be ignored, though. Here the number of observations seems sufficient for confident inferences, at least in the case of attraction. What is the likelihood that a unified-government president and/or congressional majority party leaders can convert former bill supporters into bill opponents? Only one in six (.166), which is down significantly from the overall rate of nearly one in four.[14] In the broader context of party strength, this is a rather shocking discovery. Unified government regimes are by definition periods in which majority-party status in Congress and majority-party occupancy of the White House coincide. Nevertheless, it is precisely during this confluence of supposedly strong-party forces when party-based presidential power seems to be weaker.

Divided Government

The findings for divided government are neither plagued by small numbers problems nor surprising in light of what has already been learned. Because most observations are divided-government observations, the findings in the second and third rows of table 8.4 are necessarily similar. Again, the bite of the data comes from cross-regime comparisons within columns. In instances of potential attraction, president's-party effects are much stronger in divided government (.256) than in unified government (.116), yet the former are exactly the cases in which a minority-party president must confront ostensibly strong majority-party leaders in Congress in a bidding war for pivotal votes. Comparative retention rates, in contrast, show no real difference. From a partisan perspective, however, this, too, is puzzling. Why shouldn't there be evidence that a president is more successful at retaining his own party's supporters when his party has a majority in the legislature (unified government) than when it does not (divided government)?

CAVEATS AND CONCLUSIONS

The attraction and retention analyses underscore the two major findings of the chapter. First, party effects exist on both the attraction and retention sides of the voting ledger, and these effects occur above and beyond any expectations of the pivotal politics theory. But second, these findings do not fit well within recent arguments about the resurgence of majority-party

---

14. The comparative retention probabilities show only slight slippage (from .904 to .891), but here again is a numbers problem: there are not many potential retainees even from within the president's party ($N = 55$).

strength in Congress. The reason is that the party effects are almost surely president's-party effects—not congressional majority-party effects. Inexplicably, when partisan forces are in alignment across branches of government, U.S. presidents seem less capable—not more—of capitalizing on the ostensible good fortune of unified government. Therefore, to the extent that party government exists in the United States, it appears to be presidency based, not Congress based.

Although this is a unique and uniquely derived finding, nearly all of the caveats from Chapters 5 and 6 apply here, too. For example, the measures employed are imperfect, and there may be selection biases in the votes analyzed. Add to these qualifications those introduced in Chapter 7: the method makes a questionable (but not obviously curable) assumption about strategic uniformity of situations, and it arbitrarily singles out legislators in the veto-pivot quintile for computational purposes.

Nevertheless, on balance, and most broadly, the cumulative findings from Chapters 3–8 suggest that the outcome-consequential tensions that arise and are played out in U.S. lawmaking are due, first and foremost, to politicians who straightforwardly and individualistically express their preferences within and across two branches of government in supermajority settings. It is not disputed that majority-party leaders compete actively, aggressively, and often successfully for pivotal votes in such settings. But so do minority-party leaders and the president, and there is precious little systematic evidence supporting the hypothesis that the majority party in the Congress is disproportionately powerful at winning pivotal votes, much less noncentrist outcomes. Therefore, to the extent that lawmaking outcomes in the United States are not approximate legislative-median outcomes, the explanation seems not to be found in a theory of party strength in legislatures. Rather, the probable cause is supermajoritarian institutions which allow pivotal players to dampen only somewhat the strong tendencies toward policy moderation in weakly partisan voting bodies.

NINE

PARTISANSHIP
OR PIVOTS?

At least two lingering reservations may make it premature to conclude that the pivotal politics theory is a good, basic theory of U.S. lawmaking. One reservation is an outgrowth of the empirical finding in Chapter 8 of a qualified form of party government. Perhaps a more suitable venue exists in which to reassess the role of partisanship in lawmaking. Another reservation stems from the fact that, since the pivotal politics theory was introduced in Chapter 2, its simplifying assumptions have been downplayed or ignored. Perhaps the choice of venues for the empirical tests in previous chapters has inflated the importance of pivots and overstated their nonpartisan status.

This chapter responds to these concerns with a dual, pivots-and-partisanship application. The application highlights potentially serious omissions in the pivotal politics theory in order to assess their actual seriousness, and it compares and contrasts the pivotal politics theoretical expectations with those of a leading party-centered theory. The methods and data are distinctively different from those in previous chapters. The methods are almost exclusively qualitative rather than quantitative. The data (broadly construed) are legislative histories of recent congressional budget cycles rather than broad historical sweeps of diverse types of lawmaking activity. By focusing on budgetary situations in which partisanship loomed large, the application deliberately creates a hospitable setting for party-theoretic approaches to lawmaking and, conversely, an inhospitable setting for the pivotal politics theory. In contrast to this unbalanced setup, however, the overall objective of the chapter is neutral: to increase the likelihood that sound judgments are made as researchers move beyond basic theories of lawmaking to develop and test more elaborate theories.

OMISSIONS

I begin with an understatement. The pivotal politics theory fails to embody several features of contemporary lawmaking that are widely regarded as central to the governmental process. Although the list can be extended, five such features are emphasized repeatedly throughout the chapter.

First, *political parties* are perhaps the most conspicuous omissions from the theory. Players in the game of pivotal politics are autonomous and individualistic. If they take an action on a specific piece of legislation, they take it because it is in their interest—not because some collective entity, such as a party or a party leader, pressures the player to take such an action. A voluminous literature suggests that the omission of parties or partisan behavior from a basic theory of lawmaking is likely to be serious,[1] and the finding of party-based presidential power in Chapter 8 adds some weight to this conjecture.

Second, the pivotal politics theory does not directly accommodate the *multidimensionality* of policies and the corresponding space over which decision makers draft bills, craft compromises, and ultimately enact laws. The theory instead postulates that policies and preferences can be arrayed on a unidimensional choice space. In so doing, it precludes the consideration of analytic or empirical problems that are often regarded as central to understanding collective choice.[2]

Third, pivotal politics theory does not allow for *agenda setting* by players who are presumed to have special parliamentary endowments. In the end, some players in the theory are pivotal, of course. Their special pivotal status, however, derives solely from their relative positions in the array of preferences—not from restrictive procedures or special parliamentary authority. In other words, the pivotal politics theory is perfectly egalitarian in the assignment of legislative rights. Considered jointly with the real-world feature of multidimensionality, the omission of agenda setting implicitly rules

---

1. See Cooper and Wilson 1994 for a recent review and extensive citations.

2. See the brief discussion of majoritarian chaos theories in Chapter 1. See Riker 1980 for a comprehensive review.

out the prospect for clever and creative cross-issue bundling strategies that are often characteristic of legislative and presidential politics.[3]

Fourth, although it was often applied or interpreted in a quasi-dynamic manner, the pivotal politics theory is fundamentally a finite horizon model. Real-world lawmaking, in contrast, is almost invariably a *dynamic process* of back-and-forth bargaining through repeated offers and counteroffers with few or no limits on the number of such offers.[4]

Finally, the pivotal politics theory portrays the status quo, lawmakers' preferences, and the president's preferences as exogenous, stable, and known with certainty by all players. These assumptions abstract away the very real possibility that decision makers in government operate in environments better characterized by *uncertainty* about the consequences of existing policies (the status quo), the consequences of legislation under consideration, and the preferences of legislators or the president.[5] Such uncertainties are closely related to the electoral connection. How, for example, are the preferences of politicians induced via electoral competition, campaign contributions, interest groups, lobbyists, and new information about the consequences of policies?

In its entirety, this is a formidable list. Indeed, one common inclination may be to reason that if parties, multidimensionality, agenda setting, dynamics, and uncertainty are salient features of most lawmaking in the United States, and if a so-called basic theory of U.S. lawmaking has *none* of these features, then the basic theory must be basically useless. This conclusion is not necessarily wrong, but the reasoning is somewhat misguided. As discussed in Chapter 2, the argument is *not* that the world—like the pivotal politics theory—is *strictly* nonpartisan, unidimensional, procedurally egalitarian, static, and certain. Rather, the nature of the study is to assess whether a useful approximation of complex real-world behavior and outcomes can be obtained by making simplifying assumptions such as these. Although the general thrust of Chapters 3–6 is that this is possible, it is

---

3. Seminal studies on agenda setting include McKelvey 1976; and Romer and Rosenthal 1978. Subsequent stability-inducing theories (see Chap. 1) likewise employed assumptions of asymmetric parliamentary rights, such as committee gatekeeping, restrictive amendment rules, and ex post vetoes.

4. See Baron and Ferejohn 1987 for a theory of bargaining in legislatures. See Cameron 1998 for a comprehensive study of executive-legislative bargaining.

5. Theories of legislative signaling are reviewed and tested in Krehbiel 1991. See Groseclose and McCarty 1996; Matthews 1989; Martin 1997; McCarty 1997; and for theories of legislative-executive decision making under incomplete information.

nevertheless informative to put the theory through a final and more tortuous application in which the theory must confront head-on the items on the list of omissions.

Budgetary politics during the first four years of the Clinton administration has all of the requisite features of tortuous test cases. The players were partisans. The issues at stake were multidimensional. Early stage actors set the agenda for subsequent budgetary decisions. Bargaining transpired in a complex dynamic environment. And politicians were often uncertain about the consequences of their actions.

THE BUDGET PROCESS AND RECENT BUDGET CYCLES

As it has evolved after the 1974 Budget and Impoundment Act, the congressional budget process usually takes place in two or three major phases. First, the Congress enacts a budget resolution that sets overall targets for revenue and spending. Second, appropriations bills are passed that must conform to the overall targets but may deviate from the budget resolution recommendations on a program-by-program basis. Third, often but not always, a reconciliation bill is passed that brings revenues and spending into conformity with the goals of the budget resolution.[6] Depending on the nature and scope of reconciliation instructions inserted into the budget resolution, the reconciliation bill may make programmatic changes in taxes and entitlement programs. For example, the 1990, 1993, and 1995 reconciliation bills contained major changes in taxes and entitlements, and the 1996 reconciliation bill enacted welfare reform. More specifically, the four budget cycles in the first term of the Clinton administration went as follows.

In 1993 (fiscal year 1994, 103d Congress, 1st session), the new president succeeded in implementing what, by most accounts, was major deficit reduction: $496 billion over five years. This feat was accomplished during unified government, and no minority party members voted for either the budget resolution or reconciliation bill. The victory was extremely costly to the White House and fractious within the Democratic party. Several key concessions were made until, on the crucial budget reconciliation bill, the thinnest possible winning coalitions formed in both the House and the Senate. Forty-one Democratic representatives and six Democratic senators defected from their party's position and the president's position.

In 1994 (fiscal year 1995, 103d Congress, 2d session), budgetary politics

6. See Schick 1995 for a comprehensive and uniquely accessible overview.

was calm by comparison. As Leon Panetta, director of the Office of Management and Budget, expressed it, "The real purpose of this budget is to stay on track with what was done last year."[7] For the most part, Congress did stay the course. The Congressional Budget Resolution called for about $13 billion in cuts below Clinton's initial request. Thereafter, most congressional action consisted of making small increases in one program while making roughly equivalent reductions in another.

By 1995 (fiscal year 1996, 104th Congress, 1st session), the partisan makeup of the Congress had changed dramatically. According to most journalistic accounts—and the accounts of many politicians and political scientists—the 1994 midterm election was potentially revolutionary. For the first time in 40 years, Republicans enjoyed a seat advantage in both chambers: 230–205 in the House and 53–47 in the Senate. Without exception, 1995 was regarded as a highly contentious and bitterly partisan year in Washington. The quintessential example was the budgetary showdown that heated up in the summer, erupted in the fall, and simmered through the spring and summer of the following year. In short, Republicans threatened to shut down the government if their budget priorities were not enacted, and President Clinton called their bluff. Portions of the government indeed were shut down for several weeks. The general consensus was that in the corresponding public relations battle, the president won and congressional Republicans lost. As for another bottom line—the war, arguably—the story is different. In accordance with Republicans' wishes, federal outlays fell.

In 1996 (fiscal year 1997, 104th Congress, 2d session), Republicans seemed to be stinging from their 1995 losses in the arena of public opinion. "Overreach" was a commonly used word by a few repentant congressional leaders and by many Washington pundits as they looked back at the previous year and looked forward to the election in November. While many Republicans moderated their rhetoric in hopes of maintaining control of Congress and recapturing the White House, Democrats countered with countless speeches about "protecting our values" on issues such as "Medicare, Medicaid, education, and the environment." Relative to the policy changes in 1993 and 1995, changes in 1996 were small with one key exception. In its reconciliation phase, Congress passed and President Clinton eventually signed a welfare reform bill.

Although this brief overview omits an enormous quantity of details,

7. *Congressional Quarterly Almanac* (1994), 67.

many of these will come out as a more structured discussion unfolds. Meanwhile, to help structure the discussion, consider two broad generalizations about recent budget cycles.

Partisan Behavior

First and foremost, budget politics from the Reagan through the Clinton administrations appears to have been highly partisan. Although it is impossible to quantify the rhetorical ruffles and flourishes that characterized this period, it is relatively easy to compile roll call voting data that are widely interpreted as supportive of the generalization that budget politics is partisan politics. Tables 9.1 and 9.2 do this for the four budget cycles in the first Clinton administration, first for the unified-government 103d Congress and second for the divided-government 104th Congress. For each session of Congress, the tables present final votes at three stages in the budget process: committee vote to report, floor vote to pass, and floor vote to pass conference report. In each case, roll calls are reported at the budget resolution phase and the budget reconciliation phase. The key columns for assessing the partisan nature of budgetary votes are those labeled defections. In terms of raw numbers and percentages, defections are clearly rare.

Incrementalism in Outcomes

A second and necessarily softer generalization concerns aggregate outcomes of the budget processes. The magnitude of the changes in overall discretionary spending seems, in the end, to be quite small, at least in percentage terms. Table 9.3 quantifies this in terms of budget authority and outlays for defense, international, and domestic categories as defined and reported by the Office of Management and Budget.[8] Incremental change is surely consistent with studies of budgetary politics in an earlier period (e.g., Wildavsky 1964). The absence of large changes, however, seems surprising in

---

8. Budget authority refers to the legal authority of federal agencies to spend or otherwise obligate money. This is accomplished through appropriations bills enacted into law. Outlays refer to money actually spent in a given fiscal year (as opposed to money appropriated that year but not spent until a later year). Budget authority in one year may result in outlays over several years. Likewise, outlays in a given year are determined by a mix of budget authority granted in that and prior years. Due to these complexities, the numbers in table 9.3 should be taken lightly as measures of outcomes associated with congressional decisions in a specific year. Moreover, there are additional complexities associated with federal budgeting that make inferences even more tenuous. For an excellent description with concrete examples, see Cogan and Muris 1994.

Table 9.1

Voting on Budget Measures during the 103d Congress: Unified Government

	Seats D-R	Budget Resolutions							Budget Reconciliation						
		Votes				Defections			Votes				Defections		
		Y	N	D	R	%D	%R	TOTAL	Y	N	D	R	%D	%R	TOTAL
	259ª–176							**1993 (Fiscal 1994)**							
House	26–17														
Committee		27	16	0	0	0.0	0.0	**0.0**	24	14	0	0	0.0	0.0	**0.0**
Floor		243	183	11	0	4.5	0.0	**2.6**	219	213	38	0	17.4	0.0	**8.8**
Conference Report		240	184	12	0	5.0	0.0	**2.8**	218	216	41	0	18.3	0.0	**9.4**
Senate	57–43														
Committee	12–9	12	9	0	0	0.0	0.0	**0.0**	11	9	0	0	0.0	0.0	**0.0**
Floor		54	45	2	0	3.7	0.0	**2.0**	50	49	6	0	12.0	0.0	**6.1**
Conference Report		55	45	2	0	3.6	0.0	**2.0**	51	50	6	0	11.8	0.0	**5.9**
								1994 (Fiscal 1995)							
House	26–17								(No reconciliation bill)						
Committee		26	17	0	0	0.0	0.0	**0.0**							
Floor		223	175	11	0	4.9	0.0	**2.8**							
Conference Report		220	130	17	0	7.7	0.0	**4.9**							
Senate	12–9														
Committee		13	8	0	1	0.0	12.5	**4.8**							
Floor		57	40	0	2	0.0	5.0	**2.1**							
Conference Report		53	46	4	2	7.5	4.3	**6.1**							
TOTAL		**1,223**	**898**	**59**	**5**	**4.8**	**0.6**	**3.0**	**573**	**551**	**91**	**0**	**15.9**	**0.0**	**8.1**

ª Includes one independent.

Table 9.2
Voting on Budget Measures during the 104th Congress: Divided Government

	Seats D-R	Budget Resolutions							Budget Reconciliation						
		Votes				Defections			Votes				Defections		
		Y	N	D	R	%D	%R	TOTAL	Y	N	D	R	%D	%R	TOTAL
								1995 (Fiscal 1996)							
House	230–205[a]														
Committee	24–18	24	14	1	0	4.2	0.0	**2.6**	24	16	1	0	4.2	0.0	**2.5**
Floor		238	193	8	1	3.4	0.5	**2.1**	227	203	4	10	1.8	4.9	**3.3**
Conference Report		239	194	8	1	3.3	0.5	**2.1**	235	192	5	1	2.1	0.5	**1.4**
Senate	53–47														
Committee	12–10	12	10	0	0	0.0	0.0	**0.0**	12	10	0	0	0.0	0.0	**0.0**
Floor		57	42	3	0	5.3	0.0	**3.0**	52	47	0	1	0.0	2.1	**1.0**
Conference Report		54	46	0	0	0.0	0.0	**0.0**	52	47	0	1	0.0	2.1	**1.0**
								1996 (Fiscal 1997)							
House															
Committee	24–18	23	18	0	0	0.0	0.0	**0.0**	23	14	1	0	4.3	0.0	**2.7**
Floor		226	195	5	4	2.2	2.1	**2.1**	256	170	30	4	11.7	2.4	**8.0**
Conference Report		216	211	4	19	1.9	9.0	**5.4**	328	101	98	2	29.9	2.0	**23.3**
Senate															
Committee	13–11	13	11	0	0	0.0	0.0	**0.0**	14	10	1	0	7.1	0.0	**4.2**
Floor		53	46	0	0	0.0	0.0	**0.0**	74	24	23	1	31.1	4.2	**24.5**
Conference Report		53	46	0	0	0.0	0.0	**0.0**	78	21	25	0	32.1	0.0	**25.3**
TOTAL		**1,208**	**1,026**	**29**	**25**	**2.4**	**2.4**	**2.4**	**1,375**	**855**	**188**	**20**	**13.7**	**2.3**	**9.3**

[a] Includes one independent.

Table 9.3

Discretionary Spending during Clinton's First Term

Fiscal Years:	Billions				% Change			
	1994	1995	1996	1997[a]	1994	1995	1996	1997[a]
Budget authority								
Defense	262.2	262.9	265.0	263.1	-2.58	0.13	0.40	-0.36
International	20.9	20.2	18.1	18.1	-22.88	-1.70	-5.48	0.00
Domestic	231.9	219.1	219.3	224.6	3.76	-2.84	0.05	1.19
TOTAL	515.0	502.2	502.4	505.8	-0.91	-1.26	0.02	0.34
Outlays								
Defense	282.3	273.6	266.0	268.0	-1.76	-1.57	-1.41	0.37
International	20.8	20.1	18.3	19.6	-1.89	-1.71	-4.69	3.43
Domestic	240.8	252.0	250.1	262.5	2.97	2.27	-0.38	2.42
TOTAL	543.9	545.7	534.4	550.1	0.28	0.17	-1.05	1.45
Outlays in fiscal 1992 dollars								
Defense	271.5	256.9	242.3	238.1	-2.86	-2.76	-2.92	-0.87
International	19.4	18.4	16.2	16.9	-3.72	-2.65	-6.36	2.11
Domestic	227.8	232.6	224.8	230.0	1.65	1.04	-1.71	1.14
TOTAL	518.7	507.9	483.3	485.0	-0.96	-1.05	-2.48	0.18

SOURCE: U.S. Office of Management and Budget, 1997, table 8.9.

[a] Figures in this column are estimates.

light of three mutually reinforcing contemporary facts. First, the budget process attracted a large proportion of legislators' attention in the early to middle 1990s. Second, as noted above, budget politics was widely pronounced (and denounced) by the press as a bitterly partisan ordeal. Third, the issues seemed to interest groups and the public more generally to be extremely important. Nonetheless, bottom-line change seems incremental.[9]

Do existing theories account for the generalizations of partisanship and incrementalism? Initial observations are inconclusive but nevertheless helpful in identifying sharper questions and hypotheses about more specific events in recent budget cycles. In order, we consider party-centered theories and the pivotal politics theory.

PARTY THEORIES AND BUDGET GENERALIZATIONS

In light of the first generalization (partisanship) and first item on the omission list (parties), a promising first step is to reconsider party-oriented theories of lawmaking. A credible contender for a better account of budgetary lawmaking is the notion of collective responsibility within parties. As discussed briefly in Chapter 1, this perspective has both normative and positive dimensions. Normative arguments for responsible party government are articulated by scholars such as Schattschneider (1942). Positive arguments about party behavior have been increasingly numerous and forceful in the last decade, particularly among researchers in the rational-choice tradition.[10] Because the focus here is on predictions rather than prescriptions, the more recent, positive strand of research is especially germane.

As discussed by V. O. Key (1964) and Sorauf (1964), and spelled out more formally by Cox and McCubbins (1993) and Aldrich (1995), legislators in effect play two games at once. They play a game of lawmaking within the legislature, which has been the focus in this book. In addition, they play a game of vote getting within an electoral environment, which has been mostly ignored in this book. In practice, of course, these two games may be intricately related. The force of party-oriented theories comes largely from their presumption (in varying degrees of explicitness)

9. A qualification to this interpretation is that the Budget and Enforcement Act of 1990 set limits on discretionary spending that were still in effect in the Clinton administration. A determined and disciplined unified-government Democratic majority could have undone these, however. That they chose not to surely says something about political pressures toward moderation and incrementalism.

10. See Aldrich 1995; Cox and McCubbins 1993; Dion and Huber 1997; Kiewiet and McCubbins 1991; Rohde 1991; and Sinclair 1992.

that the two games *are* intricately related in a manner in which political parties are crucial links. For example, the key concepts that Mathew McCubbins and his colleagues introduce to link the lawmaking game with the electoral game are *brand names* and *collective dilemmas*.[11]

In the case of brand names, the argument is essentially a metaphorical application of the theory of marketing by a multiproduct firm. The following summary is clear and persuasive.

> In our view, the key rationale congressional members have for organizing as parties is the common investment they have made in the informational content (and thus electoral value) of the party label. Voters decide between candidates according to their expectations about how they will perform in office. Although individual characteristics of candidates weigh heavily in the formation of these expectations, so too do the positions they adopt on important issues of national policy. A party label thus serves members in the same way as does a "brand name" for a multiproduct firm. The firm's reputation, as conveyed through its brand name, spills over across the whole product line. As firms with well-known brand names expand into new product lines, consumers can infer the characteristics of new products on the basis of their experience with the company's other products. The more homogeneous the products are in style, price, and quality, the higher the informational value of the label. The same is true for parties. (Kiewiet and McCubbins 1991, 39–40)

In the case of collective dilemmas, the argument is an application of some standard insights from the well-known prisoners' dilemma game. A recent review summarizes the thesis as follows.

> Cox and McCubbins begin their analysis with a series of collective dilemmas, problems faced by individual legislators who, acting alone, cannot capture the gains from legislation for their district. The problems are familiar—public goods, externalities, coordination. In the tradition of the new economics of organization, they argue that members faced with these problems will devise mechanisms to capture potential gains. This logic about institutions is familiar; what is new is the focus on party and party institutions as a means of achieving improvements in legislator welfare. (Shepsle and Weingast 1995, 18)

11. See Cox and McCubbins 1993 on collective dilemmas; see Kiewiet and McCubbins 1991 on brand name. See also Cox and McCubbins on "party position" (1993, 110–12), which bears a strong resemblance to Kiewiet and McCubbins's "brand name." Other works in this genre seem comfortable with and laudatory of the work of McCubbins et al. (see, e.g., Rohde 1991; Aldrich 1995; Sinclair 1994; Cooper and Wilson 1994), so this exercise is intended as an assessment of a large and influential school of thought—not as a targeted assessment of just two works.

When woven together, these two strands of thought—parties as brand names, party leaders as solutions to collective dilemmas—make for a theoretical approach that covers a lot more territory than lawmaking, which is the focus of the pivotal politics theory. In summary, parties—and especially the majority party or Cox and McCubbins's "legislative leviathan"—use institutional prerogatives to bring about coordinated action in lawmaking. Coordinated collective action in lawmaking results in majority-party-favored laws that help to maintain a brand image. The brand image resonates well with the electorate. The electorate responds to the party's brand image by voting to keep the party's candidates in the majority. And the cycle repeats itself.

Predictions and Evidence

An immediate empirical expectation that arises from the party framework is party discipline. To preserve the party's brand name and reap electoral rewards, the leadership of a strong majority party must be able regularly to persuade, cajole, or coerce fellow party members to vote consistently with the designated party position. Furthermore, leaders must do this especially when backbenchers' votes are needed to move the policy in a majority-party-preferred direction.[12] This yields the general empirical expectation of *party votes*—roll calls on which a large percentage of one party opposes a large percentage of the other party—which are often cited as evidence of partisanship or party strength.[13]

A quick and conventional way of testing this expectation is to return to tables 9.1 and 9.2 and ask: On decisive or near-decisive votes on budgetary matters, how likely are individual legislators to defect from (ex post ascertained) party positions? The answer is: Not at all likely. The average Republican defection rate is consistently below 3 percent over the four-year period. Democratic defection rates are also low, although greater in the reconciliation phases (14–16 percent) than the on budget resolutions (2–

---

12.   More precisely, for the policy shift to be unambiguously partisan, the *magnitude* of the shift must be greater than that predicted by a baseline nonpartisan model. Elsewhere, I have used the median voter model as the baseline (Krehbiel 1993; Krehbiel 1996b). Here it makes more sense to think of the pivotal politics theory as the baseline. Then the issue becomes whether a suitably defined, outcome-consequential party theory makes predictions that differ meaningfully from the pivotal politics theory.

13.   See, for example, Collie 1988 and dozens of sources cited therein.

5 percent). Therefore, party-centered theories seem to account very well for the generalization of partisanship in budget politics.

To understand more deeply the behavioral mechanics of party theories and proceed to a prediction about budgetary outcomes, several additional questions must be addressed.

First, why is such intraparty cohesion possible? The short answer of most recent party theorists is, simply, because it's rational. The longer answer, fortunately, is more illuminating. Because of the key assumption that there is a potential brand-name-based benefit that a party can capture in the electoral arena, the party's problem of obtaining discipline within the lawmaking game is portrayed as a "collective (or prisoners') dilemma." Furthermore, the lawmaking and electoral games are repeated. Given that legislators have long time horizons, leaders may have sufficient punishment mechanisms to make disciplined behavior by backbenchers optimal. If so, then backbenchers will resist short-term incentives to "defect" from the party plan by voting consistently with their immediate policy preferences; instead, they will vote for their party's program.[14]

Now comes the linchpin of the theory. Why is such cohesion beneficial not only to the party as a collective entity but also to individual party members who have short-term incentives to deviate from party-disciplined behavior? The party-theoretic argument is that it is in the interest of individuals not to deviate from party strategies because cohesive behavior results in lawmaking that communicates credibly the party's brand name to electorate and therefore increases individual party members' vote shares or reelection probabilities.

What, then, are the implications of these theories for the nature and magnitude of policy change? Taking the party-oriented theories at face value, the answer is clear. Policy shifts should always be directionally consistent with the majority party in Congress,[15] and the magnitude of such shifts should be proportional to the strength (in the sense of discipline) of the majority party. In its strongest form, then, by which is meant maximum

---

14. Although this is a standard result in this class of games—so much so that it is called a *folk theorem*—there is another substantively important component of the folk theorem. Not only is "all cooperate" an equilibrium under specifiable conditions. So, too, is "all defect" an equilibrium, as well as a wide range of more moderate strategies. Therefore, while the collective dilemma approach effectively rationalizes one kind of party-like behavior, it does not generate this as a unique prediction. Some proponents of this approach to studying parties are aware of this problem (see, e.g., Cox and McCubbins 1993, 86n.4); however, they do not provide a theoretical argument for why party members play "all cooperate" strategies rather than any of countless other equilibrium strategies.

15. The theories are ambiguous when party control varies across chambers, for example, 1981–86.

party discipline, party theories predict *abrupt and large swings in policy whenever party control changes*.

In contrast to the behavioral prediction of party discipline, this outcome-centered party-theoretic prediction seems to fare less well in the budgetary arena. Between the famous "read my lips" showdown during the Bush administration in 1990 and the end of the President Clinton's first term in 1996, two abrupt changes in governmental regimes occurred: the return to unified government after the 1992 election, and the change back to divided government after the 1994 election. Therefore, the 1993 and 1995 budget cycles should have produced not only party discipline but also major policy shifts in a Democratic and Republican direction, respectively. Did they? The evidence is mixed.

In support of the prediction, table 9.3 indicates that changes in spending priorities were approximately as expected when measured by budget authority or outlays. Consistent with Democratic priorities broadly, defense outlays declined by about 3 percent (in constant dollars) after the 1993 (fiscal 1994) process, while domestic outlays increased by somewhat under 2 percent. Whether the magnitude of the change is significant, however, is questionable.[16]

Other aspects of aggregate outcomes are also open to question. Specifically, although the 1993 budget resolution and corresponding reconciliation bill were widely scored as comeback-kid successes for President Clinton,[17] the content of the legislation was remarkably similar to that produced by divided government three years earlier.[18] So although Democrats claimed eventually to have secured this hard-fought "victory," the direction and magnitude of polity change in their self-proclaimed historic 1993 reconciliation bill was anything but clear. The left wing of the party complained

---

16. For example, part of the defense decrement is undoubtedly due to across-the-board changing perceptions regarding defense needs after the collapse of the Berlin Wall, the emerging market economies of Eastern Europe, etc. Likewise, there can be no doubt that President Clinton and his Democratic allies in the Congress wanted to raise domestic expenditures more. Exhibit A is the fledgling economic stimulus package discussed in Chapter 2.

17. See, for example, Cohen 1994; Drew 1994; and Woodward 1994.

18. Brady and Volden provide a concise summary: "The final bill that passed Congress and was signed by the President bore a remarkable resemblance to that passed by the 101st Congress in 1990. Both bills called for savings of half a trillion dollars over five years. Both contained tax increases on individual incomes in the highest brackets and spending cuts on defense. The same areas that were left alone in 1990 maintained their untouchable status in 1993. This is no surprise. As the members of Congress and their positions did not change dramatically, the bill outcomes are expected to be in the same range as before" (Brady and Volden 1997, 152).

bitterly that their president had sold them out. The right wing of the party complained, too, but, unlike the left wing, conservative Democrats credibly threatened not to uphold party positions unless they were changed. And many of them were.[19]

A party-theoretic response to these observations on 1993 might be: but the 1990–93 comparison is an instance of regime change in national government broadly—from divided to unified—not an instance of regime change within the Congress, which was Democratic throughout this period. These are, after all, theories of *congressional* decision making. True enough. So it is perhaps better to focus on the congressional regime change brought on by the 1994 midterm election.

After Republicans obtained majority party status in the 104th Congress, apparent party discipline became even stronger than under Democratic control. Republican defections on the 1995 budget resolution, for example, numbered only two, while defections on the more controversial reconciliation bill increased only slightly, to 13 (see table 9.2). Overall, this seems consistent with party-theoretic expectations about behavior.

The aggregate outcome data, however, are again murky. Domestic and defense budget authority remained constant, but outlays in both categories decreased. In the case of domestic spending, the direction of the change is broadly consistent with Republican wishes, however the magnitude of the overall reduction is smaller than journalistic coverage and political rhetoric suggested. In the case of defense outlays, the overall decrease is inexplicable in terms of the change to Republican majority status. This, however, may have a different and broader party-in-government rationale, namely, a Democratic president battling effectively against a Republican Congress.

In summary, a focus on parties seems to provide a perfect theoretical fix for addressing some broad patterns in recent budget cycles. Why is voting on important budgetary measures so partisan? Because parties use the salience of budgetary issues to build and maintain their brand name. Why do (some) broad shifts in federal expenditures comport with majority party control of the Congress? Because, by definition, the majority party has the votes to enact budgetary legislation, and because, more subtly, majority party leaders can acquire these votes in the crunch. Why can majority party leaders acquire these votes in the crunch in budgetary showdowns? Because cohesive party behavior enhances individual party members' electoral images and thereby helps the party to maintain or increase its seat share in the Congress.

---

19. Details are provided in the next section.

These are compelling arguments on the surface, and they have important implications regarding behavior in the electoral arena—an arena about which the pivotal politics theory is silent. Before continuing to scratch beneath this surface, we return to the pivotal politics theory to assess its comparative strengths and weaknesses in explaining the two budgetary generalizations.

PIVOTAL POLITICS AND BUDGET GENERALIZATIONS

As noted in the introduction to this chapter, the on-the-surface case for pivotal politics theory is clearly worse than that for party-centered theories. The causes of skepticism were stated in terms of five omissions from the model: parties, multidimensionality, agenda setting, dynamics, and uncertainty. What should be inferred from such a blatant mismatch between assumptions and reality? Opinions differ widely. On one end of the spectrum, the mismatch can be regarded as a devastating critique. On the other end of the spectrum, the mismatch is beside the point. The real vulnerability of a formal theory is not its simplifying assumptions; it is the theory's predictions.[20] With no hope of resolving this enduring issue in the philosophy of science, I shall simply concede outright that the mismatch exists but request that judgment be suspended about whether the mismatch is devastating. Meanwhile, we proceed to predictions, paralleling the focal points identified and discussed above for party-theoretic approaches.

Predictions and Evidence

The first budgetary generalization identified above was partisan behavior, and the findings in tables 9.1 and 9.2 indicate clearly that budget votes break sharply on party lines. On the surface, these findings seem to favor party-centered theories. There is one condition, however, under which such evidence should not be construed as strong support for party-centered theories or as convincing refutation of the pivotal politics theory. The condition is that preferences and partisanship are highly correlated. As a general matter, most observers of congressional politics think that budgetary preferences and partisanship are strongly correlated. As a practical matter, this condition raises a formidable methodological problem. Evidence such as that presented in tables 9.1 and 9.2 has either of two plausible interpretations.

---

20. For seminal works on this view of positivism, see Popper 1992; and Friedman 1953. Although widely accepted and practiced, this perspective is still controversial in some circles.

First, it may be that budgetary preferences and party identification are nearly perfectly correlated. If so, then legislators' party identification brings no marginal predictive power to the table above and beyond what a purely preference-driven theory, such as the pivotal politics theory, already captures. In other words, voting may be an instance of straightforward, individual preference revelation, independent of collective dilemmas, party persuasion, cajoling, and coercion. Under these circumstances, the findings in tables 9.1 and 9.2 should not be construed as inconsistent with the pivotal politics theory.

Second, however, it may be that the voting patterns in tables 9.1 and 9.2 emerge even in the presence of unmeasured but significant heterogeneity of intraparty budgetary preferences. If so, then party-centered theories stand ready to explain behavior that the pivotal politics theory and other nonpartisan theories cannot explain: disciplined roll call voting in situations in which the existence of party discipline has potentially major consequences for outcomes relative to a baseline of nonpartisan behavior.

The problem—which arguably constitutes *the* major challenge for future tests of theories of lawmaking—is that, given current measures, it is essentially impossible to discern which of these two conditions holds.[21] It should be increasingly evident, though, that we should not cite data such as these as immediate and direct support for party discipline. Nor should we cite data such as these as immediate and direct support for nonpartisan preference revelation. We should instead develop better measures of preferences in the long term and turn to other evidence in the short term.

The second budgetary generalization, incrementalism, also raises some sticky issues and new challenges. What is the prediction of pivotal politics theory regarding dramatic versus incremental change? It is tempting to reason that gridlock is much like incrementalism, so, to the extent that gridlock is common in pivotal politics theory, incrementalism in budgetary outcomes is to be expected. And, according to the aggregate data in table 9.3, it is. But this reasoning is not only sloppy; it also masks the untapped potential of the pivotal politics framework to be modified for situations, such as the budget process, that have peculiar institutional features. Proper application of the theory, then, requires that these features be spelled out, that the theory be applied with the special budgetary features in mind, and, finally, that more refined predictions be extracted and tested.

---

21. Strictly speaking, of course, it is not a dichotomy. The problem is that we cannot know *how much* so-called party voting is due to party pressures and *how much* is due to homogeneous primitive preferences within parties and heterogeneous primitive preferences across parties.

PIVOTAL POLITICS AND BUDGET OUTCOMES

The basic claim of pivotal politics theory is that most lawmaking can be usefully approximated by a few points and a line. The special challenges posed by lawmaking in the budgetary domain can be summarized accordingly. As for points, nonpartisan pivots such as p, f, m, and v may not be sufficient for predicting and understanding budgetary lawmaking that appears to be partisan. Perhaps a better theory needs an r and d (e.g., Republican and Democratic median) as well.[22] As for lines, the extreme complexity of budgetary lawmaking suggests that many lines are needed rather than the one onto which the pivotal politics theory collapses all such conflict. In other words, perhaps a better theory should be of the multidimensional variety. Before jumping to these conclusions, it seems prudent to apply and assess more thoroughly the pivotal politics theory in its current, nonpartisan state, albeit with a modicum of tailoring to make it budget ready. Two modeling strategies can be envisioned.

First, one might attempt to develop a relatively realistic model of the three-phase process outlined above in which players have preferences over a multidimensional choice space. In the first, budget-resolution phase, players would chose overall budget targets to guide second-phase appropriations, and they would also choose whether to play the third, budget-reconciliation game.[23] In effect, this latter choice would determine whether to bring tax changes or entitlements into the budget cycle. Conceptually this is promising, but operationally it is problematic. Such a model would entail solving the third phase first, and, unfortunately, we have no such multidimensional theory of budget reconciliation.[24]

A second, simpler strategy is to transport the pivotal politics theory into the budgetary domain almost as is but to take into account some distinctive features of budget situations when applying the theory. Distinctive features correspond to two of the three phases of the process as outlined above. First, the budget resolution is strictly a congressional document adopted by majority vote. The president, although he is statutorily obliged to propose a budget to Congress, is therefore not a veto player in this first phase of

---

22. See, for example, Aldrich 1995.

23. In practice this is determined by the inclusion or exclusion of reconciliation instructions in the congressional budget resolution.

24. A very rough approximation of such a model can be found in Ferejohn and Krehbiel 1986, but this model, while multidimensional, has no taxation, entitlements, president, or supermajority pivots. Some other models take on multidimensionality and a president, but they tend to employ restrictive assumptions about the status quo and/or tend to yield examples rather than general results.

the game. Similarly, Senate rules set time limits on budget resolutions, so the filibuster pivot is not a player in this stage either. Second, the appropriations phase of the process is procedurally consistent with the pivotal politics theory as portrayed elsewhere in this book. That is, appropriations bills are subject to filibusters in the Senate, and they require the president's signature or a veto override prior to enactment. Third, the reconciliation phase is a unique blend of the resolution and appropriations phases. Like appropriations bills, reconciliation bills require the president's signature, so theoretically the veto pivot v and the president's ideal point p are significant. Like the budget resolution, however, reconciliation bills are protected from filibusters by standing rules of the Senate, so the pivot point f has no special significance at the end of the process.[25]

How do these observations translate to the pivotal politics framework? First, we need an assumption that is admittedly strong, arguably unrealistic, but ultimately an empirical matter. The assumption is that budgetary decision making occurs as if the Congress and the president make collective choices on an independent, dimension-by-dimension basis. Many such decisions will be of the form: How many dollars will be appropriated for program X in year Y? Others may be of the form: Should we change the tax code in year Y and, if so, how? Or, similarly: Should entitlements such as Medicare or Medicaid be altered to achieve budgetary savings, and, if so, how and how much? There are two keys to understanding the difference between these two kinds of budgetary choices and to extracting predictions from the pivotal politics theory. One key concerns the different parliamentary and thus pivot situations in which appropriations versus entitlements decisions are made, while the other concerns the comparative extremity of status quo points in the two classes of situations.

First, consider appropriations as simplified in figure 9.1. For this kind of lawmaking, all the normal rules are in effect: senators may filibuster bills; the president may veto bills. However, what happens if a bill is not enacted? The literal answer is unequivocal: the government ceases to write out checks for the authorized programs in question. Consequently, the status quo, in dollar terms, is zero.[26] The corresponding implication of the pivotal

25. For example, this simple-majority parliamentary situation was a key to Democrats hard-fought victory in the 1993 budget process (note the simple-majority winning coalitions in table 9.1). Republicans undoubtedly would have filibustered the Clinton-Democratic reconciliation bill if they had been permitted to do so. But they weren't, so they didn't.

26. Elsewhere researchers studying the appropriations process have adopted an assumption that the status quo, or *reversion point*, is the minimum of the previous year's appropriation, the House-passed amount, or the Senate-passed amount (Kiewiet and McCubbins 1991), and have defended this with reference to empirical regularities such as continuing resolutions. But what happens if

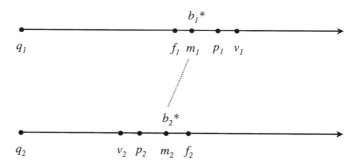

Figure 9.1
The appropriations hypothesis: median tracking

politics theory is given by the interval-I prediction from figure 2.7. The normal pivots are not constraining,[27] so full convergence to the median legislator's ideal point m occurs. This establishes the first of two pivotal politics budget hypotheses:

> *The Appropriations Hypothesis:* Appropriations outcomes will lie at the congressional median voter's ideal point and will track shifts in the congressional median over time.

Notice that this prediction is independent of party control of the White House and the Congress.

Next, consider entitlements as simplified in figure 9.2. Two questions must be addressed here, too. Who are the relevant pivots? How extreme are entitlements status quo points relative to these pivots? Since we are considering entitlements that are addressed within the reconciliation process, the filibuster pivot is out of the picture: a minority of 41 in the Senate cannot put a halt to reconciliation bills.[28] The president, however, may

---

continuing resolutions are vetoed and not overridden (e.g., in 1995)? The answer is: The government stops writing checks, that is, zero dollars.

27. The constraining pivot is f if the president prefers more spending than the median legislator and the lower of v or p if the president prefers less spending than the median legislator. A minor technical qualification is that the usual pivots are not constraining provided that the status quo is sufficiently far from the median voter and the pivots. For Euclidean preferences sufficiency is expressible as $q < 2x - m$, where $x = \min(f, \max(p,v))$.

28. The filibuster pivot is effectively out of the picture for appropriations, too, but for a different reason: extremity of the status quo leaves the pivot in a position with a parliamentary right, but without a credible threat.

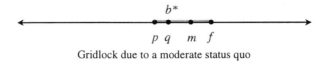

Gridlock due to a moderate status quo

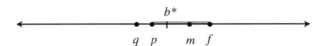

Dampened change due to a pivotal president

Figure 9.2
The entitlements hypothesis: gridlock or pivot-dampened change

veto reconciliation packages, so the president and veto pivot, p and v, *may* constrain or preclude policy change. Whether these pivots *do* constrain or preclude policy change depends on the location of the status quo, q. Herein lies the key to the entitlements hypothesis. Unlike the appropriations situation, the reversion point q for entitlements is likely to be moderate except in extraordinary situations. The intuition is straightforward. For example, what happens to tax rates if no new tax bill is passed? In contrast to appropriations, taxes do *not* revert to zero in the absence of a new law. Rather, the core features of the tax code remain intact at previously legislated levels.[29] Similarly, what happens to Medicare, Medicaid, or welfare expenditures in the absence of new legislation that defines the conditions for the entitlement? The answer is the same: the government continues to implement the entitlement programs in accordance with the conditions established in prior laws.

The resulting hypothesis is not derived and stated rigorously because of the limited scope of the empirical analysis that follows. However, it can easily be made rigorous by exhausting the cases of relative locations of four points (q, p, v, and m) on a line.

The Entitlements Hypothesis. Policy change in entitlements via reconciliation will be dampened by a pivot (usually the president) and therefore will not lie at or

---

29. Some provisions in the tax code occasionally have expiration dates, such as taxes on airline tickets. These are usually small ticket items, however.

track median legislator ideal points. Gridlock in entitlements will be common due to typically moderate status quo points in entitlements.

Consistent with the dominant theme of the chapter, plenty is missing from these pictures: partisanship, multidimensionality, agenda setting, dynamics, and uncertainty. Naturally, these omissions raise doubts about the degree to which the pivotal politics budget hypotheses will be borne out. For example, consider the events of 1995 (with analytic subtext). The strategy of the fortified Republican leadership rested crucially on the use of procedures to bundle together a diverse set of large ticket items in a way such that President Clinton would be forced to take a lot of bitter with a little sweet (partisanship, multidimensionality, agenda setting). Republicans gambled that eventually this would play well with the electorate which, after all, had just recently promoted them to majority status (uncertainty, dynamics). Specifically, the Republican-initiated budget resolution called for reconciliation that effectively brought taxes and several major entitlement programs onto the agenda. By the time the fiscal year began in October, only two minor appropriations bills had been sent to the White House, and the federal government was expected to exceed its debt limit in November.[30] So, the expected scope of the reconciliation bill became larger still. Republicans had hoped to wrap together appropriations, tax cuts, Medicare and Medicaid savings, student loans, farm programs, and welfare, and then to attach these to the presumably must-have measure to raise the debt ceiling.

In spite of the fact that most of these real-world events lie outside the formal boundaries of the pivotal politics theory, it is instructive to see how well the budget version of the pivotal politics theory accounts for the outcomes of this admittedly complex process.

First Glances

Initial observations are not encouraging. The aggregate data in table 9.3 fail to provide consistent support for the hypothesis that changes in appropriations track changes in congressional median preferences. This is true at the bottom of the table as well as in rows in which budget authority or outlays are broken down by broad categories.

A more bothersome inconsistency (as opposed to the null or no-pattern

---

30. David Rogers, "Huge Backlog of Appropriations Bills Remains in Congress as Fiscal '95 Ends," *New York Times,* September 29, 1995.

finding) arises upon inspection of the legislative histories of appropriations politics during the 104th Congress. The pivotal politics appropriations analysis in figure 9.1 led to the prediction that neither gridlock nor vetoes will occur. Yet, coincident with months of harsh rhetoric and partisan bickering, gridlock was alleged and vetoes did occur. As 1995 came to a close, three regular appropriations bills were still stuck in Congress for one reason or another. Additionally, President Clinton had vetoed three regular appropriations bill plus the massive reconciliation bill.[31]

The existence of vetoes in the appropriations settings is arguably more damning than in other instances of lawmaking, such as those that formed a large portion of the data set analyzed in Chapter 6. In nonappropriations instances, which typically have relatively moderate status quo points, real-world vetoes may arise simply due to a miscalculation on the part of legislators on the location of the veto pivot or president's ideal point.[32] In appropriations instances, however, I have argued that the appropriate way to characterize the status quo is as zero dollars, in which case there is rarely any uncertainty—and surely not in 1995—that the president prefers a wide range of appropriations amounts to zero. Given this analysis, the events of the fall and winter of 1995 are glaring anomalies within the pivotal politics framework.

Two kinds of responses can be adopted in the presence of glaring anomalies. One response focuses on the "glaring" and shifts attention away from the subtleties, intrigue, and nuance of the lawmaking *process* to assess instead whether, in spite of abstracting away from real-world subtleties, intrigue, and nuance, the basic theory nevertheless seems to predict *outcomes* more or less correctly. Adopted in the budget context, this response requires moving beyond the broad spending categories of table 9.3 to program-specific outcomes and entitlements. If the basic theory turns out to predict outcomes more or less correctly, then at least some of the glare in the anomaly will have been reduced. Another response focuses on the "anomaly" and tries

---

31. David E. Rosenbaum, "Battle over the Budget: The Details," *New York Times,* December 29, 1995.

32. Of course, as an analytic matter, miscalculation does not occur in these models. A more rigorous but somewhat tedious way of making the same point is to incorporate uncertainty into the pivotal politics theory, so that players do not know the exact location of one another's ideal points but rather know the probability density function of pivots' ideal points and thus calculate the expected locations and play accordingly. Under these conditions, vetoes occasionally occur in equilibrium, and the other basic predictions of the pivotal politics theory as presented above go through as well. It should be stressed, however, that this incorporation of uncertainty is not the same as others' incorporation of asymmetric information into congressional-legislative settings (see Matthews 1989; Groseclose and McCarty 1996; McCarty 1997; and Cameron 1998).

to identify the behavioral or structural features in the complex world that seem to differ from those of the simple theory. In turn, this may lead to better theories in which today's anomaly becomes tomorrow's prediction. This is an instance of Kuhn's (1962) "normal science" and can be expected in future studies *if* the pivotal politics theory comes to be seen as useful at a basic level.

Harder Looks

The hypotheses focus on tracking of legislative medians in appropriations situations and on gridlock or pivot-dampened change in entitlements. The legislative histories of 1993 and 1995 make it clear that, as a practical matter, disparate policy choices often become bundled together. It remains to be seen, however, whether this partisan multidimensional agenda setting in a dynamic and uncertain environment severely undermines the empirical validity of these relatively simple hypotheses. To ascertain this requires delving into details, the quantity of which can become overwhelming. As a preview to a fact-intensive discussion, consider three generalizations with which most facts are ultimately consistent.

1. *Median tracking: limits to agenda-setting effectiveness.* Early stage proposals by partisan agenda setters (e.g., the president, majority party leaders, or majority party members on the Budget Committees) may constitute over-reaching. By the time the multistage budget process culminates in law, however, substantial convergence toward the legislative median voter occurs. Over time, the median tracking in appropriations seems to occur.
2. *Median tracking: a variation.* To the extent that preferences change within Congresses (e.g., due to new information and corresponding percep-tions by legislators that their strategies are not well-received by the vot-ing public), second-session decisions seem to track these changes in (in-duced) lawmakers' preferences, too.
3. *Entitlements: more limits to agenda-setting effectiveness.* Agenda setters some-times engage in strategies to attempt to obtain nonmoderate outcomes on one dimension by tying this policy to other must-have legislation (e.g., debt extensions, continuing resolutions). The evidence that this strategy works on entitlements is scanty. That is, final entitlement outcomes seem usually to be either instances of gridlock or pivot-dampened change.

Median Tracking: Limits to Agenda-Setting Effectiveness
The headline in the budget section of the *Congressional Quarterly Almanac* doesn't say it all, but it does say quite a lot about the process and outcome

of the 1995 divided-government budget wars: "Republicans Seek Total Victory, End Year Empty-Handed."[33] The budget strategy of the new congressional majority party had three components: (1) to pass a huge package of rescissions early on to set a tone of seriousness about budget cutting, (2) to pass the 13 regular fiscal 1996 appropriations bills in the summer to implement deep cuts in discretionary spending, and (3) to bring the budget cycle to a grand conclusion in the fall by passing a massive reconciliation bill. According to the budget resolution passed in June, the combined effect of this plan would have been to reduce the federal deficit by $894 billion over seven years.

Many things refused to go as Republicans had planned. A rescissions bill was passed, but only after it had been vetoed and then significantly scaled back.[34] Appropriations bills proved much more difficult to craft in a manner that Republican leaders, freshmen conservatives, and a chamber majority could simultaneously accept, so most of these were not passed by the October 1 deadline. Most dramatically, the budget reconciliation bill led to a classic congressional-presidential eye-to-eye confrontation in which the president refused to blink. For all three prongs of the Republican strategy, the public record indicates the same pattern. Early-stage partisan agenda setting was followed by later-stage significant moderation of bills in order to gain support of pivotal lawmakers.[35] Below I confine my attention to the third and most significant prong of the strategy: reconciliation.

The largest measure ever of its kind, the 1995 budget reconciliation bill was the "*raison d'être* for the new GOP majority, a vehicle for remaking government in a Republican image."[36] The bill proposed to cut projected spending by $894 billion and lower taxes by $245 billion by fiscal 2002.

---

33. *Congressional Quarterly Almanac* (1995), 2–3. The subtitle reinforces the basic theme: "Single-mindedness resulted in sweeping legislation and guaranteed a presidential veto." (This is a reference to the reconciliation bill.)

34. See George Hager, "Rescissions Bill Runs Aground," *Congressional Quarterly Weekly Report*, July 1, 1995, p. 1904.

35. See Jerry Gray, "Moderates Seek Delay on Tax Plan," *New York Times*, March 25, 1995; Jackie Calmes, "Conservative 'Blue Dog' Democrats in the House Believe Their Bark Is 'Useful' and 'Influential,' " *Wall Street Journal*, March 28, 1995; David Rogers, "Gingrich Seems to Bolster Tax-Cut Link to Competing Goal of Balancing Budget," *Wall Street Journal*, April 3, 1995; David Rogers, "Clinton Joins Balanced-Budget Talks; GOP Leaders Call Meeting 'Constructive,' " *Wall Street Journal*, October 20, 1995; David Rogers, "Panetta Accuses GOP over Plan on Budget Cuts," *Wall Street Journal*, October 23, 1995; "Some in G.O.P. Defy Leaders," *New York Times*, October 27, 1995; and Jerry Gray, "Senate Moderates Gain Concessions in Big Budget Bill," *New York Times*, October 28, 1995.

36. *Congressional Quarterly Almanac* (1995), 2–44.

The biggest savings were proposed in Medicare, Medicaid, and an array of welfare programs for which the bill sought to transform several federal entitlements into block grants. Other cuts were made in the earned income tax credit, student loans, veterans' benefits, and housing. Finally, some provisions were included primarily for their appeal to conservatives rather than their budgetary consequences, such as termination of the Commerce Department, opening the Alaskan wilderness to oil and gas drilling, repeal of laws prized by organized labor, consolidation of foreign aid programs, and easing regulations on banks.

With an agenda-setter constructed package of provisions this large to contend with, it is not possible to detail all of the changes that were made as the bill wended its way through committees and onto the floors of the House and Senate. With very few exceptions, though, if the provisions were changed, they were changed to appeal to moderates and to soften the blow from often-caustic Democratic attacks. In the House, for example, the following changes seemed to be crucial for passage. Thirty moderate Republicans wrote Speaker Gingrich and persuaded him to limit child tax credits to families making less than $95,000 per year. The House Budget Committee's final version of the bill dropped the repeal of the Davis-Bacon (labor) Act. The bill backed off the proposed elimination of the Federal Housing Authority's foreclosure-relief program and settled for revision. A provision was dropped that would have authorized the sale of the Southeastern Power Administration by the Energy Department. Leaders eliminated a section of the bill that would have required the secretary of interior to submit a plan that would have recommended closure of some national parks. And Speaker Gingrich was persuaded to negotiate with state authorities concerned with Medicaid, the consequence of which was restoration of $12 billion.

A typical write-up of the House's eventual passage of the reconciliation bill was: "With the lockstep discipline and the zeal of crusaders, House Republicans passed the budget reconciliation bill October 26 by a vote of 227–203."[37] Such coverage is extremely misleading, however, when the more complete history is considered. Similar to President Clinton's so-called comeback victory two years earlier, the Republicans' "lockstep discipline and the zeal of crusaders" almost surely would not have been secured without the acceptance of many major substantive changes to the original right-of-center proposal.

37. Ibid., 2–48.

The situation and events in the Senate were much the same. Dilution of original provisions was much more common than strengthening. In many cases, the Senate outdid the House in moderating the content of the bill. "After hours of behind-the-scenes negotiations, Senate Republicans succeeded in appeasing the moderate wing of the party and rallied a majority of their members behind the reconciliation package."[38] The concessions that firmed up support to pass the bill almost invariably involved avowed Senate moderates: Chafee, Kassebaum, Jeffords, Campbell, Snowe, Hatfield, Specter, and Cohen. For example, a Roth (R–Delaware) amendment restored about $13 billion in spending for health programs; a Kassebaum (R–Kansas) amendment restored $5.9 billion for education; and a Chafee (R–Rhode Island) amendment adopted a definition of "disabled" that would ease the eligibility requirement for the Supplemental Security Income benefits.

Although the vast majority of the changes in the bill were moderating changes, these were not sufficient for President Clinton to back down from his veto threat. His December 6 message continued along the path of partisan rhetoric established months earlier, accusing the Republicans of adopting an "extreme" approach that would "hurt average Americans and help special interests."[39] A government shutdown resulted, and the 1995 budget cycle rolled over into 1996.

Who won? More to the point, did outcomes, if not rhetoric, track legislative preferences as hypothesized? These are quite difficult and quite different questions. The consensus of pundits seems to have been that the president won the budget showdown in the court of public opinion, because the public seemed to blame the Congress rather than the president for the government shutdowns brought about by the vetoes of ostensibly extreme legislation.[40] However, the government shutdowns were not permanent. Continuing resolutions were repeatedly both passed and signed, and cumulatively these bills embodied the real, substantive outcome of the tedious process. After the well-publicized vetoes of 1995 came the relatively sub-

---

38. Ibid., 2–50.

39. In retrospect, the veto message was also a dry run for a successful reelection campaign in which these themes loomed large.

40. For example, in mid-November of 1995, an estimated 51 percent of Americans blamed Republicans for the partial government shutdown, while only 28 percent blamed Clinton (CBS/New York Times poll as summarized in "Opinion Outlook: Views on Presidential Performance," *National Journal,* December 2, 1995, p. 3000). See also William Schneider, "Clinton Could Still Win Budget War," *National Journal,* November 25, 1995, p. 2954.

dued headlines of 1996: "With or Without a Budget Pact, the G.O.P.'s Fiscal Squeeze Is On," and "Historic Budget Battle Ends with a Whimper, as Congress Approves Funding Deal for 1996."[41] The content of articles such as these goes to the heart of the median tracking hypothesis. For example:

> The President and Democrats in Congress cheered last week when they reached agreement on a stopgap spending bill that avoided another shutdown of much of the government. But now as they analyze its fine print, they are discovering that the terms are much more stringent than they realized. Republicans are using the power of the purse to shrink the government—to scale it down rather than shut it down.[42]

Supporting evidence included references to 15 percent cuts in the Occupational Safety and Health Administration budget, and to spending for the Departments of Interior, Labor, Education, and Health and Human Services that was "no higher than the 1995 level or the lower of the levels approved for 1996 by the House and the Senate."[43] Several programs were singled out for 25 percent cuts, including the Office of Consumer Affairs, the Advanced Technology Program, and President Clinton's much cherished Americorps.

Congress finally finished its fiscal 1996 business in the spring of 1996 with one last, five-month continuing resolution. Its substance was much the same as in previous stopgap measures. Cuts from fiscal 1995 levels included $5.5 billion for Housing and Urban Development, $3.4 billion for Health and Human Services, $2.3 billion for education, $1.6 billion for Labor, $1.5 billion for Foreign Operations, and so on. In percentage terms, the story is similar. The EPA finally emerged with a $6.6 billion budget— a cut of about 9 percent. Federal housing funds were cut by more than 20 percent. Total funding for the Department of Education amounted to approximately a 9 percent reduction. One apparent exception is not really an exception, given the pattern of preferences across parties: Pentagon

41. From Robert Pear, *New York Times,* January 31, 1996; and Jackie Calmes and David Rogers, *Wall Street Journal,* April 26, 1996, respectively.

42. Robert Pear, "With or Without a Budget Pact, the G.O.P.'s Fiscal Squeeze Is On," *New York Times,* January 31, 1996.

43. Ibid. There were some exceptions to this pattern, but the exceptions, too, seem consistent with the 1994 changes in legislative composition. For example, the Department of Justice budget went up by 20 percent, with most of the new money going for the Immigration and Naturalization Service, the Drug Enforcement Administration, and the F.B.I.

spending went up $7 billion over the president's request. On the other hand, there were some instances in which Republicans clearly and significantly scaled back their original ambitions. The Commerce Department, which many Republicans wanted to eliminate, survived with only a $358 million cut. And last-minute compromises spared labor programs, such as $1.1 billion for dislocated workers and $625 million for teenage jobs.[44]

In summary, the outcomes of the 1995 process were not evident until well after the period of peak partisan behavior in the winter of 1995–96. But when all was said and, more important, done, a general pattern emerges that seems to be consistent with the pivotal politics median-tracking prediction. Changes in program support ranged from medium to large. Only rarely, if ever, were changes as large as the new congressional majority seemed initially to want. And rarely, if ever, did the funding decisions end in gridlock or go in the direction opposite what pivotal voters (moderates within the Congress) wanted. In brief, overreaching seems to describe the partisan ambitions and agenda-setting *attempts* of the new Republican majority, while congressional median tracking seems to describe the ultimate spending *outcomes*.[45]

Median Tracking: A Variation

Controlling for other factors, David Mayhew (1991) identified a seemingly robust first-of-term bump in legislative productivity within presidential interelection periods. An interpretation offered in Chapter 3 was that this may be due to election-induced shocks in politicians' preferences which, figuratively, leave relatively many $t - 1$ status quo points outside the gridlock interval in time $t,$ and thus leaves those old policies ripe for new lawmaking action. In the intra-administration period, in contrast, there are usually fewer preference shocks, hence fewer opportunities for lawmaking, hence fewer important new laws passed after the beginning of the term.

If the pivotal politics theory is useful for understanding budgetary lawmaking, then we might observe an analogous systematic pattern within Congresses, albeit with an important difference consistent with the budget-tailored theory as introduced above. The difference is that now the issue

44. Jackie Calmes and David Rogers, "Historic Budget Battle Ends with a Whimper, as Congress Approves Funding Deal for 1996," *Wall Street Journal,* April 26, 1996. These estimates exclude rescissions passed in 1995.

45. It remains a judgment call, though, whether final outcomes tended to lie closer to the congressional median or to the Republican median, so this summary is not to be construed as clearly inconsistent with party-theoretic approaches. We return to this issue in the next section.

is not the presence or absence of gridlock but rather the relative magnitude of changes in funding for various programs. (Again, this expectation is indirectly due to the zero-dollars reversion point assumption.) The similarity is that between session 1 and session 2 of a given Congress, preferences do not change much, so neither should budget outcomes. In contrast, between, say, the 103d and 104th Congresses, the set of preferences in the Congress changed significantly, so we should see comparatively large changes in budget outcomes. When the data are inspected at the program level, this is the approximate finding.

As for two-year intra-Congress periods, the evidence is mixed in an enlightening way. First, within the 103d unified-government Congress, the expectation is borne out quite nicely. A comprehensive and program-specific comparison of fiscal year 1994 and 1995 budgets is not undertaken here. However, the 1994 *Congressional Quarterly Almanac's* bottom line is that, relative to the dramatic first session, the second-session budget process was one of staying the course.

The support for intra-Congress effects is less clear-cut in the case of the 104th Congress. On the positive side, as stressed above, changes in the first session were predictably dramatic (although less dramatic than Republican leaders promised and wanted). On the negative side, however, Congress seemed not to stay the course in 1996. One headline proclaimed, "Spending Pact Marks Major Retreat by GOP Leaders," and quantified the situation with aggregate expenditure data.

> The numbers tell the story. When Republicans took over in 1995, Democrats were spending about $508 billion a year for general government. In a series of stormy battles last year, the GOP achieved historic cuts, reducing this figure to about $488 billion for [fiscal] 1996. Now, for [fiscal] 1997, the number will be back up close to $503 billion, not counting another $2 billion in last-minute expenditures to battle terrorism and fire and natural disasters.[46]

Specific examples included $4.8 billion restored for the Department of Education, a $270 million increase in EPA funding, 8 percent growth in the National Park and Fish and Wildlife Services budgets, a $1.27 billion increase for transportation, and survival of the Commerce Department yet again.

A probable cause for this "retreat" is that Republican legislators became

---

46. David Rogers, "Spending Pact Marks Major Retreat by GOP Leaders," *Wall Street Journal,* September 30, 1996.

somewhat shell-shocked when they began to see how their aggressive budget strategy was playing to the electorate.[47] New information about the attitudes of interest groups and the electorate toward spending cuts accordingly translated into moderation in legislators' induced preferences. If this is true, then pivots moved even though congressional and presidential membership remained constant.[48] In one respect, this illustrates an important limitation to the pivotal politics theory: it is a complete information theory, yet this is an instance in which incomplete information was evidently significant. In another respect, though, the observation does not severely undermine the theory as a theory of budgeting or lawmaking more generally. As a theory of lawmaking, the pivotal politics theory only says that *given* a shift in pivots' preferences, outcomes will change in a specifiable way. In 1996, they did. It does not say where such preferences come from, although an extended theory with an explicit electoral connection component could and should do this.[49] In the meantime, and subject to the caveat concerning incomplete information which admittedly is outside the pivotal politics theory framework, the evidence of median tracking continues to mount.

Entitlements: More Limits to Agenda-Setting Effectiveness

The major exception to the expectation of median-tracking concerns entitlements. These issues are conceptually tractable to the extent that entitlement programs reside comfortably on the liberal-conservatism spectrum, but they are operationally difficult for two reasons. First, it is not obvious a priori where the status quo lies relative to preferences. Second, as noted above and illustrated below, the budget process offers opportunities to complicate the basic unidimensional model by providing incentives for agenda setters to bundle entitlements changes with presumably must-pass legislation.

To illustrate, consider the conflicting theoretical views of welfare reform as depicted in figure 9.3. First, take at face value President Clinton's claimed desire to "end welfare as we know it." If the president wants to change the status quo in a conservative direction, then $p > q$. Second, Republicans,

47. See, for example, James A. Barnes, "The GOP's High-Wire Budget Act," *National Journal,* June 3, 1995, p. 1364.

48. A handful of legislators changed parties, but few died or retired. Moreover, if a party-based prediction were to be extracted on the basis of those who changed parties, the prediction would be the opposite of the pattern in budget data.

49. See Persson, Roland, and Tabellini 1997, for example.

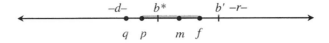

Figure 9.3
Partisan and pivot-based views of welfare reform

of course, shared this directional preference but undoubtedly desired a greater change than did the president. Therefore, let $r > p$, where r is, say, the median of Republicans in the Congress. Third, Democrats tended to be to the left of the president, so let $d < p$. Because it is not clear whether the pivotal Democrats preferred the status quo to all conservative changes (and because in the end it will not matter), d is denoted as an interval rather than a point, and likewise for r on the right side of the spectrum.[50]

The Republican agenda-setters' multidimensional bundling strategy was consistent with bundling strategies generally. Agenda setters combined Democrat-opposed changes in entitlements (welfare, Medicare, and Medicaid) with the huge budget reconciliation act that included a supposedly must-pass provision to raise the federal debt limit. The strategy rested on the following plausible logic. When opponents of entitlement cuts are given a choice between a bundle consisting of entitlement cuts *and* a debt extension versus no entitlement cuts and the federal government defaulting on its loans, they will consider the choice a virtual no-brainer and choose to take the bitter (entitlements reductions) with the sweet (no default). In terms of figure 9.3, then, the bundle theoretically allows Republican agenda setters to obtain significantly more entitlements changes than would otherwise be possible. For example, the point b' on figure 9.3 represents the expected outcome under this kind of agenda setting, while the point $b\star$ represents the prediction of the unidimensional pivotal politics theory.

How well agenda setting works in practice is, of course, an empirical question. Events in the fall of 1995 provide a probable counterexample of effective agenda setting as long as some fairly straightforward assumptions about preferences are made. Support for the agenda-setting theory would consist of passage of a reconciliation bill that included not only sweeping entitlements changes but also the tax cut that Speaker Gingrich frequently called the crown jewel of the Contract for America. Republican leaders attempted to do this but failed. This leaves two sets of questions. First,

50. It seems natural to think of partisan pivots, d and r, as intraparty medians, but this is not essential. For instance, they instead could be positions of party leaders.

was the 1995 cycle peculiar? Second, does another theory account for the entitlements outcomes in 1995–96 more satisfactorily than this straightforward application of agenda-setting theory?

The question about peculiarity cannot be resolved in what is essentially a case study. About all that can be said is that some characteristics of the 104th Congress were unusual (such as the first Republican majority in 40 years, and a highly partisan environment following a more or less uniquely coordinated election campaign), but others were not (the culmination of the budget process in omnibus bills in which party leaders at least *try* to exploit agenda setting opportunities).

The question of whether an alternative theory is available is relatively easy, though not open-and-shut. The pivotal politics theory makes predictions regarding entitlements outcomes by treating the situation as if it were unidimensional. This means that if the status quo, q, lies in the gridlock interval, entitlements will not change. If q lies outside the gridlock interval, entitlements will change, but only to the point at which the pivotal lawmaker is indifferent between q and the new bill, that is, to $b\star$ in figure 9.3. In the case of the 104th Congress, subjective evidence supports two interpretations. First, for most entitlements (including the originally proposed tax cut), the status quo was probably left-of-center but not so far left-of-center that the requisite supermajority could be assembled to override the veto of the president who claimed to be determined to "protect our values." Evidence further supportive of this interpretation is that Republicans could have come back in the second session of the 104th Congress to propose entitlements reforms in Medicare and Medicaid as stand-alone bills, but they chose not to do so. Second, in the case of welfare reform, Republicans did take up the issue again in the second session. Their original bill was weaker than that previously bundled into the 1995 reconciliation bill, and it became diluted more and more as it went through committees, parent chambers, and conference. In spite of these significant moderating changes, it remained unclear until the eleventh hour whether the president would sign the bill. In the end he did, and there is little doubt that his threat not to sign it was in part responsible for dampening the magnitude of the change. This is roughly consistent with the entitlements hypothesis, the simple unidimensional approach in figure 9.2, and the point $b\star$ (representing the pivotal politics prediction) in figure 9.3.

The reason this interpretation is not open-and-shut is that without good measures of preferences in these settings—the normal state of the field, regrettably—it is almost always possible to rationalize specific outcomes in terms of the pivotal politics theory. The power of this ostensible test, then, is so weak that it ought not to be considered a test. It is merely an illustration of what might be a sound and simple theoretical basis for a very complicated set of events.

PARTY POLITICS AND THE ELECTORAL CONNECTION

The study of budget politics in the first term of Bill Clinton's presidency exposes several weaknesses as well as a few strengths of the pivotal politics theory. The chief weaknesses fall under the rubric of realism. The politics surrounding budgetary lawmaking is explicitly partisan, dynamic, multi-dimensional, and uncertain; the pivotal politics theory has none of these properties. The chief strengths fall under the rubric of predictions. The pivotal politics theory, when tailored to address budgetary situations, predicts median tracking on issues involving discretionary spending, and it predicts gridlock or pivot-dampened change on entitlements and taxation. Broadly speaking, and with plenty of subjectivity surrounding interpretations, this is what we have seen in recent years.

Theories of collective party responsibility, although relatively less formal, embody most or all of the attributes of realism that are omitted in the pivotal politics theory: explicit partisanship, dynamics, multidimensionality, agenda setting, and uncertainty. These theories, too, have some predictive strong suits. Most notably, harsh partisan rhetoric, sharp partisan splits in budgetary roll call voting, agenda setting attempts by party leaders, and electoral jockeying over time are all salient in budget lawmaking, and they are all broadly consistent with this theoretical approach. An additional comparative advantage of party-theoretic approaches is their explicit attention to the electoral connection. Theoretically, as discussed in detail above, this larger repeated game within the electorate is essential in providing the behavioral impetus for partisanship within the smaller repeated game of lawmaking within the government.

If we wish to move beyond basics in a theory of U.S. lawmaking, then embedding a basic theory of lawmaking within a larger electoral context is, in principle, a promising development. The more specific question worth raising and addressing presently, however, is whether such an approach necessarily ought to have an explicit and exogenous partisan component. To obtain some constructive ideas about this question, reconsideration of the approach adopted by Mathew McCubbins and his colleagues is helpful. Recall the key component in their electoral connection: that legislators will behave as cohesive partisan entities in the lawmaking game because to do so improves their brand name which, in turn, translates into electoral successes.

Does it? To find out, we first search for evidence that an arguably necessary condition is met in the partisan electoral-connection argument. Specifically, do reelection seekers use their party labels and partisan voting records from the lawmaking arena when they compete in the electoral arena? The answer to this question is qualitative and somewhat soft. Second, we look at more systematic evidence of the electoral consequences of partisan lawmaking behavior. Specifically, do legislators with party-tending records within the lawmaking arena do better in the electoral arena than legislators who are more inclined to gravitate to moderate positions? The answer to this question is quantitative but preliminary.

Use of the Party Brand Name

The distance that Democrats attempted to put between themselves and President Clinton in the 1994 midterm election was amazing not only outside the beltway but also within, where, by some accounts, it reached the status of an official policy. "Acknowledging that the Democrats face a grim political environment this fall, President Clinton's pollster [Stanley Greenberg] is advising that those seeking re-election should emphasize their own records rather than link themselves too closely to Mr. Clinton or even their own party."[51] The memorandum in question, "Strategic Guide to the 1994 Election," stressed that "there is no reason to highlight [accomplishments] as Clinton or Democratic proposals. Voters want to know that you are fighting to get things done for them, not that you are advancing some national agenda."

Evidence that Democrats heeded this distancing doctrine is easy to find. Rep. Sam Coppersmith (D-Arizona) ran a nonpartisan ad promoting his virtues while the words "Independent Voice" flashed on the screen. Sen. Jeff Bingaman (D-New Mexico) featured a constituent who said, "I believe he votes for what he believes in, not just for the party." Sen. Jim Sasser (D-Tennessee) ran a 30-second spot into which was crammed a proclamation of support for welfare reform, deporting illegal aliens, mandatory life sentences for violent criminals, and prayer in the schools—not to mention

---

51. Richard L. Berke, "Advice for Democrats in Fall: Don't Be Too Close to Clinton," *New York Times,* August 5, 1994.

the obligatory attack on government fraud. This left no time for information regarding his party identification of his fairly liberal voting record.[52] Sen. Kent Conrad (D–North Dakota) was slightly more forthcoming about his voting record, perhaps because his electoral threat was small. One of his ads quibbled with the charge that he votes with President Clinton most of the time. His response? "That's a meaningless statistic. Most votes are non-partisan. A majority of the time I vote with Republican Leader Bob Dole."[53]

True, there were some exceptions to this pattern, as illustrated by a report that began: "When Rep. Mike Synar of Oklahoma refers to President Clinton, he uses the word 'we.' When Rep. Nathan Deal of Georgia talks about the president, he pointedly says 'he.' "[54] It is noteworthy, however, that Deal won reelection with 58 percent of the vote, and Synar was defeated in the Democratic primary.

Was 1994 an exceptional year in terms of majority party legislators distancing themselves from their party leaders and party label? Judging from the experiences on the campaign trail two years later, it was not.[55] The majority party label, of course, was different in 1996. However, when it came to using their party label for electoral gain, Republican candidates behaved much the same in 1996 as Democrats in 1994: party labels were conveniently misplaced. For example, two years after the GOP's Contract with America campaign, Rep. Phil English (R–Pennsylvania) ran for reelection. In 1996, though, his fliers did not even hint that he was a Republican

52. Gerald F. Seib, "As GOP Candidates Target Clinton in Campaign, Many Democrats Stress Their 'Independence,' " *Wall Street Journal,* July 8, 1994. Sassar's ADA ratings in 1993 and 1994 were 75 (70th percentile among senators).

53. Fred Barnes, "Donkey Kong," *New Republic,* November 14, 1994. See also Paul A. Gigot, "Dan Quayle: The Democrats' New Idea Man," *Wall Street Journal,* September 23, 1994, for similar examples from the campaigns of Rep. Bob Carr (D-Michigan), Sen. Richard Bryan (D-Nevada), and several Republicans whose campaigns tried to get Democrats to do what Democrats refused to do on their own—run as Democrats.

54. Jeffrey H. Birnbaum, "Tale of Two Democratic Lawmakers: One Links Himself to Clinton, the Other Keeps His Distance," *Wall Street Journal,* August 11, 1994.

55. In what may seem like unconscionable selection bias, I forgo an extensive discussion of the relatively coordinated Republican campaign of 1994, after which many pundits acted as if the Contract with America played a decisive role in Republicans' obtaining majority status. In light of public opinion data, this is a hard claim to defend. Prior to the election, polls from the *Wall Street Journal*/NBC and from the *Los Angeles Times* reported, respectively, that 70 percent and 73 percent of respondents who planned to vote Republican had never heard of the Contract. After the election, a *New York Times*/CBS poll said that only 38 percent of respondents (not 38 percent of Republican voters) had read or heard anything about the Contract.

except for their mention that he opposed his party leaders by supporting a minimum-wage increase. "Independent Voice; Pennsylvania Values" was his motto, in spite of the fact that he voted with the GOP majority more than 90 percent of the time.[56] Pat Roberts (R-Kansas), in his successful bid to move from the House to the Senate, likewise "pointedly distance[d] himself from House Speaker Newt Gingrich and the GOP Contract With America: 'I was one of the first to say that the contract was much too ideological.' "[57] Greg Ganske (R-Iowa), also a signer of the Contract, proved to be a loyal follower of Speaker Gingrich in the House. Not so on the campaign trail, though. "Along with other Gingrich Republicans running for re-election, he has tried to distance himself from the Speaker on some issues, including Medicaid financing for rural hospitals."[58] Still other Republicans had the temerity to highlight their successes with the Democratic president. Peter Blute of Massachusetts put it this way in 1996: "It's me and Clinton against my opponent. Congress can work with Clinton. We've already shown it." Peter Torkildsen, also of Massachusetts, boasted that he had compiled "one of the smallest records of support for Republican leadership of any Republican."[59]

By election day of 1996, distancing had again become a national strategy. Jay Dickey of Arkansas was a Republican "not-Newt." Despite a 93 percent party-loyalty rating, his creative declaration of independence was: "Newt canceled a fund-raiser in my district."[60] Other not-Newts spoke even more boldly in their acts partisan disassociation. Rep. Sam Brownback of Kansas, running for the U.S. Senate: "I am not a clone of Newt Gingrich. I am not going to be asking him to come into the state on my behalf." Rep. Scott Klug of Wisconsin: "If people tell you I'm Newt Gingrich, you tell them they got the wrong picture." Sen. Jim Jeffords of Vermont: "It would be a mistake to have him as Speaker again."[61]

To argue by anecdote is tenuous. Even so, at some point anecdotes be-

---

56. David Rogers, "Democrats Find Pennsylvania House Seats Are Elusive," *Wall Street Journal,* September 16, 1996.

57. Dennis Farney, "With Many Hot Races, Politics Is Now Putting Kansas on the Map," *Wall Street Journal,* September 25, 1996.

58. Don Terry, "Surprise Winner in '94 Becomes a Target in '96," *New York Times,* August 22, 1996.

59. Christopher Georges and John Harwood, "Some GOP Congressional Incumbents Emphasize Their Ability to Work with President Clinton," *Wall Street Journal,* September 10, 1996.

60. Dana Milbank, "No Newt Is Good News: GOP Congressmen Sprint to Set Their Distance from Unpopular Speaker," *Wall Street Journal,* June 14, 1996.

61. Albert R. Hunt, "Democrats to Newt: Thanks," *Wall Street Journal,* October 17, 1996.

come data, and it is difficult to imagine that a randomly selected sample of anecdotes would nullify these observations of widespread distancing in recent congressional campaigns. Nor is the apparent regularity confined to the legislative branch. The Morris-Clinton "triangulation" strategy for reelection was similarly silent about partisan attachments. Indeed, it was more like conspicuous partisan detachment. In summary, it seems likely that the key condition in party-theoretic attempts to incorporate the electoral connection into a theory of lawmaking is not met. The notion of a brand name is intuitive and appealing, particularly in economic theory and marketing practice. In practical politics, however, the party label seems more like a bad-luck charm than a treasured brand name.

Electoral Consequences

The discussion of distancing is limited not only by its anecdotal nature but also because it is silent about the consequences of the strategies adopted. If, for example, Mike Synar and other friends of Bill like him had won and Nathan Deal and other distancers from Bill had lost, then this would be evidence that the party brand name is electorally valuable after all. Likewise, it would suggest that the anecdotes were composed mostly of peculiar candidates who adopted unwise strategies and suffered accordingly. The unsettled issue, then, is whether distancing helps or hurts in the electoral arena.

A direct answer is not possible due to the absence of a direct measure of distancing. However, an empirical study by David Brady and colleagues creatively works around this problem in an analysis of all House incumbents since the 1956 election. Of the many interesting questions raised, the one most central to this discussion is whether losing incumbents tend to have voting records that are too liberal or too conservative relative to their districts.[62] Consider specifically the midterm election of 1994. The finding is that, on average, losing Democratic incumbents were eight ADA units too liberal for their districts.[63] Furthermore, of the 34 Democrats who lost, 68 percent were too liberal for their districts.[64]

---

62. To determine this, Brady, Canes, and Cogan 1997 regress members' transformed ADA scores on their districts' Democratic presidential vote. (Presidential vote is presumed to be an unbiased measure of district ideology.) Then they calculate residuals for each member. Transformations and coding are such that a negative residual means the member's voting record was too liberal for his district, while a positive residual means his voting record was too conservative for his district.

63. The authors interpret this as "presidential pull," akin to the measure of presidential power in Chapter 7 but, obviously, calculated much differently.

64. For Democrats in 1996, the number of losers, three, was too small to make any confident quantitative assessments. Since the authors focus on Clinton and Democrats, they do not perform comparable analyses of Republicans in 1996.

In summary, the study by Brady et al. is preliminary but suggestive. The suggestion is that when legislators gravitate away from the preferences of their electoral constituents and toward their off-center president, the electoral consequences tend to be negative. This finding is consistent with the notion that reelection-seeking candidates *should* try to distance themselves from their president (or party leaders, if the pattern is similar across the aisle). It is consistent with the anecdotal evidence above that candidates *do* try to distance themselves from their president (or party leaders). And it is consistent with the classic Downsian view that elections in two-party systems tend to provide incentives for candidates to converge to moderate positions within their districts. It is not consistent, however, with the key contention in party-centered theories that legislators benefit from strengthening their party's brand name in the lawmaking game to reap periodic benefits in the electoral game.

CAVEATS AND CONCLUSIONS

The methodological approach in this chapter was to stack the deck against the pivotal politics theory by surveying lawmaking in an arena in which the uncontested absence of realism of the theory poses a serious challenge to its ability to explain behavior and outcomes. The arena is budgetary politics, and two conclusions are warranted, again subject to caveats. First, when tailored slightly for the budget process, the pivotal politics theory performs reasonably well as an interpretive, if not predictive, device. As such, a stronger claim can be made that its assumptions are not outrageously simple, at least for purposes of a basic theory. Second, budget-process applications of party theories yielded relatively mixed results—generally strong in terms of rhetorical and voting *behavior* during the lawmaking process, generally weak in terms of lawmaking *outcomes,* and weaker still in terms of the electoral connection. Some broader implications of these findings are taken up in Chapter 10.

The main caveats of the chapter are also twofold. First, the data and style of the argument were softer than in previous chapters. Although very much theory driven, this exercise should be seen as an empirical application rather than an empirical test. Second, here as elsewhere in the book, it is possible that I have not selected the best possible party theory as a basis for comparison, or that I have not extracted hypotheses correctly from the theory selected. Therefore, this is yet another area in which future theory-motivated empirical research is welcome.

IV

CONCLUSION

··· TEN

BEYOND BASICS

The theory of pivotal politics is not the only game in town. To the extent that the arguments advanced in this book have been persuasive, however, it might be considered one of the better *basic* theories of U.S. lawmaking. Would relaxation of its simplifying assumptions make for a more realistic theory? Unquestionably. However, the task of moving beyond basics in theorizing about lawmaking should be guided less by worries about realism of assumptions than by the need for parsimonious and lucid explanations of behavior and outcomes. Basic theories should explain basic facts. Beyond-basic theories will, in all likelihood, explain basic facts better.

When considered collectively, the theory, findings, and applications in this study not only make a case that the pivotal politics theory is a good basic theory; they also produce suggestions about which assumptions in the theory to modify if basic facts about U.S. lawmaking are to be explained better. Although these suggestions are impressionistic and perhaps controversial, a brief summary helps to set the stage for some final, broader conclusions about lawmaking in the United States. The summary is organized around the five omissions highlighted in Chapter 9.

IMPLICATIONS FOR BEYOND–BASIC THEORIES

Parties

Political scientists like to say, "parties matter," and I do not disagree. The important issue in studies of lawmaking, however, is not whether parties matter generally but rather how majority-party status matters specifically, and whether it ultimately matters in ways that are predictable and *outcome consequential*. Party-centered theories deserve serious consideration, and, accordingly, this project has reached out to a wide range of such theories to test their hypotheses alongside those of the pivotal politics theory. With only a few exceptions, however, the party findings have been unconvincing or negative.[1] Existing party theories are unable to account for basic facts of lawmaking (e.g., gridlock, large bipartisan coalitions), and they also stumble when it comes to other predictions which, while intuitive, seem not to be borne out (e.g., agenda setting and corresponding noncentrist outcomes in government, running successfully under the party label in elections). In short, parties may well matter, but it simply does not follow that they need to be incorporated into a good theory of U.S. lawmaking.

Multidimensionality and Agenda Setting

The study of budgetary decision making reinforces what had already been conceded: lawmaking politics is multidimensional, and leaders *try* to exploit multidimensionality via agenda setting which, if successful, can lead to noncentrist outcomes (of a majority-party tending sort). But recent budgetary lawmaking also suggests that such plans are much easier to envision than they are to execute. The core reason for this, I suspect, is twofold. First, the kinds of restrictive procedures that are needed to make such plans work in theory are endogenous in reality. Second, even in the occasional real-world instances in which restrictive procedures are chosen and used effectively to obtain noncentrist outcomes, the resulting policies are not likely to stick in the long run. This is because as quickly as the consequences of noncentrist policies are realized, a large majority of reelection-seeking lawmakers has strong incentives to revisit those policies, and they possess the requisite parliamentary rights to moderate noncentrist policies upon their revisitation. Therefore, to the extent that endogenous rules and multiperiod decision making trump multidimensionality and agenda setting in practice, good theories of lawmaking do not have to be multidimensional, nor must they postulate agenda setters or, more generally, nonegalitarian parliamentary rights.

---

1. The most convincing evidence supporting the claim that parties matter was the partisan basis for presidential power discovered in Chapter 8. The corresponding problem is that the divided-unified government differences in such power are inconsistent with theories of majority party strength in Congress.

Dynamics and Uncertainty

By comparison, real-world dynamics and various forms of uncertainty seem to have a lot to do with the shortcomings of the basic pivotal politics theory. We see filibusters in reality that the theory does not predict. We see vetoes in reality that the theory does not predict. And we see bills that, in various combinations, are vetoed, overriden, sustained, tabled, revisited, modified further, and sometimes ultimately passed after long delays spanning Congresses and administrations. Plausible interpretations of these anomalies rest heavily on uncertainty and/or differential patience of lawmakers. Of the many off-center legislators on any given issue, who is the real filibuster pivot or veto pivot? What does he or she want? Are they willing to wait? Are coalition builders willing to wait? These are the sorts of questions lawmakers implicitly ask all the time, yet, beyond their most basic forms, they are not questions that the pivotal politics theory accommodates.[2] As beyond-basic theories incorporate these salient real-world complexities, an improved and enriched understanding of lawmaking will almost surely result.[3]

IMPLICATIONS FOR UNDERSTANDING LAWMAKING

While waiting for, or embarking upon advancements to, beyond-basic theories of lawmaking, it is useful to take stock of the current understanding of lawmaking, as perhaps it has been modified by this study. How does the pivotal politics theory, backed by various forms of corroborative evidence, affect today's received wisdom about lawmaking in U.S. national government? Topic-specific answers are offered to this question.

Gridlock and Government Regimes

As noted in Chapter 1, the topic of gridlock has positive and normative angles. The conventional positive angle is (or was until recently) that grid-

---

2.   See Arnold 1990, chapter 5, for an excellent discussion of these issues.

3.   Indeed, considerable progress along these lines has been made concomitant with the development of this project. See, for example, Baron's ongoing work on dynamic theories of lawmaking regarding collective goods, beginning with Baron 1994; Groseclose and McCarty's 1996 "blame-game" executive-legislative model with uncertainty; and Cameron's 1998 comprehensive theoretical and empirical study of vetoes which has both dynamic and uncertainty components; McCarty's 1997 theory of presidential reputation building; and Canes's 1997 theory of executive strength via "going public."

lock is caused by divided government, bitter partisanship, or both. The conventional normative angle is that gridlock is symptomatic of unresponsive, antimajoritarian government and is, therefore, bad.

As a positive matter, we have seen not only that gridlock occurs in unified and divided government alike but also *why* gridlock is essentially neutral with respect to regimes. Gridlock occurs regularly because of moderate status quo policies, supermajority procedures, and heterogeneous preferences. It occurs in unified as well as divided government because the most basic rules of U.S. lawmaking are identical in divided and unified government. Therefore, even though styles of behavior may differ across regime types, the evidence that outcomes differ predictably is thin at best. The pivotal politics theory and corroborative evidence therefore complement and reinforce Mayhew's empirical findings. Partisanship and party control seem here to be secondary or tertiary factors when it comes to legislative productivity.[4]

As a normative matter, only one confident recommendation can be offered based on this study. Critics should stop looking for ways to break gridlock by minimizing the probability of divided government, because this recommendation is an instance of treating a suspected cause rather than an actual cause. Instead, results-oriented critics of gridlock should advocate fundamental reforms in the Constitution and in Senate rules to make lawmaking more of a pure-majority enterprise.

That having been said, such reforms are not advocated here for two reasons. First, as conceded in Chapter 1, normative analysis is not my *forte.* Second, if figuratively forced to play *piano,* I would strike a different chord in a short interlude. Instead of instinctively adopting the premise that gridlock is bad, we should perhaps dispassionately try to identify and weigh benefits as well as costs of the U.S. system of lawmaking. The cost of gridlock, of course, is that by making it difficult to change the status quo, supermajority procedures often frustrate simple majorities within government who wish to change status quo policies. The benefit of gridlock, however, is that many actors outside of government, while not perfectly satisfied with somewhat off-center policies, nevertheless prefer a known and stable policy regime to frequent and often unpredictable changes. In the marketplace, for example, stable regulatory environments can encourage decision making for the long term, smooth out investments and consumption, and more

---

4.   Elsewhere the debate over the consequences, if any, of divided government goes on. See, for example, Alt and Stewart 1990; Bond and Fleisher 1995; Edwards, Barrett, and Peake 1995; Epstein and O'Halloran 1996; Gibson 1994; Goldfinger and Shull 1995; Howell, Adler, and Cameron 1997; King and Ragsdale 1988; Royed and Borrelli 1995; Taylor 1996; and Wirls 1993.

generally help to capture efficiencies that could not be captured if, say, regulatory policy changed abruptly and significantly after each election. If this reasoning is approximately correct, then, as Charles Jones argues, our separation-of-powers system "ain't broke" (Jones 1995). Rather, the system is operating in a more or less normal fashion to address a straightforward trade-off between stability and responsiveness. More specifically, our system is neither perfectly responsive to changes in preferences nor utterly impervious to such changes. Instead, the system guarantees that policies will be *nearly* centrally located and stable *most* of the time. In exceptional times when, for whatever reasons, policies are bumped outside of the typically moderate gridlock interval, our system is both *responsive* and *central tending*. Therefore, supermajoritarianism seems to manage quite well the inherent tensions between policy stability and policy responsiveness. The resulting mix of incremental changes, moderate policies, and gridlock is not such a bad thing.

Presidents

The causes, nature, and degree of presidential power in the U.S. system are matters of ongoing controversy—so much so that it is difficult to identify received wisdom in this area. The probably small affect of the findings of this study on received wisdom in presidential studies is simply to elevate somewhat the role of the veto as a component of presidential power. The veto in the pivotal politics theory does either of two things, and it does these whether it is employed or not. It contributes to policy stability (pejoratively, gridlock) in instances in which the status quo is moderate (in the gridlock interval), and it dampens the degree of convergence to the median legislator's ideal point when the status quo lies just outside the gridlock interval on the president's side of the ideological spectrum.

Additionally, this study reinforces what has long been suspected but seldom quantified—that presidents vary in the degree to which they exert persuasive influences over legislators. More specifically, in veto situations presidents reap net benefits in gaining and retaining votes, and part of this power has a distinctive partisan underpinning, particularly in divided government.

Congress

The body of research on legislative decision making is also one for which conventional wisdom is hard to pin down. One contingent of congressionalists has argued that the median voter theory remains a useful approximation for many kinds of legislative decision making; another contingent holds that congressional committees bias outcomes in a procommittee direction; and yet another contingent holds that political parties are mechanisms that facilitate both nonmedian and majority-party-tending outcomes.[5] Although the pivotal politics theory is not intended to challenge any of these directly, the theory and empirical findings have at least some indirect implications for theories of legislatures.

An implication of pivotal politics theory for the strong form of the median voter theory—which claims that lawmaking outcomes are *always* median-legislator outcomes—is that this form is too strong. In exceptional cases, such as appropriations situations in which the status quo is extreme, the pivotal politics theory and median voter theory predictions are identical. In more common circumstances, however, outcomes are likely not to lie exactly at the median voter's ideal point but rather in a narrow band that includes the median voter's ideal point. Even in this refinement, the median voter should be seen as a powerful gravitational force within the legislature: when policies change, they are always pulled in his or her direction. Such convergence, however, often is not complete for reasons now well-known: pivotal lawmakers (f, p, and v) are important forces that dampen policy convergence to the median legislator's ideal point.

A comparably close relationship between the pivotal politics theory of lawmaking and committee-power theories of legislatures can be seen by considering spatially the basic substantive claim of committee power theories. Generically, committee-power theories argue that by using an array of parliamentary advantages (e.g., gatekeeping, closed rules, ex post vetoes), preference-outlying committees can pass and keep in place policies that are near committee (or committee-median) ideal points but far from legislative median ideal points. For purposes of illustration—and consistent with the approach taken in Chapter 9—let us not worry about the literal truth or falsity in controversial assumptions in committee-power theories, such as that committees are composed of preference outliers and that they possess unequivocal parliamentary advantages. Likewise, let us assert that, for whatever reasons, legislative outcomes are sometimes near committee-median positions and far from legislative-median positions. Under these conditions, gridlock will occur in committee-power theories. More specifically, as

---

5. The contingents are neither mutually exclusive nor exhaustive. See Shepsle and Weingast 1995 for a recent survey and diverse collection of related essays.

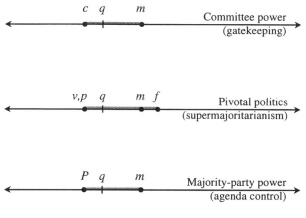

Figure 10.1
Three theoretical interpretations of gridlock

shown in figure 10.1, the nonmedian status quo policy, *q,* will remain in effect. The interesting theoretical question is, Why? At least two (and soon three) explanations can be offered. Committee-power theories offer explanations that rest on various and often elaborate arguments about legislative organization, gains-from-exchange, self-selection onto committees, and an assortment of special parliamentary rights granted to some but not all legislators. Regardless of the specifics, however, the bottom line of these arguments is that the committee *c* will exercise a special parliamentary right, such as gatekeeping, to keep the status quo, *q,* in effect.

The pivotal politics theory, in contrast, offers a more parsimonious explanation that rests only on supermajoritarian procedures. Specifically, as shown in the middle of figure 10.1, gridlock again occurs, but this time it has nothing to do with committees or to so-called rules that grant special parliamentary advantages to committees.[6] The point, then, is that what sometimes may appear to be committee power via committee gatekeeping may instead be yet another manifestation of the implicit power of supermajority pivots in a much more open and egalitarian legislative setting.

6. "So-called" because, strictly speaking, committees do not have gatekeeping rights (the House has a majority-driven discharge procedure), restrictive rules are endogenous (and always require a majority vote to take effect), and conference committees do not have a guaranteed ex post veto (chamber majorities can circumvent conference committees in any number of ways). Institutional specifics can be found in Krehbiel 1995, 1997a, and 1987, respectively.

Likewise, a nearly identical spatial argument suggests a way in which the power of pivots can be misconstrued as the power of the majority party. Majority-party committee-stacking claims provide one possible answer to the question of how the committee, *c,* in the top of figure 10.1, might have become a preference outlier: *c* is simply an agent of the principal force in the legislature—the majority party, *P.* The corresponding party-theoretic interpretation of gridlock, then, parallels the committee-power interpretation: the majority-party contingent on the committee exerts its agenda control to block any and all lawmaking efforts to move policy to *m.*

The pivotal politics theory again provides a different and relatively parsimonious account. Whether the committee exercises agenda-setting powers to block attempts at moderation, and whether it does so because of majority-party pressures, are incidental to the more basic fact that attempts to change the status quo are doomed from the start. According to the pivotal politics theory, they are doomed from the start because of the relative locations of the status quo and the supermajority pivots.

Because figure 10.1 lends itself only to observational-equivalence arguments, choosing between different theories of legislatures should be made on grounds other than this simple illustration. Although no attempt has been made to test committee-power theories in this study, attempts to test party theories have occupied significant portions of several chapters. To recapitulate: the relationship between divided government and gridlock was small at best in Chapter 3; party hypotheses failed to account for large, bipartisan coalitions in Chapter 4; some party-specific switching tendencies were discovered in Chapters 5 and 6, but they were not closely related to extant party theories; a distinctive president's-party effect in presidential influence was discovered in Chapter 8, but it is stronger when the president's party is the minority party in Congress than when the president has a congressional majority; and in Chapter 9 the notions of collective party responsibility via collective-dilemma-solving and brand-name-leveraging received mixed support at best. When these party-centered findings as a whole are contrasted with the modest but consistent support for the pivotal politics theory, the differences seem substantial.

CONCLUSION

The thesis of this book has been that behavior and outcomes in complex processes of lawmaking in the U.S. can be explained by a simple formal model. To put it informally, a few points on a line can effectively represent much of what happens in Washington, D.C. While inspecting this claim,

I have emphasized both strong suits and soft spots associated with the theory and data. Strong suits of the pivotal politics theory include its ability to account for stylized facts and variation. Stylized facts that are consistent with the theory include gridlock usually but not always, and winning coalitions that tend to be large and bipartisan (Chaps. 1 and 2). Variation explained by the theory includes changes in legislative productivity (Chap. 3) and in coalition sizes (Chap. 4), the prominence of the filibuster pivot in cloture situations in the Senate (Chap. 5), the prominence of the veto pivot in veto situations in the House and Senate (Chap. 6), and specified forms of median tracking, dampened change, and gridlock in budgetary decision making (Chap. 9). Soft spots usually pertain to measures and/or methods and were highlighted in chapter summaries. The general approach was to clarify and concede the limitations in the analysis and to invite additional research that improves measures and methods.

Until a new, improved, beyond-basic theory emerges, the pivotal politics theory can help to sort through the otherwise overwhelming complexities of modern lawmaking. In the spirit of "the proof is in the pudding," readers are encouraged to test this thesis for themselves whenever they feel the urge to watch laws (not sausage) being made. The prescribed method is reducible to four steps that focus on preferences, procedures, pivots, and the status quo. Applying the method is essentially a no-lose proposition. Whenever it works, we not only gain confidence *that* the underlying theory works, but we also gain a deeper understanding of *why* it works: because supermajoritarian procedures, in effect, determine who is pivotal in lawmaking. Whenever the method fails, we not only learn *that* the underlying theory is fallible, but we also are well-positioned to focus on factors outside the theory that are probable causes of its fallibility. The method:

1. *Preferences*. For a given lawmaking situation, identify a single, primary dimension of conflict. Which and how many lawmakers (including the president) want to change policy, and in which direction?
2. *Procedures*. Confirm the relevance of presidential veto and senatorial cloture. Unlike the abstract constructs used in many formal theories, the constitutionally granted presidential veto and the Senate's Rule 22 are concrete and enduring features of U.S. government that unquestionably constrain lawmaking attempts. Consequently, when they are in effect, the existence of a supermajority that favors change is a necessary condition for breaking gridlock.
3. *Pivots*. Identify the supermajority pivots—p, v, and f—in light of the configuration of preferences and the supermajority procedures in effect.
4. *The status quo*. Discern the approximate location of the status quo, q,

relative to the pivots. Predict whether (or explain why) change will occur. If change is expected, predict (or explain) the magnitude of such
change.

Finally, be forewarned that in most instances of breaking gridlock—
specifically, when *non*extreme status quo policies are updated—most lawmakers and many of their constituents are likely to be unhappy for one
reason or another. Lawmakers who opposed the change will have been
made worse off by definition. Lawmakers near the pivot will have been
made approximately indifferent between the old policy and the new policy.
And most lawmakers who favored the change will have wanted a more
significant change than they were able to enact, thus underscoring one last
time the importance of pivots in politics.

BIBLIOGRAPHY

Aldrich, John H. 1995. *Why Parties? The Origin and Transformation of Party Politics in America.* Chicago: University of Chicago Press.

Aldrich, John H., and David W. Rohde. 1995. Theories of the Party in the Legislature and the Transition to Republican Rule in the House. Paper presented at annual meeting of the American Political Science Association, Chicago.

Alesina, Alberto, Morris Fiorina, and Howard Rosenthal. 1991. Why Are There So Many Divided Senate Delegations? Harvard University. Typescript.

Alesina, Alberto, and Howard Rosenthal. 1995. *Partisan Politics, Divided Government, and the Economy.* New York: Cambridge University Press.

Alt, James, and Charles Stewart. 1990. Parties and the Deficit: Some Historical Evidence. Harvard University. Typescript.

American Political Science Association. 1950. *Toward a More Responsible Two-Party System.* Washington, D.C.: APSA.

Arnold, R. Douglas. 1990. *The Logic of Congressional Action.* New Haven: Yale University Press.

Arrow, Kenneth J. 1951. *Social Choice and Individual Values.* New York: Wiley.

Asbell, Bernard. 1978. *The Senate Nobody Knows.* Garden City, N.Y.: Norton.

Austen-Smith, David, and Jeffrey Banks. 1997. Positive Political Theory I: Collective Preference. Northwestern University. Typescript.

Austen-Smith, David, and John R. Wright. 1994. Counteractive Lobbying. *American Journal of Political Science* 38:25–44.

Bailey, Stephen K. 1950. *Congress Makes a Law: The Story behind the Employment Act of 1946.* New York: Columbia University Press.

Baron, David P. 1989. A Noncooperative Theory of Legislative Coalitions. *American Journal of Political Science* 33:1048–84.

———. 1991. Majoritarian Incentives, Pork Barrel Programs, and Procedural Control. *American Journal of Political Science* 35:57–90.

———. 1994. A Sequential Choice Perspective on Legislative Organization. *Legislative Studies Quarterly* 19:267–96.

Baron, David P., and John A. Ferejohn. 1987. Bargaining and Agenda Formation in Legislatures. *American Economic Review* 77:303–9.

———. 1989. Bargaining in Legislatures. *American Political Science Review* 89:1181–1206.

Barone, Michael, and Grant Ujifusa. 1995. *The Almanac of American Politics*. Washington, D.C.: National Journal.

Baumer, Donald C. 1992. *Senate Democratic Leadership in the 101st Congress,* ed. Allen D. Hertzke and Ronald M. Peters. Armonk, N.Y.: M. E. Sharpe, Inc.

Becker, Gary S. 1983. A Theory of Competition among Pressure Groups for Political Influence. *Quarterly Journal of Economics* 98:371–400.

Beer, Samuel H. 1976. The Adoption of General Revenue Sharing: A Case Study in Public Sector Politics. *Public Policy* 24:127–95.

Beth, Richard S. 1995. What We Don't Know about Filibusters. Congressional Research Service. Typescript.

Binder, Sarah A., and Steven S. Smith. 1997. *Politics or Principle? Filibustering in the United States*. Washington, D.C.: Brookings Institution Press.

Black, Duncan. 1958. *The Theory of Committees and Elections*. London: Cambridge University Press.

Bond, Jon R., and Richard Fleisher. 1986. Presidential-Congressional Relations on Economic Votes, 1957–1980. *Journal of the Northeastern Political Science Association* 18:498–513.

———. 1993. Clinton and Congress: End of Gridlock. *Extension of Remarks*. November: 6–7.

———. 1995. Clinton and Congress: A First-Year Assessment. *American Politics Quarterly* 23:355–72.

Brady, David, Brandice Canes, and John Cogan. 1997. The Electoral Connection Revisited: The Impact of Roll Call Voting on the Reelection Quest. Stanford University. Typescript.

Brady, David, and Craig Volden. 1997. *Revolving Gridlock*. Stanford University. Typescript.

Burns, James MacGregor. 1963. *The Deadlock of Democracy: Four-Party Politics in America*. Englewood Cliffs: Prentice-Hall.

Cameron, Charles M. 1998. *Veto Bargaining: Presidents and the Politics of Negative Power*. New York: Cambridge University Press.

Cameron, Charles M., and Susan Elmes. 1994. Sequential Veto Bargaining. Columbia University. Typescript.

Cameron, Charles M., and William Howell. 1996. Measuring the Institutional Performance of Congress in the Post-War Era: Surges and Slumps in the Production of Legislation, 1945–1994. Columbia University. Typescript.

Canes, Brandice J. 1997. Presidents' Legislative Influence from Going Public. Stanford Graduate School of Business. Typescript.

Carter, John R., and David Schap. 1987. Executive Veto, Legislative Override, and Structure Induced Equilibrium. *Public Choice* 52:227–44.

Chamberlain, J. P. 1936. *Legislative Processes: National and State*. New York: D. Appleton-Century.

Clausen, Aage R. 1973. *How Congressmen Decide: A Policy Focus*. New York: St. Martin's Press.

Cogan, John F., and Timothy J. Muris. 1994. Changes in Discretionary Domestic Spending during the Reagan Years. In *The Budget Puzzle: Understanding Federal Spending,* ed. John F. Cogan, Timothy J. Muris, and Allen Schick. Stanford: Stanford University Press.

Cohen, Richard E. 1994. *Changing Course in Washington: Clinton and the New Congress.* New York: Macmillan.

Collie, Melissa P. 1988. Universalism and the Parties in the U.S. House of Representatives, 1921–80. *American Journal of Political Science* 32:865–83.

Cooper, Joseph, and Rick K. Wilson. 1994. The Role of Congressional Parties. In *Encyclopedia of the American Legislative System,* ed. Joel H. Silbey. New York: Scribner's.

Copeland, Gary W. 1983. When Congress and the President Collide: Why Presidents Veto Legislation. *Journal of Politics* 45:696–710.

Cox, Gary W., and Mathew D. McCubbins. 1993. *Legislative Leviathan: Party Government in the House.* Berkeley: University of California Press.

Cutler, Lloyd N. 1988. Some Reflections about Divided Government. *Presidential Studies Quarterly* 17:485–92.

Dearden, James A., and Thomas A. Husted. 1990. Executive Budget Proposal, Executive Veto, Legislative Override, and Uncertainty: A Comparative Analysis of the Budgetary Process. *Public Choice* 65:1–19.

Denzau, Arthur T., and Robert J. Mackay. 1983. Gatekeeping and Monopoly Power of Committees: An Analysis of Sincere and Sophisticated Behavior. *American Journal of Political Science* 27:740–61.

Dickson, Paul, and Paul Clancy. 1993. *The Congress Dictionary: The Ways and Meanings of Capitol Hill.* New York: WIley.

Diermeier, Daniel. 1997. Explanatory Concepts in Positive Political Theory. Graduate School of Business, Stanford University. Typescript.

Dion, Douglas, and John Huber. 1996. Party Leadership and Procedural Choice in Legislatures. *Journal of Politics* 58:25–53.

———. 1997. Sense and Sensibility: The Role of Rules. *American Journal of Political Science* 41:945–57.

Downs, Anthony. 1957. *An Economic Theory of Democracy.* New York: Harper and Row.

Drew, Elazabeth. 1994. *On the Edge*. New York: Simon and Schuster.

Edwards, George C., III, Andrew Barrett, and Jeffrey Peake. 1995. The Legislative Impact of Divided Government: What Failed to Pass in Congress? Texas A&M University. Typescript.

Edwards, George C., John H. Kessel, and Bert A. Rockman, eds. 1993. *Researching the Presidency*. Pittsburgh: University of Pittsburgh Press.

Epstein, David, and Sharyn O'Halloran. 1996. Divided Government and the Design of Administrative Procedures. *Journal of Politics* 58:373–97.

Ferejohn, John A. 1986. Logrolling in an Institutional Context: A Case Study of Food Stamp Legislation. In *Congress and Policy Change,* ed. Gerald C. Wright, Leroy N. Rieselbach, and Lawrence C. Dodd. New York: Agathon Press.

Ferejohn, John A., and Keith Krehbiel. 1987. The Budget Process and the Size of the Budget. *American Journal of Political Science* 31:296–320.

Fiorina, Morris P. 1996. *Divided Government*. Boston: Allyn and Bacon.

Friedman, Milton. 1953. *Essays in Positive Economics*. Chicago: University of Chicago Press.

Gibson, Martha L. 1994. Politics of Divided Government. University of Connecticut. Typescript.

Goldfinger, Johnny, and Steven A. Shull. 1995. Presidential Influence on Major Legislation. Duke University. Typescript.

Greenstein, Fred. 1982. *The Hidden-Hand Presidency*. New York: Basic Books.

Grier, Kevin B., Michael McDonald, and Robert Tollison. 1994. Electoral Politics and the Presidential Veto. George Mason University. Typescript.

Groseclose, Timothy. 1995. An Examination of the Market for Favors and Votes in Congress. *Economic Inquiry* 30:320–40.

Groseclose, Timothy, Steve Levitt, and James Snyder. 1996. An Inflation-Adjusted ADA Measure. Massachusetts Institute of Technology. Typescript.

Groseclose, Timothy, and Nolan McCarty. 1996. Presidential Vetoes: Bargaining, Blame Game, and Gridlock. Ohio State University. Typescript.

Groseclose, Timothy, and James M. Snyder. 1996. Buying Supermajorities. *American Political Science Review* 90:303–15.

Gross, Bertram M. 1953. *The Legislative Struggle*. New York: McGraw Hill.

Grossman, Gene M., and Elhanan Helpman. 1994. Protection for Sale. *American Economic Review* 84:833–50.

Hammond, Thomas H., and Gary J. Miller. 1987. The Core of the Constitution. *American Political Science Review* 81:1155–74.

Heckman, James J., and James Snyder. 1996. Linear Probability Models of the Demand for Attributes with an Empirical Application to Estimating the Preferences of Legislators. University of Chicago. Typescript.

Herring, Pendleton. 1940. *Presidential Leadership*. New York: Farrar and Rinehart.

Hill, Kim Quaile, and John Patrick Plumlee. 1982. Presidential Success in Budgetary Policymaking: A Longitudinal Analysis. *Presidential Studies Quarterly* 12:174–85.

Hinckley, Barbara. 1990. *The Symbolic Presidency*. New York: Routledge.

Hoff, Samuel B. 1991. Saying No: Presidential Support and Veto Use, 1889–1989. *American Politics Quarterly* 19:310–23.

Howell, William, Scott Adler, and Charles Cameron. 1997. Institutional Causes of Legislative Productivity in the Post-WWII Era. Stanford University. Typescript.

Huntington, Samuel P. 1965. Congressional Responses to the Twentieth Century. In *The Congress and America's Future,* ed. David B. Truman. Englewood Cliffs: Prentice-Hall.

Ingberman, Daniel, and Dennis Yao. 1991. Presidential Commitment and the Veto. *American Journal of Political Science* 35:357–89.

Jones, Charles O. 1975. *Clean Air: The Policies and Politics of Pollution Control*. Pittsburgh: University of Pittsburgh Press.

———. 1994. *The Presidency in a Separated System*. Washington, D.C.: Brookings Institution Press.

———. 1995. It Ain't Broke. In *Back To Gridlock?* ed. James L. Sundquist. Washington, D.C.: Brookings Institution Press.

Kelly, Sean Q. 1993. Research Note: Divided We Govern? A Reassessment. *Polity* 25: 475–84.

Kernell, Samuel. 1986. *Going Public*. Washington D.C.: Congressional Quarterly Press.

Key, V. O. 1964. *Politics, Parties, and Pressure Groups*. New York: Crowell.

Kiewiet, D. Roderick, and Mathew D. McCubbins. 1988. Presidential Influence on Congressional Appropriations Decisions. *American Journal of Political Science* 32:713–36.

———. 1991. *The Logic of Delegation: Congressional Parties and the Appropriations Process*. Chicago: University of Chicago Press.

King, David C., and Richard J. Zeckhauser. 1996. Options on Congressional Votes: Why Leaders Win by a Little and Lose by a Lot. Harvard University. Typescript.

King, Gary, and Lyn Ragsdale. 1988. *The Elusive Executive*. Washington, D.C.: Congressional Quarterly Press.

Kingdon, John W. 1984. *Agendas, Alternatives, and Public Policies*. Boston: Little, Brown.

Kramer, Gerald H. 1986. Political Science as Science. In *Political Science: The Science of Politics,* ed. Herbert Weisberg. New York: Agathon Press.

Krehbiel, Keith. 1987. Why Are Congressional Committees Powerful? *American Political Science Review* 81:929–35.

———. 1988. Spatial Models of Legislative Choice. *Legislative Studies Quarterly* 8: 259–319.

———. 1991. *Information and Legislative Organization*. Ann Arbor: University of Michigan Press.

————. 1992. Constituency Characteristics and Legislative Preferences. *Public Choice* 76: 21–37.

————. 1993. Where's the Party? *British Journal of Political Science* 23:235–66.

————. 1995. Cosponsors and Wafflers from A to Z. *American Journal of Political Science* 39:906–23.

————. 1996a. Institutional and Partisan Sources of Gridlock: A Theory of Divided and Unified Government. *Journal of Theoretical Politics* 8:7–40.

————. 1996b. Committee Power, Leadership, and the Median Voter: Evidence from the Smoking Ban. *Journal of Law, Economics, & Organization* 11:237–59.

————. 1997a. Restrictive Rules Reconsidered. *American Journal of Political Science* 41: 919–44.

————. 1997b. Response to "Sense and Sensibility." *American Journal of Political Science* 41:958–64.

Krehbiel, Keith, and Douglas Rivers. 1988. The Analysis of Committee Power: An Application to Senate Voting on the Minimum Wage. *American Journal of Political Science* 32:1151–74.

Kreps, David M. 1990. *A Course in Microeconomic Theory*. Princeton: Princeton University Press.

Kuhn, Thomas S. 1962. *The Structure of Scientific Revolutions*. Chicago: University of Chicago Press.

Light, Paul C. 1991. *The President's Agenda: Domestic Policy Choice from Kennedy to Reagan*. Baltimore: Johns Hopkins University Press.

Lohmann, Susanne, and Sharyn O'Halloran. 1994. Divided Government and U.S. Trade Policy: Theory and Evidence. *Industrial Organization* 48:595–632.

Londregan, John. 1996. Estimating Preferred Points in Small Legislatures: Why We Can't Remain Agnostic. University of California, Los Angeles. Typescript.

Lowell, A. L. 1901. The Influence of Party upon Legislation in England and America. *Report of the American Historical Association*, 319–542.

Luce, Robert. 1922. *Legislative Procedure*. Boston: Houghton Mifflin.

McCarty, Nolan M. 1997. Reputation and the Veto. *Economics and Politics* 9:1–16.

McCarty, Nolan M., and Keith T. Poole. 1995. Veto Power and Legislation: An Empirical Analysis of Executive and Legislative Bargaining from 1961 to 1986. *Journal of Law, Economics, and Organization* 11:282–312.

McConnell, Grant. 1966. *Private Power and American Democracy*. New York: Vintage Books.

McKelvey, Richard D. 1976. Intransitivities in Multidimensional Voting Models and Some Implications for Agenda Control. *Journal of Economic Theory* 12:471–82.

Manley, John F. 1970. *The Politics of Finance: The House Committee on Ways and Means*. Boston: Little, Brown.

Mann, Robert. 1996. *The Walls of Jericho*. New York: Harcourt Brace.

Martin, Elizabeth. 1997. An Informational Theory of the Legislative Veto. *Journal of Law, Economics, and Organization* 13:319–43.

Matthews, Steven A. 1989. Veto Threats: Rhetoric in a Bargaining Game. *Quarterly Journal of Economics* 103:347–69.

Mayhew, David R. 1974. *Congress: The Electoral Connection.* New Haven: Yale University Press.

———. 1991. *Divided We Govern: Party Control, Lawmaking, and Investigations, 1946–1990.* New Haven: Yale University Press.

———. 1993. Reply: Let's Stick with the Longer List. *Polity* 25:485–88.

———. 1995. Clinton, the 103d Congress, and Unified Party Control: What are the Lessons. Yale University. Typescript.

Merriam, Charles E., and Harold Gosnell. 1929. *The American Party System: An Introduction to the Study of Political Parties in the United States.* New York: Macmillan.

Neustadt, Richard E. 1960. *Presidential Power.* New York: Wiley.

Niemi, Richard G., John E. Mueller, and Tom W. Smith. 1989. *Trends in Public Opinion: A Compendium of Survey Data.* New York: Greenwood Press.

Niemi, Richard, and Harold Stanley, eds. 1989. *Vital Statistics on American Politics.* Washington, D.C.: Congressional Quarterly Press.

Odegard, Peter, and E. Allen Helms. 1938. *American Politics.* New York: Harper and Brothers.

Oppenheimer, Bruce I. 1985. Changing Time Constraints on Congress: Historical Perspectives on the Use of Cloture. In *Congress Reconsidered,* ed. Lawrence C. Dodd and Bruce I. Oppenheimer. Washington D.C.: Congressional Quarterly Press.

———. 1995. The Importance of Elections in a Strong Congressional Party Era: The Effect of Unified v. Divided Government. Vanderbilt University. Typescript.

Ornstein, Norman J., Thomas E. Mann, and Allen Schick. 1984. *Vital Statistics on Congress.* Washington, D.C.: American Enterprise Institute.

Patterson, Samuel C. 1989. Party Leadership in the U.S. Senate. *Legislative Studies Quarterly* 14:393–413.

———. 1995. The Congressional Parties in the United States. Ohio State University. Typescript.

Patterson, Samuel C., and Gregory A. Caldeira. 1988. Party Voting in the United States Congress. *British Journal of Political Science* 18:111–31.

Patterson, Samuel C., Gregory A. Caldeira, and Eric N. Waltenburg. 1995. Cloture Voting in the United States Senate, 1919–1989. Ohio State University. Typescript.

Peltzman, Sam. 1976. Toward a More General Theory of Regulation. *Journal of Law and Economics* 17:211–40.

Persson, Torsten, Gerard Roland, and Guido Tabellini. 1997. Separation of Powers and Political Accountability. Harvard University. Typescript.

Peterson, Mark. 1990. The President and Congress. In *The Presidency in the Political System,* ed. Michael Nelson. Washington, D.C.: Congressional Quarterly Press.

Plott, Charles. 1967. A Notion of Equilibrium and Its Possibility under Majority Rule. *American Economic Review* 57:787–806.

Poole, Keith T., and Howard Rosenthal. 1985. A Spatial Model for Legislative Roll Call Analysis. *American Journal of Political Science* 29:357–84.

————. 1997. *Congress: A Political-Economic History of Roll Call Voting.* New York: Oxford University Press.

Popper, Karl R. 1992. *The Logic of Scientific Discovery.* London: Routledge.

Ragsdale, Lyn. 1996. *Vital Statistics on the Presidency.* Washington, D.C.: Congressional Quarterly Press.

Redman, Eric. 1973. *The Dance of Legislation.* New York: Simon and Schuster.

Reid, T. R. 1980. *Congressional Oddyssey: The Saga of a Senate Bill.* San Francisco: Freeman.

Rieselbach, Leroy N. 1993. It's the Constitution, Stupid: Clinton and Congress. *Extension of Remarks.* November: 10–11.

Riker, William H. 1962. *The Theory of Political Coalitions.* New Haven: Yale University Press.

————. 1977. The Future of a Science of Politics. *American Behavioral Scientist* 21:11–38.

————. 1980. Implications from the Disequilibrium of Majority Rule for the Study of Institutions. *American Political Science Review* 74:432–46.

Ripley, Randall B. 1969. *Majority Party Leadership in Congress.* Boston: Little, Brown.

Rivers, Douglas, and Nancy L. Rose. 1985. Passing the President's Program: Public Opinion and Presidential Influence in Congress. *American Journal of Political Science* 29:183–96.

Rohde, David W. 1991. *Parties and Leaders in the Postreform House.* Chicago: University of Chicago Press.

————. 1994. Parties and Committees in the House: Member Motivations, Issues, and Institutional Arrangements. *Legislative Studies Quarterly* 19:341–59.

————. 1995. Consensus, Conflict and the Domain of Partisanship in House Committees. Michigan State University. Typescript.

Rohde, David W., and Dennis M. Simon. 1985. Presidential Vetoes and Congressional Response: A Study of Institutional Conflict. *American Journal of Political Science* 29:397–427.

Romer, Thomas, and Howard Rosenthal. 1978. Political Resource Allocation, Controlled Agendas, and the Status Quo. *Public Choice* 33:27–43.

Royed, Terry J., and Stephen A. Borrelli. 1995. Testing Mandate Theory in the U.S.: Social Welfare Policy from Carter to Bush. University of Alabama. Typescript.

Safire, William. 1993. *Safire's New Political Dictionary.* New York: Random House.

Schap, David. 1986. Executive Veto and Informational Strategy: A Structure-Induced Equilibrium Analysis. *American Journal of Political Science* 30:755–70.

Schattschneider, E. E. 1942. *Party Government.* New York: Holt, Rinehart.

Schick, Allen. 1995. *The Federal Budget: Politics, Policy, Process.* Washington D.C.: Brookings Institution Press.

Schickler, Eric, and Andrew Rich. 1997. Controlling the Floor: Parties as Procedural Coalitions in the House. *American Journal of Political Science* 41: n.p.

Schofield, Norman. 1978. Instability of Simple Dynamic Games. *Review of Economic Studies* 45:575–94.

Shepsle, Kenneth A. 1979. Institutional Arrangements and Equilibrium in Multidimensional Voting Models. *American Journal of Political Science* 23:27–60.

———. 1986. Institutional Equilibrium and Equilibrium Institutions. In *Political Science: The Science of Politics,* ed. Herbert Weisberg. New York: Agathon Press.

Shepsle, Kenneth A., and Barry R. Weingast. 1981. Structure-Induced Equilibrium and Legislative Choice. *Public Choice* 37:503–19.

———. 1987. The Institutional Foundations of Committee Power. *American Political Science Review* 81:85–104.

———, eds. 1995. *Positive Theories of Congressional Institutions.* Ann Arbor: University of Michigan Press.

Shields, Todd G., and Chi Huang. 1995. Presidential Vetoes: An Event Count Model. *Political Research Quarterly* 48:559–72.

Sinclair, Barbara. 1992. The Emergence of Strong Leadership in the 1980s House of Representatives. *Journal of Politics* 54:657–84.

———. 1994. House Special Rules and the Institutional Design Controversy. *Legislative Studies Quarterly* 19:477–94.

Snyder, James M. 1991. On Buying Legislatures. *Economics and Politics* 3:93–109.

Sorauf, Frank J. 1964. *Political Parties in the American System.* Boston: Little, Brown.

Spitzer, Robert J. 1988. *The Presidential Veto: Touchstone of the Presidency.* Albany: State University of New York Press.

Stigler, George. 1971. The Theory of Economic Regulation. *Bell Journal of Economics* 2: 3–21.

Stimson, James A. 1991. *Public Opinion in America: Moods, Cycles, and Swings.* Boulder, Colo.: Westview Press.

Sundquist, James L. 1981. *The Decline and Resurgence of Congress.* Washington, D.C.: Brookings Institution Press.

———. 1988. Needed: A Political Theory for the New Era of Coalition Government in the United States. *Political Science Quarterly* 103:613–35.

Taylor, Andrew J. 1996. Explaining Government Productivity. North Carolina State University. Typescript.

United States Office of Management and Budget. 1987. *The Budget for Fiscal Year 1998*. Washington, D.C.: Government Printing Office.

Waldman, Steven. 1995. *The Bill: How Legislation Really Becomes Law: A Case Study of the National Service Bill*. New York: Penguin Books.

Watson, Richard A. 1988a. *Presidential Vetoes and Public Policy*. Lawrence: University of Kansas Press.

————. 1988b. The President's Veto Power. *Annals of the American Academy of Political and Social Science* 499:36–46.

Weingast, Barry R. 1979. A Rational Choice Perspective on Congressional Norms. *American Journal of Political Science* 23:245–62.

————. 1989. Floor Behavior in the U.S. Congress: Committee Power under the Open Rule. *American Political Science Review* 83:795–816.

————. 1996. Rational Choice Perspectives on Institutions. In *A New Handbook of Political Science,* ed. Robert E. Goodin and Hans-Dieter Klingemann. Oxford: Oxford University Press.

Whalen, Charles, and Barbara Whalen. 1985. *The Longest Debate*. Washington, D.C.: Seven Locks Press.

Wildavsky, Aaron B. 1964. *The Politics of the Budgetary Process*. Boston: Little, Brown.

Wirls, Daniel. 1995. United Government, Divided Congress?: The Senate and the Democratic Agenda in the 103d Congress. University of California, Santa Cruz. Typescript.

Woodward, Bob. 1994. *The Agenda*. New York: Simon and Schuster.